THE MUSIC BUSINESS

SECOND, REVISED, UPDATED EDITION

THE MUSIC BUSINESS

Career Opportunities and Self-Defense

DICK WEISSMAN

Three Rivers Press, New York

Published by Three Rivers Press, a division of Crown Publishers,
Inc., 201 East 50th Street, New York, New York 10022. Member of
the Crown Publishing Group.

Random House, Inc. New York, Toronto, London, Sydney, Auckland
http://www.randomhouse.com/

THREE RIVERS PRESS and colophon are trademarks of Crown
Publishers, Inc.

Originally published by Crown Publishers, Inc. in 1979. A first
revised edition was published in 1990.

Printed in the United States of America

Design by Cynthia Dunne

Library of Congress Cataloging-in-Publication Data

Weissman, Dick.
    The music business : career opportunities and self-defense / Dick
Weissman.
        p.   cm.
    Includes bibliographical references and index.
    Summary: Discusses the music industry and describes a wide variety
of careers, focusing on popular music
    1. Music—Vocational guidance.   2. Music trade—United States.
[1. Music—Vocational guidance.   2. Vocational guidance.   3. Music
trade.]   I. Title.
    ML3790.W4   1997
    780'.23'73—dc21   97-12275
                                                                        CIP
                                                                    MN AC

ISBN 0-517-88784-3 (pbk.)

10 9 8 7 6 5 4 3 2

Second Revised Edition

Contents

GLOSSARY OF MUSIC BUSINESS TERMS

ANNOTATED BIBLIOGRAPHY

Introduction, or How I Got into the Music Business and Why I Wrote This Book

$\mathcal{W}$hen I was seven years old and my brother was eleven we started out together to take piano lessons. He was a more serious individual than I, and my parents assumed that he would take lessons and I would tag along. It turned out that he was virtually tone deaf, so he quit after a couple of weeks, and I ended up taking piano lessons for about seven years. We lived in northwest Philadelphia in a section called Mount Airy, and every Tuesday I would take the railroad train downtown for my lesson. I played classical music only, and all of the music was written. There was no improvisation. I played the Mozart Sonata no. 3, scales, and exercises, and so on. I never had any idea about what chords I was playing or any other aspect of music structure. I would practice each piece until I had learned it reasonably well, and then go on to the next one. By the last year of my lessons I had reduced them to every other week, and had pretty much given up practicing.

About the same time that I gave up on the piano I heard Pete Seeger play the banjo. This was in 1948, and I was thirteen years old. I had never heard of American folk music, and found it kind of intriguing. At that time the music that was played on Philadelphia radio was a boring collection of insipid love songs, performed by such musical luminaries as Vaughn Monroe, Patti Page, Doris Day, Guy Mitchell, etc. Soon after this, 78 rpm records were phased out, and I discovered an army-navy surplus store that sold 78s by Pete Seeger, Brownie McGhee, Lonnie Johnson, Woody Guthrie, and other folk and blues singers. I bought quite a few of these records at about a quarter a record, and through reading the liner notes of one album I sent for Pete Seeger's book *How to Play the 5-String Banjo.*

At this point I was going to an academically oriented and boring high school in Philly called Central High. I hated it so much that I went to summer school so that I could graduate in three and a half years. I decided not to go to college right away because I felt tired of school. I got a job running a mimeograph machine in a downtown department store. Sometime during that year (1951) I bought Pete Seeger's first LP, *Darling Corey,* a 10-inch LP for Folkways Records. I used to listen to that record every night before going to sleep—in fact, to this day it is the only LP that I have ever worn out. Under the spell of the book and the record I decided to go out and buy a banjo. Following Pete's instructions, I went to a pawn shop and bought a banjo for $25. I took it home, breathless with excitement, and proceeded to break two of the strings while trying to tune them to the piano. I had never seen anyone tune a stringed instrument before, and didn't know how to match the pitch to the piano. I took the banjo and put it in a closet. It stayed there for about a year and a half.

A year later I entered Goddard College, a small progressive college in north-central Vermont that had no marks, no tests, and almost no students. I met a girl there named Lil Blos, who played the banjo, and she offered to show me how to play. That Thanksgiving I went home to Philadelphia and got the banjo.

For the next two years I played the banjo almost incessantly, much to the discomfort of anyone within earshot. One friend of mine used to re-

fer to it as the tin can with strings. I was quite ruthless about my practicing, sitting in front of the campus community center playing hour after hour, destroying the peace of the Vermont countryside by playing in
the woods, and dragging the banjo to parties and picnics. At no time
during this period did I decide to become a professional musician. My
interests were in the social sciences and literature, and my dream was to
write the Great American Novel. I had a friend named Burrill Crohn
who played the trumpet, and he and I started jamming, with me playing
piano. Burrill played blues and Dixieland jazz. I had never played any piano without reading music, but I had learned how to play the banjo
without any written music at all. I managed to find a couple of jazz piano books, including one by Mary Lou Williams that included helpful
hints about chord structure.

By the time I was ready for my junior year of college, I realized that
I didn't want to stay at Goddard for four years. At that time it was very
difficult to transfer credits because Goddard was not yet accredited by
the regional accrediting association. I arranged to divide my junior year
between New York and New Mexico. In the fall I went to the New
School for Social Research in New York, and in the spring I went to the
University of New Mexico. As part of my fall plan, I persuaded Goddard
to agree to my taking six credits of banjo and guitar lessons. I remember
the registrar writing me a very serious note saying that these credits
might not be applicable to a graduate school transcript should I go on
for an advanced degree. Since I am now teaching both banjo and guitar
for college credit at Colorado Women's College, and there are guitar
programs at almost every major American college, it seems funny in retrospect. In those days guitar was considered a bit suspect in the American academic world, and banjo was not recognized as an instrument
worthy of serious study.

I took four months of banjo and guitar lessons from Jerry Silverman
at the Metropolitan Music School in New York City, and I also had
some theory and ear-training classes. In the spring I went on to Albuquerque and took some sociology and anthropology classes. I also met a
marvelous banjo player named Stu Jamieson, who lived in the nearby
Sandia Mountains. I spent two long evenings at his house listening to
him play, and I did a number of goofy things in Albuquerque, such as
playing on KOB-TV in Albuquerque with Glen Campbell's uncle, Dick

Bills, dressed in full but borrowed cowboy regalia, and a couple of concerts at the university. When I returned to Goddard for my senior year I started work on my senior thesis, which combined sociology and what is now called black studies (but was then called Negro history) with my interest in folk music. It concerned the relationship between the life and the music of Huddie Ledbetter (Leadbelly), the black folksinger-composer. Mostly I focused on a content analysis of the lyrics of his songs.

That spring I wrote a suite called *A Day in the Kentucky Mountains*. It was a five-part piece for the banjo with a song in the middle, and although I had written a few songs by that time, this was the first original work I had tried to compose for the banjo. I played the piece at a graduation concert, and settled by the end of the summer in New York City.

I decided to go to graduate school, and after being rejected by the New York School of Social Work, I entered Columbia University in the graduate sociology program. This was a rough period in my life because I didn't think I had the talent to make it as a writer of fiction, I still hadn't conceived of the possibility of becoming a musician, and I really had no idea of how I could earn a living. I didn't especially want to go into the army, which was breathing fairly close down my neck, so I finally decided to pursue some kind of social science research.

I found graduate school to be an elaborate rerun of my high school experiences. I never could understand what my fellow students were talking about, due to my limited background in formal sociology. In fact, I found them harder to understand than my teachers. I didn't know too many people in New York, and I didn't like my academic compatriots much. I started to support myself by teaching banjo and guitar. During the year and a half I was taking courses at Columbia some friends and music store owners told some other musicians and arrangers that I could play the five-string banjo, and I got a few good jobs doing commercials and playing on some records. Before long I was taking my banjo with me to classes, leaving classes early to play jobs, or not going to classes at all. Finally it came time to write my thesis. I wanted to write about a number of blind black street singers, some still alive and some dead. I had a theory that blind street singers who were basically nonliterate people reflected and upheld the traditions that were alive when they were children, rather than changing their beliefs and attitudes as the society itself changed. I tried to explain what I wanted to do to my adviser. He looked at me with some confusion, probably at least partly the fault of my explanation, and acknowledged that he didn't know much about what I was talking about. He informed me that his wife was an artist. In other words he was used to dealing with eccentrics. The sociology department at Columbia mostly welcomed very structured statistically oriented studies of voting behavior, consumer product choices, etc. This kind of study was statistically sound, used specific data, and didn't involve abstractions or much in the way of loose theorizing. In other words they were safe. Sometime during this conversation with my adviser I decided to become a full-time musician. I realized I would never write a thesis at Columbia. I didn't officially quit school, but I started teaching guitar and banjo six days a week, four in New York and two in my hometown of Philadelphia. I got some jobs teaching classes at Ys, neighborhood art centers, and so on. Gradually more calls came in for studio work, and I studied some jazz guitar, worked on reading music for guitar, and met some good professional musicians, particularly my guitar teacher, Dan Fox. In 1960 I met John Phillips, and he and I and Scott Mackenzie formed a group called the Journeymen. We recorded three albums for Capitol, did college concerts and played nightclubs all over the United States and Canada, and did some commercials and television. Without any real foresight or planning I had become a professional musician.

HOW AND WHY I WROTE THIS BOOK

Anyone writing a book seeks a certain amount of recognition or some degree of financial success. I also have some other specific motivations in mind that should be of greater value to the reader. I hope that everyone reading this book will be able to learn from a few of the unfortunate experiences I have had in the music industry over the last thirty-five years, and I hope that some of the more positive experiences will be of interest and value.

In 1959–60 I was a member of what probably was the world's first folk-rock group. It was a collection of singers and musicians called the Citizens, put together by two Broadway songwriters named Sid Jacobson and Lou Stallman. By Broadway songwriters I mean a corps of professional writers of that time who literally wrote two or three songs a day most days of the week, year after year. Sid and Lou had written a few hits, and were the owners of a huge bunch of demonstration records and lead sheets of their songs. They had put together a concept album consisting of a group of songs describing life in New York City. They auditioned a number of singers and musicians and I was accepted into the group as the principal guitarist, banjo picker, and occasional singer. Lou and Sid had a deal with Laurie Records, the company that recorded Dion and the Belmonts, the Chiffons, and others. Lou and Sid gave us contracts, which signed us to them as our personal managers. I no longer remember whether we were under contract to Lou and Sid as independent record producers or whether we had a direct contract with Laurie Records. In the record deal it was stated that we could not record for any other record label. Since I was starting to make a good part of my living doing free-lance recording for various record companies, I insisted that this provision be changed so that I could continue to record for other labels. Lou and Sid agreed to revise this part of the contract. Considering my lack of experience at the time, in retrospect I am amazed I even read the contract that carefully. Anyway, the contract was not revised, so I never did sign it. We finished the record, but Laurie held on to it for a long time before issuing it. Perhaps they didn't think it would sell, wasn't any good, or whatever. While this was dragging on I had met John Phillips, and he and I and Scott Mackenzie ended up signing a recording contract with Capitol. One day the phone rang, and Sid called to remind me that I was still under a contract with them as managers, and that they would expect to get 20 percent of my earnings. I reminded Sid that I had never signed the contract because they had failed to rewrite it. I mention this because if I had signed the contract, I would indeed have had to pay Sid and Lou commissions. The moral of this story is to be very careful about the contracts that you sign because some months or years later you may find yourself in a situation that you never anticipated. In this instance I was very lucky.

When the Journeymen got together we went through the Schwann LP catalog and decided on eight record companies that we thought were likely prospects. John, who was the smoothest talker in our group, called them on the phone and asked to speak to the artist and repertoire department. None of them was willing to have us do a live audition except MGM Records. Since we had very little money, and we all had some recording experience, we didn't want to go to the time, trouble, or expense to do a demonstration tape. We sang and played for MGM and they liked us and offered to sign us. Meanwhile John and Scott were under contract to Decca Records because they had been in a group called the Smoothies, who recorded for Decca. None of us wanted to record for Decca, which we felt was a dated and musically unsympathetic company, so we adopted the following strategy. The Smoothies' producer was a man named Milt Gabler, a noted jazz buff who, according to John, hated banjos. We positioned ourselves with me slightly in front of the other members of the group and with my banjo pointed directly at Milt's head. John then had me play as loud as I could so that I virtually drowned out anything else. John and Scott got their release from Decca after we sang two or three songs.

In the midst of our negotiations with MGM we picked up a manager named Rene Cardenas, who was in a sort of limited partnership with Frank Werber, who then managed the Kingston Trio. The Trio was at that time the most successful pop-folk group around. The Kingston Trio recorded for Capitol, and Werber and Cardenas felt they would have no trouble getting us a deal with Capitol if that proved necessary. We went back to MGM with Rene Cardenas. He asked for a guarantee of two albums a year, and a $5,000 guarantee for promotion of the first album. Besides the three of us and Rene, two people represented MGM at this meeting. One of them was Danny Davis, who later became a producer for RCA and then left to form the Nashville Brass, and Jim Vienneau, who now produces records in Nashville. Danny was very friendly but not optimistic about the deal that Rene had outlined. Vienneau played the bad guy (which he did quite well) and looked us straight in the eye and said, "You'll never get a deal like that in the record business." Ten minutes later we walked into the New York office of Capitol Records, and sang a few songs for Andy Wiswell, their eastern production chief. He called Capitol's head office in Hollywood in our presence, and within a half hour of Vienneau's speech we got exactly the deal that he had described as impossible. At that moment and forever more I learned not to believe people in the music industry when they describe a deal as impossible, or a contract as nonnegotiable.

The sequel to this story has a less happy conclusion. After some months of management by Werber and Cardenas, we became convinced that our careers were not progressing as quickly as we had hoped. The Kingston Trio was breaking up, and we felt that most of our manager's energies were directed toward finding a replacement for Dave Guard, who was leaving the Trio. Since the Trio was an exceptionally valuable show business property, this was somewhat understandable. We spent several months starving in San Francisco, and Scott and I moved into a $9-a-week Chinese hotel in North Beach, while John worried a lot because he had relocated his wife and two children to Mill Valley, California, from their home in Virginia. We got about six weeks of work on our own at a club in San Jose, and finally Werber and Cardenas got us a couple of jobs in Spokane and Phoenix. Most of the money was eaten up in travel expenses, but we were happy to be working at all. In Phoenix we were fired from the steak house in which we were playing, because the owner thought we were arrogant and was annoyed that we weren't drawing customers.

Just about this time our first Capitol single came out. It began to get heavy radio play in New York City. Our original booking agency, International Talent Associates (ITA), had been in New York, but Werber and Cardenas had pulled us out of that agency and started trying to book us themselves, and in the case of the abortive Phoenix job through another outfit called ABC (Associated Booking Corp.). We got in touch with the people from ITA, who had been hearing our record on the way to work every day and thought it possibly would be a hit. They offered to book us again, and we fired our managers and went back to New York. Unfortunately, we had a binding contract with Werber and Cardenas, which we had to buy out of with cash. It cost us $6,000 and some monies they had advanced us, and a lot of anxiety and bitterness. The money was paid in deferred payments, since we were penniless. Ever since this experience I have been very careful about signing contracts. Contracts can be broken, but it is a long and expensive process, which consumes time and energy as well as money.

The Journeymen stayed together for three and a half years, did three albums for Capitol, and several hundred concerts and a bunch of nightclub gigs all over North America. By 1964 it became apparent that the folk boom was ending, and I had done about enough living out of a suitcase. I had met my future wife, and decided to leave, get married, and move back to New York. I did all of that, and resumed my career as a free-lance studio musician, also doing some songwriting and record producing. John tried to keep the Journeymen alive for a year, calling them the New Journeymen. They never got a record deal, and broke up, eventually evolving into the Mamas and the Papas. Scott Mackenzie made a number of 45s that were unsuccessful, and then scored with the big hit "If You Go to San Francisco," written and coproduced by John Phillips.

In 1972 I moved to Denver, Colorado. I had gotten tired of the New York studio scene, and decided to get a music degree and study a bit about composing and arranging. In 1975 I met Tom MacCluskey, head of the music department at Colorado Women's College. He offered me a job organizing and teaching courses in the music industry program at the school. This is one of a number of such programs at schools throughout the United States that teaches music students about jobs available in the music industry. As I started to organize the courses, I looked around for a good textbook. I found the available books either vague, technical, or purely autobiographical. In my opinion they were not valuable or clear to someone who is trying to enter the music business but lacks knowledge or experience about it. This book is my attempt to convey what goes on in the music industry to the young, aspiring musician or to the curious layperson. It tries to explain what the various people in the business do, how record companies function, what agents and personal managers do, the role of songwriters and publishers, unions, etc. Basically, I am trying to explain to a young person how to make intelligent career choices, how to get started, and how to progress.

I will also explore alternatives to going after the big money for those interested in a more personal, less popular sort of music. Other topics to be discussed are contracts, lawyers, commercials, studio work, video, new technological developments, music therapy, and arts management. I hope that this book will answer some of the questions you may have and point out some directions that will be of use to you in making a career in music.

SINCE 1979

In the eighteen years that have elapsed since the first edition of this book appeared, quite a few things have changed in the music industry and in my own career. I've written a second feature film score, produced a number of records and tapes, written three other books, and have been fortunate enough to receive a grant from the National Endowment for the Humanities. The school where I taught, Colorado Women's College, went out of business, and for several years I became very involved in working with the artist-in-residence program for the state of Colorado.

In 1987–88 I lived in Los Angeles and worked as the National Education Coordinator for NARAS, the National Academy of the Recording Arts and Sciences. I did not enjoy living in Southern California, and after a year moved back to Colorado, where I taught briefly at the Colorado Institute of Art. Since 1990 I have been teaching in the Music Management Program at the University of Colorado at Denver, one of the first schools to offer a four-year degree program in that area. I have written quite a bit of instrumental music lately, and have two albums out on the Folk Era label. My most recent CD is called *American Dreams*. It consists of instrumental music for classical guitar, five-string banjo, flute, and saxophone, played with two other musicians. We call ourselves the Uncommon Thread.

Musical fads have come and gone, and new technologies for the recording and distribution of music appear on a daily basis. I find that I still love playing and writing music. I would like to see the day when everyone who works in the music business will share that enthusiasm.

This second revised edition of *The Music Business* is intended as an update of the original and revised editions. I hope it reflects my sincere desire to communicate the things that I have learned and thought about. Thanks to Randi Perkins, Rich Sanders, and Dennis Dreith for research assistance.

part 1

THE
MUSIC
BUSINESS

Records, Agents, Managers,
Music Publishing, Commercials,
and Unions

1

Getting Started

Before I discuss the structure of the music industry, I'd like to take you through the complete process that a beginner or a near-beginner in the industry might need to experience in his efforts to start a music business career. This is only a single example of someone getting started, and the situation may not apply to you or your own problems in a starting a career. This is intended as a road map, not as a complete guide to the territory.

I am basing this part of the book on questions that people have asked me or that I have heard them ask others in the last few years. Denver, the metropolitan area where I have been living for most of the last twenty-two years, is a fairly typical American city in the sense that there are some reasonably good recording studios, a few very small record companies, a number of clubs to perform in, and a reasonably good symphony orchestra. Denver is not a center for national recording, so some of the frustrations or career roadblocks felt by the person in this example may not hold true if you live in Nashville, New York, Los Angeles, or Toronto. On the other hand, living in a major music town doesn't necessarily provide you with access to what Joni Mitchell so aptly calls the "starmaker machinery."

Let's say that you are a singer-songwriter. You live in a medium-sized town, say Dubuque, Iowa. You have had a little bit of performing experience, but nothing of an extended nature. In other words, you haven't been on the road or played outside the immediate area in which you live, but you do have twenty or twenty-five songs that you have written, and you're really not sure what to do with them. Let's further assume that you have not copyrighted the songs, you don't have an agent or a manager, don't really know anyone making a living in the music business, and are not a member of the union. I am assuming that you have made a commitment in your own mind to try to pursue a successful career in music.

The first thing that you need to do is to get as much performing experience as possible, on whatever level it is available. Offer your services, probably without charge at this point, to hospitals, homes for the elderly, schools for the retarded, public and private schools, parties, or to any other group that might enjoy watching a musical performance. As you begin to get more comfortable with performing, try to notice what is working well in your performances and what doesn't work at all. Try a few of your own songs in your shows, but don't restrict yourself to your own material. What songs do people like? Solicit comments on what you are doing, and listen to unsolicited comments. Have your friends attend some of these performances and ask them to listen to what people are saying about you. Think of this period in your career as a growth or experimental period, during which you are putting together a show that will hopefully make you some money in the future. Experiment with your material and your musical arrangements. Make some songs longer than you originally wrote them, take some instrumental solos if you can, use different tempos and try different keys, do some sections of a song louder or softer than others, and so on. If possible, tape some of your performances and some of your rehearsals, and try to be objective about the results. Tape a song before and after you have changed the arrangement and compare the results. Some things will work, other things may not.

After this period of trial and error you should have put together some kind of a coherent show, including some of your own songs. Do guest sets in clubs, and begin to start asking for money for your performances. Find some other musicians to jam with through music stores, music school bulletin boards, friends, and so forth. At this point you may want to decide whether you want to play in a band or pursue a solo career. What kind of music are you playing? If you play hard rock, you will need to have a band to get the effect you want. Do you have enough original songs of your own? Are you a great harmony singer who doesn't have a wonderful solo voice? Do you have some friends who have good sound equipment who are looking for an additional performer who plays rhythm guitar, or piano, or whatever you play?

With or without a band, you will need to make a demo tape for the club owner or school staff person who wants to hear a sample of your work. It doesn't have to be a professional tape recorded in an expensive studio. It should represent what you do well enough to give an accurate impression of your sound. Take some time in doing the tape to achieve that result. Sometimes people working in high-fidelity stores or at college radio stations have reasonably good sound equipment and enjoy recording tapes of this kind. See if you can find someone like that to do your tape. Often they will be happy to do your tape for the cost of the tape itself, or for a very small fee. A 16- or 24-track studio will cost you between $25 and $200 an hour, plus tape costs, ranging from about $45 to $450 or so, depending upon whether you use the digital or analog format. Don't go into the studio thinking you will make a cheap tape.

You should limit the number of tunes on your tape to three or four. In the early stages of your career it is unlikely that anyone will listen closely to much more than that. Don't put very long or esoteric songs on a tape for a club owner. Rather, show the range of what you can do, including perhaps a ballad, an up-tempo song, and a unique arrangement or song of your own. It is always possible to do a live audition and sing other tunes for a club owner who expresses real interest in what you are doing. You will also need some photos of yourself—you might again try your friends or someone studying photography at an art school. This will minimize your costs.

Let's say that you are now beginning to get work in some local clubs, as a solo act or as a member of a group. Should you copyright your songs? The copyright fee for each song is now $20, so that for twenty songs you are looking at $400. It is possible to copyright a group of songs under one name, such as the Jane Smith Songbook. This will cost you $20 and will protect your songs. As each song gets recorded or published in the future you will have to copyright it separately, but this will save you some money for now. To copyright a song you must include a lead sheet with the melody line, lyrics, and chords of your song (see the Appendix of this book for a lead sheet [p. 281] and the address of the Copyright Office [p. 316]). In my opinion at this stage no one is apt to steal your songs. It is possible, but unlikely, that someone will run off with your song and copyright it himself. If someone else has to write your lead sheet for you because you don't read or write music, that person will probably charge you from $10 to $35, depending on his experience. Music school students are a good source for relatively cheap lead sheets. With your demo tape you should include photocopies of any favorable reviews that you have received in local newspapers or magazines.

HOME STUDIOS

The last five years have seen a vast improvement in home semiprofessional studio equipment, with such formats as 4-track cassettes and 8-track A-DAT, or Alesis digital audiotape, recorders available at reasonable prices. With an investment of a few thousand dollars you can now put yourself in a position to make quality demo tapes at reasonable prices. Working with this equipment will also pay off in terms of enabling you to develop studio experience, which will save you time once you get into a larger studio.

VIDEOS

It is now possible to make a video demo at a local college or cable TV channel. Most local cable facilities offer some sort of community access programs.

If you can make a reasonable video demo, it will enhance your ability to get work in clubs and to get a recording contract. The difficulty lies in whether you will get a reasonable amount of editing time in a facility that has quality editing equipment. A poor video demo is probably a worse selling tool than having none at all.

About a dozen locals of the American Federation of Musicians (AFM, the musicians' union) provide free video services for their members. Once again, the value of such demos is going to depend on the quality or availability of good editing equipment.

You can now take your audio or video demo to various club owners or managers together with your photos and any good reviews of your work. Offer to do a live audition. As you start to get local club jobs and build a reputation, you will probably be approached by local booking agents, who will flatter you and make promises of work if you sign an exclusive agreement with them. Avoid signing any exclusive or long-term contracts at this time, if you possibly can. If you are headed for New York or Los Angeles, why tie yourself up with an agent in Dubuque who will continue to collect commissions on your jobs in New York, but who doesn't have the contacts to get you work outside the immediate area? Don't sign with a personal manager in a small town unless you are convinced that she is as ambitious as you or more so. Will she go anywhere it is necessary to promote your long-range career? Do take local jobs from booking agents, and pay them the required commissions on the work they get for you. If necessary, sign a relatively short-term contract, say for six months or a year, to book you exclusively. Don't do this until you have some definite offers of work. The offers should be for reasonable amounts of money in clubs that you are familiar with and should specify the number of shows, wages, and so forth. Take the advice of your booking agent about the union—you may have to join the local in your city of the AFM as you start to work in better clubs or in concerts. Before you join the union go down and talk to the officials about the dues, the initiation fee, any possible work dues, and what will be required of you as a union member.

STRATEGIES FOR LEAVING TOWN

Let's say that you are now ready to leave Iowa and try for the big time in a major recording and talent center. Before you go you may want to take a few precautions. First of all, save up a certain amount of money— enough to sustain you for at least three or four months as you attempt to become established in your new city. You can't reasonably expect to start working right away, and you will need a cushion to sustain you while you get to know the new city, make contacts, and so on. Upgrade your sound equipment. In a larger city you can't get away with inadequate equipment—the competition is too tough. Plan on getting new instruments or amplifiers if you need them—maybe even a whole new sound system. Make another demo tape. This time pay more attention to the sound quality, and be sure to include some original songs. The purpose of this demo will be to interest a major agent or manager in a big city. Have some new photos taken, put together your best reviews, and possibly buy some new stage clothes. Where will you live in the big city? Do you have any contacts in the business there? Perhaps a local agent in your hometown knows an agent, a manager, promoter, or record company employee who can put you in touch with business in your new town. Do you have any other marketable skills? In other words, do you have another way to support yourself while you are knocking on music business doors? Have you ever been a waitress, waiter, temporary office worker, or taxi driver? It may take you some time before you become self-supporting with your music in a new environment.

You have now arrived in the big city. Look for clubs that have open stage nights, songwriters' showcases, etc. Some of these clubs may be famous places, like the Roxy in Los Angeles, and some may be small unknown bars. Try to meet other composers and musicians through music stores, music schools, clubs, and ads in papers like the *Village Voice* in New York. As a member of the Iowa union you will be allowed to accept one-night jobs in union clubs in New York or Los Angeles, but you will be prohibited from accepting steady work unless you transfer your card (which usually takes six months) or unless you get a card in your new local. The larger locals of the musicians' union generally charge higher initiation fees and dues than the unions in smaller towns. There is also usually a residency requirement of some minimum amount of time. Sometimes the union will waive this residency requirement, formally or informally, if you can pay the full initiation fee or if another member of the local vouches that their group must include you in order to continue working. If you have not joined the union before, you almost certainly will need to do so now.

As you start to get jobs in clubs you will meet agents again. Most of them will dress better (or flashier), talk faster, and be harder to figure out than the agents in your hometown. Beware of signing long-term agreements based on verbal promises without actual contracts that offer specific jobs. Find out what acts the agent is currently booking, and if possible talk to the acts about the agent. If possible go through a trial period until you are convinced of what the agent can do for you. It is also a good idea at this point to make sure that the agent has a union franchise. If you are in the union, you may not work for agents unless they have a union franchise, nor can you work with nonunion musicians. If you live in a right-to-work state, none of these restrictions applies. Such states limit the ability of the union to make these sorts of rules. A number of states in the southern United States, such as Texas and Florida, are right-to-work states.

At this point you need a personal manager. While an agent solicits work for clients, a manager is a person with a career plan for his acts. A manager should have relatively few clients, while a good agency may have a number of agents and a huge roster of clients. What clients does the manager currently handle? What do they think of him? If a manager refuses to let you talk with his clients, you should beware of him. What does he have to hide? Even if a group is happy with a manager, you will have to decide whether their judgment suits your own impressions. Maybe he had done a mediocre job, but the group is too trusting, naive, or ignorant to objectively evaluate his performance.

Here are some other questions to ask. What percentage of your earnings does the manager want? Does he handle any acts with current recording contracts? Beware of managers who talk about top acts that they used to handle. Perhaps these clients left and went on to success through someone else's efforts. Agency contracts are usually fairly cut-and-dried, but no one should sign a personal management contract without having an experienced music business attorney check it out. Your lawyer should have other clients in the business and be used to dealing with managers and record companies. A hometown lawyer who is an old friend of the family won't do; after all, you wouldn't go to a heart surgeon to treat an ear infection. Don't use the same lawyer your manager uses to go over your management contract; with all the goodwill in the world he can't reasonably represent both of you. In a year or two you and your manager may end up in court. This could create a conflict of interest for your lawyer, and might leave you without proper legal help.

Be sure that your manager and agency can get along. One of the most important jobs of a manager is to make sure that the artist is getting good agency representation. This includes such matters as the choice of appropriate venues, limitations on traveling between jobs, and more. Your manager and agent should not be the same person, generally speaking, although in the early stages of your career your manager may also help you to find work.

Armed with an agent, a manager, and a lawyer, you are now ready to go after a recording contract. You should consider making a final demo tape and, if possible, a video demo as well. Perhaps your agent or manager can get a reduced rate at a studio, or even owns an interest in one. Your manager should be the key person working on a record deal, but some lawyers and agents are quite knowledgeable and experienced in dealing with record companies. Such an individual may help or spearhead the process. After a record deal is made, attention can be devoted to such matters as where the record will be produced, who the producer should be, what kind of promotional guarantees you can get out of the record company, and whether they will advance you some money to buy new instruments or sound equipment, provide some tour support to help transport you to high-exposure-but-low-money jobs, and finance a quality video. Now you are on your way.

There are some things that I have left out of this beginning portrait of the business. I haven't discussed percentages that go to agents and managers because the material can be found in later sections of the book that deal with these specific roles. Similarly I have omitted any description of music publishing or the nature of the record deal. In general it doesn't help you to make unsolicited tapes and send them to a record company where you don't know a soul. Once in a while this rule is successfully violated. The Doobie Brothers and Boston were signed on the basis of unsolicited tapes, but most of such products are thrown away or listened to very quickly by people who have no deal-making power. These people cannot sign an act to a record company, but they can reject a tape. If they like a tape, it is simply passed on to someone further up the corporate ladder. At each level your tape can experience a rejection, but you cannot get signed until you have crossed over several levels. It is the job of a personal manager to get your tape to someone at the company with deal-making power, and then to negotiate a deal together with your lawyer, the record company lawyer, and a record company executive.

In this description I don't mean to imply that you are doomed to a life sentence in a music industry center. You may well end up recording in such a town, but if you become successful, ultimately you can live wherever you wish. You will always have to maintain some kind of contact with the lifelines of the industry, which run most strongly in Nashville, New York, Los Angeles, and Toronto.

2

Records

RECORDS ARE THE VEHICLE

There are numerous ways for an artist to establish popularity with the general public, including concerts, nightclub performances, and television, but at the present time records are the lifeblood of the music industry. When I say records, I mean compact discs, cassette tapes, or LPs. Without making records, an artist's popularity is generally limited to a specific city or region of the country. This is true for every kind of music, from rap to Country & Western to heavy metal, jazz, or New Age music. Records are the catalyst for music business careers, and without them these careers will not get off the ground. Just as records have been largely replaced by CDs and cassettes, it is possible that in the future all audio products will be replaced by some video storage system, where the consumer can see as well as hear the performer. It would be a mistake to disregard that rare performer, such as Lena Horne or Ben Vereen, who has achieved comparatively little success on records but does very well in nightclub appearances. Nevertheless, at the present time an artist must generally make successful recordings in order to pursue a fruitful career in the music business.

RECORDING CONTRACTS AND HOW TO GET THEM

There are a number of ways to get a recording contract, but these methods usually follow the same general pattern. First of all, it is necessary to make some sort of contact with a record company representative and get her excited about your music. There are producers (in the old days referred to as A&R, or artist and repertoire, people) who look for talent in clubs or concerts. There are even A&R coordinators for whom this activity constitutes a large percentage of their work. Naturally, these visits will occur most frequently in the cities where record company headquarters are located, but some companies will have producers seeking talent in different parts of the country as well. Once in a while one of these people will chance upon a group or an individual performer by accident, but the chances are heavily in favor of their investigating acts that they have heard about through a manager, agent, promoter, lawyer, or another record company employee. Occasionally an employee of one record company who can't sign an act for one reason or another will pass along a tip to a friend at another record company. In Nashville, Los Angeles, and New York there are certain clubs, such as the Bluebird Cafe in Nashville, the Roxy in Los Angeles, or the Bottom Line in New York, where industry people hang out. If you should land a booking at a club like this, you will very likely be seen by some record company reps.

Sony has A&R people stationed in various cities, including Seattle, Dallas, and San Francisco, whose primary job is to investigate talent in these markets. Periodically a particular market, such as Seattle in the early and mid-nineties, develops an industry "buzz" that causes A&R personnel to cultivate agents, managers, and lawyers in the area. When this happens, companies are apt to sign acts from this area in an attempt to capitalize on consumer interest in the music being created there (like the "Seattle sound" in the above example).

As U.S. exports to South and Central America have increased, and as the Spanish-speaking population of the United States has grown, Miami has developed a similar cachet for Spanish-speaking music. A number of major record companies now have staff in Miami who are attempting to gain access to the South American market for U.S. product. For this reason it is reasonable to anticipate a continuing boom in the Miami music market.

Although albums are the key to a long-term career in the music business, most listeners look for the hit single that will establish a new act in the public eye—the song that can serve to introduce the group to the average person through the medium of radio or music video. If you pay any attention to hit records, you probably will have noted several things about their structure. First of all, most hits have some sort of introduction that serves to whet the listener's appetite for what is coming next. It may be an unusual musical figure, an instrument recorded in an unaccustomed way—anything that will serve to involve you with the song. Sometimes this figure will recur in various parts of the song, at times played in an identical way, sometimes arranged in a different manner as the song continues. This device is called a *musical hook*. It is one technique used in writing and arranging popular songs.

Another rule of thumb is that the opening cut of a demo should be your best song on the tape. Generally speaking it should be up-tempo and enthusiastic. Make sure that your first song is one that the listener will want to come back to and hear again. Don't do three consecutive songs in the same key with similar tempos and arrangements. This will expose your group's inability to do more than one thing. On the other hand, the sound of each song should be recognizably that of your group, with whatever strengths you have going represented on each cut. Too much variety may cause a company to feel that your product is not commercial. A record company wants to feel that your group has a coherent and consistent image. If in fact your group has tremendous musical diversity, it is best not to initially share this information with your record company. It will only serve to confuse them!

What songs should be on your tape? In the competitive record business of the 1990s most record companies prefer artists or groups that write their own material. If you or the members of your group don't write songs, your best bet is to seek out someone you know who does write. It may be a fellow musician in another band, an ex–band member who doesn't want to leave home, a sister or brother, or anyone else who happens along. Why do record companies like to see original songs on these demos? There are a number of reasons. If you or your group are going to sustain a career over a long period of time, it will be necessary for you to keep coming up with songs. If no one in the group writes, it means that the band, your manager, and your record producer will spend many hours looking for new songs that are suitable for your style. If you write songs, the material is already there, and probably in a style that is compatible with your group. Not being able to write songs doesn't necessarily destroy your career. Linda Ronstadt, Andy Williams, and Whitney Houston are not songwriters, but they have been very successful as performers. Sometimes a performer who writes only words or music will establish a long-term collaboration with someone who can supply the missing part of the song. Examples are Carole King's collaborations with Gerry Goffin or Neil Sedaka's work with Howard Greenfield or Phil Cody.

Another reason that record companies like the artist to be a songwriter is so they can publish the songs. This represents a considerable source of money if the artist is successful. (See chapters 22 and 25.)

You have now come to a critical point in doing your demo tape. You have decided on three or four tunes, you have a fairly good idea of how they will be arranged—who the lead singer will be, what instruments will be played, etc. How good should the tape be? Should you record on a friend's 4-track Teac tape recorder, on your cassette player, or should you go to a 32- or 48-track studio? At this point sit down and use every bit of common sense you and your fellow musicians have. What kind of sound does your group have? Is it a hard-rock band, or are you a singer-songwriter who has a friend add occasional second guitar parts? Does someone in the group have a really incredible voice, one that sounds great in person but doesn't pick up on your $35 cassette recorder? Remember, you are going to be judged on the basis of your demo. Record people get dozens of tapes that include letters excusing the quality of the tape, explaining how broke the group is, that the arrangement is sketchy, the lead singer had a cold, and so forth. Imagine yourself listening to these tapes. What would you do with them?

Do you know anyone who has good tape equipment? You may know an engineer who works for a radio station, a college student who has access to the college's brand-new recording studio (some colleges have good 24-track studios), or there may be a high-fidelity store that would love to engineer a demo by a group that could go on to fame and fortune. These are all ways of doing your tape for little or no money beyond the cost of the tape itself. Keep in mind that someone is doing you a favor. They may not be professional engineers, and your tape may take a bit longer to do and may not come out sounding like a hit record. Remember your goals. You want the tape to reflect the strongest part of your sound. Be sure to feature your strong points—instrumental solos, lead singer, or backup harmonies. What stands out about the sound of your group that would excite a record company? Be sure these qualities get on the tape. If they're not there, go back and do it again.

Assuming that your group hasn't been together for fourteen years, there are also some weaknesses that you recognize. If possible, try to keep these weaknesses from being obvious on your tape. Maybe in performance your drummer sings backup harmonies, but he can't sing all that well. On the actual recording have someone else cover the part.

Here is a checklist of some things record companies look for in an act:

- Is the group working?

- Do they have professional management?

- Do they write hit songs?

- Can the group sustain a three-to-seven-year career?

- Is the sound recognizable and new, yet marketable?

- Will the public understand the music?

- Are they good performers?

- Are they attractive or magnetic people who can make good videos?

- Do they seem to get along with one another?

- Do they respond well to constructive criticism?

- Have they developed a fan base in their own market?

- Is there anything unusual about the performers' songs, appearance, or character that will make them stand out in a crowded and competitive marketplace?

- Does the group understand how hard they will have to work to sustain a career? Are they serious enough to commit to long and tiring road tours and extensive rehearsals? Do they understand that the initial financial rewards will be small, and that the odds are against any one group "making it"?

3

THE RECORDING PROCESS

I am going to assume that you have gained access to either a 4- or an 8-track recorder through friends, relatives, or whoever. Recording is quite a different procedure from live performance. If you have ever heard a tape of yourself or your group, you know what I mean. Some things that work beautifully in performance, such as drum solos or spontaneous shouts, can sound dull and artificial on a tape or record. Weaknesses that are barely noticeable in live performances, such as rhythm sections that are not quite together or vocal harmonies that are slightly out of tune, can be much more serious defects on tape. In a live performance the audience itself is often making quite a bit of noise, and the performance may have an excitement to it that covers up minor flaws.

Modern tape recorders have a number of available tracks on each piece of tape. Semiprofessional or professional studios have machines that have anything from 4 to 48 tracks. This means that information can be recorded on different sections of the same piece of tape. If the machine has 4 tracks, four separate bits of information (we can call them programs) can be recorded on different sections of the same piece of tape. If your group has piano, bass, and drums, a lead singer, and some background vocals, you might record the bass and drums on one track, the piano on a second, the lead vocal on track 3, and the background vocals on track 4. This can be done simultaneously or one at a time. The studio can be set up in such a way that the piano track does not "leak" onto the bass and drum track. This is done through careful microphone placement or by setting up wooden *baffles*—soundproof barriers that keep the sound of one instrument from leaking into the microphones of other instruments. When these baffles are used, it is often necessary for the musicians to wear headphones so that they can hear one another. This is a strange experience if you are not used to it. Some people wear one headphone on and one off, which enables them to hear the natural sound of their own instrument while the other instruments are coming through the headphones.

If you don't like the sound that is coming out on the tape, it is possible to experiment with changing microphones, moving the microphones to different positions, or adjusting your own instruments or amplifiers to modify the sound. In the case of guitars or electric basses, it is possible to use or discard various types of picks. Drum heads may be tightened or loosened; pedals on a keyboard instrument can be used more or less; an electric bass can be recorded directly through the recording console and/or the amplifier can be miked.

The lead vocal may be recorded at the time the rhythm section plays, but the final lead vocal is usually done again afterward. Having the vocal there keeps the rhythm section more aware of the song with its lyrics and musical dynamics, but rerecording the vocal enables the performer to concentrate on getting a richer performance without distractions.

Some other recurrent studio problems: Make sure that guitar and bass strings are new enough to sound bright, but not so new that a lot of time is wasted in constant tuning; make certain that your drummer has tuned the drum set, that any keyboard instruments are in tune; and if you are using an acoustic piano, have it tuned in the recording studio, just before the session if possible (by all means buy an electronic tuner, which will save hours of tuning).

You have now finished recording your 4- or 8-track demo, and the next step is to mix it down to a stereo tape, just as you would do for a record. Don't listen to your demo for long periods of time at high volume levels or you may wear out your ears and your patience. Make sure that whatever unique qualities your group has are prominent on your final tape. At this stage of the game don't get too involved with subtleties. If the lead vocals are good, the band is coherent, and the lyrics are understandable, that should be good enough to demonstrate what your group can do. If you are having trouble making decisions, rely on the judgment of the person who did the engineering. Don't bring in friends, lovers, relatives, or other nonprofessional experts or you may get involved in time-consuming and meaningless arguments.

You will note that I have assumed that you worked out some way of doing the demo without renting a studio. My feeling is that if this is the first time you've worked in a studio with any seriousness, it is best not to spend your money there. A 4-track studio might rent for $10 to $25 an hour, and an 8-track studio might cost $25 to $50 an hour. In addition, you will be paying tape charges, which can mount up considerably, and you will be charged professional prices for copies of your demo. Very few young bands can afford to go into a studio and burn up thirty or forty hours of studio time at these prices. This is a time for experimentation and learning, not for professionalism and quickness. If you live in a small town and have no way of getting your tape done, perhaps you will be forced to rent a studio. Talk to the engineer ahead of time, explain what you are trying to do, and find out exactly what it is going to cost. In some instances it is possible to make some sort of trade-off for studio time, such as doing free studio work for the owner of the studio. Or perhaps you can sing or play on someone else's session in exchange for the studio time. Some engineers who are also musicians arrange to do free engineering in exchange for free studio time for their own projects. Don't make promises to come back and use the studio for your album, and don't give away publishing rights or a percentage of your group's record rights to the studio. Commitments of that kind could prove impossible for you to fulfill at a later date and could involve you in a lawsuit.

How good should you make your demo? Try to be realistic. A typical album today costs $150,000 to record. You are not in a position to compete with that sort of studio production. What you are trying to do is to convince a record company to invest that kind of money in your career.

Don't be intimidated by insignificant mistakes. Be sure that the main strengths of your group get on the tape and can be heard.

It is possible to make a demo that is a finished product intended for commercial release. This is called a *master*. Think of the amount of time and money this may take. Also think of your comparative inexperience. A record company can find you a producer who has experience in putting records together. String parts, horn parts, additional vocals, or other touches may get added to your record later. Unless you have experience in the studio and unrestricted use of free studio time, it is best not to think about the possibility of doing a finished product at this time.

There are some other problems that may come up in selling a demo as a master. If you have used musicians who have donated their time as a favor to you, you will now have to pay them. The studio that gave you a special deal based on the fact that you were cutting a demo may now ask for additional payment, especially if the demo is now being picked up by a large record company.

There may also be some technical difficulties. Some record companies are not buying anything that wasn't recorded in a multitrack digital format. If your product was recorded on an analog tape recorder, such a company simply will not buy it.

There is also a vast difference between getting a record deal with a demo and selling a finished product. Who is going to be shopping your master, and where are they going to take it?

This brings up another question. How good are the ears of the person who will ultimately judge your tape? Will he be horrified at the wrong bass note on the second verse of your song? The people who work at record companies vary wildly in their musical tastes and backgrounds. Some of them are ex-musicians or arrangers with tremendous ears—the kind of people who can write out the third saxophone part of a big band record after hearing it once. Others are lawyers or ex-salespeople. Some of them have a good feel for music, but wouldn't know a C from an F#. If there is a glaring deficiency in your band, such as a bad drummer, you may want to use a friend or a fellow musician to play on your tape. You may want to add an instrumental part on one song, such as a flute solo, but not have anyone in the group who plays flute. It is always possible to hire someone to play the part for you. Unless you really think the sound is vital for your demo, it is better to leave it off the tape. When you get a record deal your producer will have access to many fine flute players, and you can hear your idea in finished form.

SELLING THE DEMO

Now that you have completed your demo tape, what are you going to do with it? Let's assume that you are for the most part pleased with the fruit of your labors, and you have your cassette copies in hand ready to go. At this point you need to get your product to the record company in order to make a deal.

First off, let's deal with the subject of unsolicited tapes. Most large companies employ people who listen to unsolicited tapes that come in through the mail. Your chances of getting a record deal this way are probably about one in a million. There are always exceptions, of course.

There are some very good reasons why sending an unsolicited tape usually is unsuccessful. The people who listen to these tapes are generally very young people with very little experience. They listen to hundreds of such tapes a week. These "screeners" cannot sign an act to the company. If they do like your tape they will pass it on to the next person up the chain of command. If you're lucky, that person is a record producer and with the approval of the A&R administrator might sign you. The point is that the person who first heard your tape can pass your tape up to the next rung of the ladder or he may reject it. In no case can he make a deal. It is much better to deal with someone higher up in the record company hierarchy in the first place—someone who has decision-making power. The identity of this person will vary from company to company. An executive like Clive Davis, CEO of Arista Records, likes to involve himself with creative decisions. He will go out and sign talent personally. Some other record company presidents don't involve themselves in creative decisions, but might take your tape and give it to a company staff producer to get an opinion.

At this point you probably have already guessed the next part of this dissertation, which is that you need to have someone to sell the tape for you. Managers and lawyers are the two most likely groups that can succeed in getting you a record contract. Quality managers and lawyers know most of the record company bigwigs on a first-name basis. This is one of the reasons why it is so difficult to get a record deal starting out from a city like Boise, Idaho, using a local lawyer and manager. Most local managers or lawyers don't have the time, money, or expertise to negotiate with the high rollers of the record business. The person attempting to sell your tape must know and believe in the product. He should also have some financial stake in your success as an additional incentive.

It is better to have almost anyone try to sell the tape than a member of the group itself. Record companies do not like to talk business with artists. Most artists don't understand the way record companies work, and later they often feel that the company has taken advantage of them (which it may well have done). Unhappy artists don't make good records, and over a period of years record companies have learned that it's better for the manager and the record company executives to hammer out a deal.

Selling a demo requires as much skill, labor, and determination as recording it. The person doing the selling needs to be enthusiastic, mature, patient, and a good salesperson. A personal manager is someone with a career plan for an act and with the contracts and expertise to make it all happen. If you don't know someone with this sort of capability, you may want to put off the selling and use the demo itself to find the right person to handle your career. Don't wait too long because records become dated very quickly. Remember punk rock? Today's new sound is tomorrow's cliché. Above all, don't rely on a personal friend (it usually turns out to be someone your own age) to sell a demo. Not only are the chances minute that someone like this will sell your demo, it may destroy your friendship when he doesn't succeed.

If you are totally unsuccessful in finding a record company that expresses any interest in your product, it is always possible to manufacture your own product and to put it out in your local market. If you can get it played on local radio—a big if—and if you can get record stores to carry it, then you have a chance to break the product in your own market without the assistance of a record label. If you are successful in this strategy, there is an excellent chance that one of the local record company promotion or sales people will report your success, and you may end up with a major record deal. Hootie & The Blowfish started out as independent artists in South Carolina. They moved from local fame on their own label to multiplatinum success on Atlantic Records.

It is sometimes possible to get in touch with record companies through people who work at a local branch of a record company or at an independent distributor. Major companies have such sales and promotion branches in most major cities. The problem in having such a person help you is that he may be great at selling or promoting records, but the home office may not have any particular respect for his opinions of talent. If the local person really has a good relationship with a record producer who works for the company, that might work in your favor. Sometimes people in the record business have a tendency to exaggerate, and your idea of friendship might not be the casual relationship that they in fact have with the producer. Everyone in the music business seems to be on a first-name basis with everyone else, but this does not necessarily mean that they are really close to one another.

Be sure to include some photos and any favorable reviews with your demo, much as you did in selling the group long ago to local club owners. If you can write out music, include lead sheets with the melody line, words, and chords written out. Since so few pop musicians are musically literate, this itself may impress the person examining the tape. If you can't write out the music, at least include typed copies of the lyrics. Be sure that these lyric sheets or lead sheets are neat and readable. Include some leader (blank tape) between the songs so that whoever is listening to the tape can go back and find each song without wasting any time. Write the names and author or authors of each tune on the tape box so that the listener knows which songs are originals. You might also type out a brief history of the group. Also use a copyright notice (© John Doe, 1997).

Remember to be patient. Record people often put off appointments or inquiries from people they don't know, or even people they do know, when things get busy. When I worked as a record producer at ABC, I once listened to a tape of a group from West Virginia. The seventeen-year-old boy who came to see me was one of the members of the group. A producer at RCA had made him wait eight hours before he would listen to the tape, even though the poor fellow had received an appointment after writing to this particular producer.

The person selling your demo is representing you and your group.

He should make a good first impression and be able to answer any questions that the company may have about the group—where it has worked, the ages of the members, career plans, education, or anything else the record company wants to know. Often when a good manager doesn't know the answers to questions like these, he will make up a convincing story.

4

THE RECORD INDUSTRY:
A BRIEF HISTORY

*T*he first phonographs date back to the nineteenth century. Thomas Edison in the United States and Charles Cros in France both came up with similar ideas independent of each other in 1877. In 1893 a phonograph cost $193, a considerable sum at that time. In the early days, records had music on only one side; the other side was blank. In 1904 a German company called Odeon produced the first double-sided records. The first big record star was Enrico Caruso, the opera singer. According to Roland Gelatt,* Caruso made over $2 million in royalties, and his estate collected about as much after his death. Some Caruso recordings are still available today. The first jazz recordings were by the Original Dixieland Jazz Band, a white group that recorded in 1917. Freddie Keppard, a

---

* Much of the material in this chapter was extracted from an excellent book, *The Fabulous Phonograph: 1877 to 1977*, by Roland Gelatt.

black New Orleans trumpeter, had been offered the chance to record, but he refused, feeling that other musicians would steal his ideas.

The early recordings did not use microphones. Edison had a solid brass horn, which was 135 feet long and tapered to 1 inch wide where the sound was actually being recorded. The records were wax cylinders, and the horn was attached to them. If a mistake was made, the process would start over again. Victor introduced electrical recording with microphones in 1925. By 1931 Victor had come up with the idea of long-playing records, but none were produced until after World War II.

Sales of records moved right along and got as high as 987,000 records in 1927. Shortly thereafter the Depression struck, and sales plummeted to 40,000 in 1932. Gradually the country recovered, and record sales started to go up again. In 1948 Columbia Records introduced the 33⅓ rpm long-playing record. Victor tried to compete with the 45 rpm disc, resulting in several years of costly competition until a compromise was reached, and singles were issued on 45 with albums on 33⅓.

Three other innovations changed the character of the record business. The 10-inch LP was eliminated in favor of the 12-inch record, and stereo, or 2-channel, sound was introduced. Many small companies were badly hurt because they were left with overstocks of 10-inch and monaural records. By 1958 stereo had taken over 69 percent of the business. In the late sixties Columbia tried to introduce quadraphonic sound but met with consumer resistance. Many people do not have a room suitable for 4-channel sound, or don't wish to buy four speakers and an additional amplifier. Whenever I think of quad, I think of my friend Ron Lockhart, who used to be a producer for the Columbia Record Club. I remember him sitting in his cubiclelike windowless office with the walls covered by four speakers, a room smaller than the average kitchen. Possibly if the CBS people had seen Ron's office they wouldn't have pursued quad sound.

The most fundamental change of all in the business was the switch to tape recorders, which were brought back from Germany after World War II. The first tape recorders used only one track, but in the early days of rock 'n' roll someone discovered a process called overdubbing. In overdubbing, after you finish recording, you run two tape recorders at one time, and besides recording the information on the first recorder onto the second machine, you can also add whatever additional sounds you wish at the same time. This was revolutionary for its time, but as you went from one tape recorder to the next, you went to what is called another generation of sound, with a resulting loss of fidelity. This didn't necessarily bother some rock producers, notably Phil Spector, because they were seeking new sound techniques to play with, and an overall thickness of texture in the sound was their goal, not clarity as such.

The next step was the introduction of 2-track tape recorders, quickly followed by 3- and then 4-track machines by the early sixties. With these multitrack machines, by recording in the sync mode, which is marked on the machine, the new information could be put onto other tracks of the same tape without any loss of fidelity in adding generations, as was necessary in overdubbing. This is the way modern recording is done. Although the process is called sel synchronization, many people still refer to it as overdubbing.

Tracks soon jumped from 4 to 8, briefly to 12, and then came the major leap to 16 tracks in the middle sixties. With 16 tracks the technology that we know today was born. Not only could most instruments have their own tracks, but some instruments, such as the piano, were recorded on 2 tracks initially, with the high notes of the piano on one track and the low notes on another track. The drum set was separated on as many as 5 or 6 tacks; each track was devoted to a different part of the drum set. All of this also required a necessary refining of microphone techniques so that leakage could be avoided from one track to another. In the middle and late sixties noise-reduction systems came into use to remove tape hiss. The first system that became popular was the Dolby system. Then came DBX, and today Telefunken and others are also in use. These systems work in somewhat different ways, and different engineers and producers prefer one or another. Many studios have only one of the systems because each one of them represents a considerable expense, since the noise reduction must be added to each track separately. When you use one of the systems on a record, if you mix the record in another city you must use a studio that has the same noise-reduction equipment.

Today 24-track studios are common, and 32- and 48-tracks are also being manufactured. At times two 24-track machines are linked together. The linkage uses up 2 tracks, thereby keeping 46 available tracks. I suppose the technology will continue until someone records a symphony with 105 tracks, one for each instrument.

It is a wonderful thing to have so many tracks to experiment with, but it has a tendency to make a producer put off decisions about the final product until the very end of the process. In the final mix the producer, together with an engineer, and sometimes the artist, must mix down the 24 tracks to a stereo tape. Generally speaking, the original tape is recorded flat—that is, no echo or special effects are added on the original tape—but at this point in the process it is possible to add echo, and to add or subtract the high, medium, and low frequencies on the top. This is called equalization, or EQ. Many producers spend hours and hours equalizing the various tracks, especially if there is some sound that they don't like on the original tracks.

Other special effects are available through the use of a graphic equalizer, limiters, tape-delay devices, and the Aphex aural exciter. It isn't that you can't make good records without these devices, but not having the technology puts you at a competitive disadvantage.

In the mid-1980s digital tape recorders were introduced. The proponents of digital recording claim that it produces a cleaner sound with more musical range at the top and bottom than the "old-fashioned" analog tape. Some engineers and producers still prefer analog tape, arguing that it has a warmer and gutsier sound.

By the early nineties digital recording in the A-DAT format was readily available.

Once your tape is completed and approved by the record company, it is taken or sent to a mastering studio. At this point it is still possible to influence the sound of the tape, but the decisions are on a different level. Again, you can add or subtract from the high, middle, and low ends of the sound spectrum. However, at this point your information is on 2 tracks only. If you don't like the sound of the bass and you boost the bass frequently, everything else on that channel (left or right) will also have its bass frequencies boosted. It is therefore fairly radical surgery to make this kind of decision at this time. It is advisable to have someone at the mastering session who worked on the record, preferably a producer or engineer. The mastering engineer usually does nothing but master records for eight or more hours a day and will not be familiar with your record. If you have one cut on your record that is too loud, for example, the engineer may simply set all the volume levels low. Consequently, your record will sound dull and lifeless, especially on the radio.

What actually goes on in the mastering is that the engineer is cutting your tape onto a record. This lacquer then gets covered with silver nitrate. From this "mother" record is made a stamper, and the stamper is mounted onto a hydraulic press that turns hot plastic into records. Dozens of these presses work at one time, and each stamper is good for about 500 records, after which another stamper must be made from the mother. By the midnineties many recording studios had the ability to cut CD reference disks. These can be sent directly to the pressing plant, thereby eliminating the use of a separate mastering studio.

Today LPs have been largely replaced by cassette tapes and CDs. Although the manufacturing process is different in each case, there still needs to be a finished 2-track master tape in order to manufacture the tapes or CDs. DATs were introduced to a minor extent in the late 1980s. The large record companies are terribly afraid of the DAT format, because they fear that ultimately the consumer will be able to make a perfect copy of a compact disc. Although there is little doubt that many consumers copy records onto tapes for use in their car stereos or on Walkman recorders, there is no conclusive evidence as to how many consumers pirate albums to tapes for friends or relatives. Since many of the major record companies have invested millions in new CD plants, they have a justifiable concern about what the DAT format will do to the CD.

Other technological experiments include running tape recorders at double speed (30 ips) without noise reduction and recording direct to disc, without the use of tape. Who knows what the formats of the future will be.

5

RECORD COMPANIES

$\mathcal{T}$here is a wide variety of record companies in North America. Some of them are small specialty labels that may press as few as 500 copies of a record at a time, but there are six giant, multinational record companies that record virtually all styles of music and have worldwide distribution. They are BMG, the German-owned Bertelsmann Music Group, which bought RCA; CBS-Sony; EMI, owner of Capitol Records; MCA, 80 percent Canadian- and 20 percent Japanese-owned; Polygram, 80 percent Dutch- and 20 percent German-owned; and the lone American company, the WEA group, which includes Warner Brothers, Elektra, Atlantic, and Asylum Records. Even in these companies there may be specific areas of concentration; for example, WEA consigns its classical music to the small Nonesuch label, which is itself a subsidiary of Elektra.

Many of the giant labels bought up medium-size operations during the 1980s and have continued to do so in the '90s. For example, Polygram owns Island and A&M. When the multinationals buy labels, they may fold them into the larger operations, or, as in the case of Island, the bought company may continue to operate in much the same way as it did when it was independent, only with better financial muscle. In the 1960s and '70s medium-size labels generally distributed their product through independent record distributors, but today the multinationals' distribution wings control 80 to 90 percent of the American market, though the figure varies from year to year. Occasionally the multinationals will buy a company, as Warner Brothers did with Tommy Boy, and allow the label to continue to use independent distributors. The thinking here is that the larger label may not understand the style of music that the smaller label produces, and also the smaller label may have effective ways of marketing to alternative markets that the larger companies may not comprehend.

Why do larger labels pay huge sums to acquire these labels rather than continue to compete with them? Large labels tend to operate by committee and often are a bit behind the actual music changes taking place "on the street." Often labels acquire other companies or establish subsidiaries in order to deal with specialized markets and to be able to bring seemingly different products to radio stations. To avoid any semblance of impropriety, a radio station probably will not want to play fifteen new Polygram releases, but if the labels say Island, or its subsidiaries, Mango or Quango, or A&M, this concern will be averted. Often different promotion personnel will bring these various albums to the station, even though technically the ownership may be the same.

An independent label may wish to sell its company to a major label for two reasons: (1) The label wants to obtain some cash. Even successful companies often have to reinvest their money in the business, so that the owners are sitting on tremendous assets without having much cash. (2) The smaller label may want to acquire better financing in order to enter the bidding race for acquiring major-league talent that is leaving their current label and seeking new deals.

When these deals are made, the old management is usually retained, and the larger company always uses the rhetoric that the company will still have the same image and policies that it had when it was an independent. Despite these assurances, it is not unusual for the old management to leave after a few years. Often they find it difficult to work with a more corporate and less flexible company. In the case of Polygram's acquisition of A&M and Island, Chris Blackwell remains as

CEO of Island, but Herb Alpert and Jerry Moss no longer work at A&M.

The smallest record companies rely on independent record distributors to handle their distribution and sales. Obviously their promotional efforts cannot compete with the giants of the industry. Independent record distributors now deal primarily with specialized product—jazz, classical, ethnic music, some rap, Latin, folk, and New Age product.

Some specialty labels use what are called P&D (production and distribution) deals, where a major label presses the CDs and distributes the product for the smaller label in exchange for a percentage of the gross income. There are also "boutique" labels, wherein a company sets up a label for a superstar or a producer, and covers or shares in the expenses and also participates in the products. Madonna's Maverick label has such a deal with WEA, and in 1995–96 the label experienced tremendous success, especially with Grammy-winning artist Alanis Morissette.

The following breakdown expresses the current method of record distribution.

MULTINATIONALS	MEDIUM-SIZE INDEPENDENT COMPANIES	SMALL SPECIALTY LABELS
(CBS-Sony, WEA-Time and their subsidiaries.)	Rounder, Rykodisc	Shanachie
Distribute own product and product of medium-size and sometimes smaller companies	Self-distributed, or use independent distributors	Distributed by independent record distributors in various cities.

The largest record companies have a fairly complex operating structure. Companies like WEA or CBS have someone at the top of the structure who sits on the board of directors of the parent company (CBS-Sony or Warner Communications Time-Life). This executive is responsible for the overall supervision of the record division of the company. The president of a major company may have a creative background, coming from work as an artist, musician, songwriter, arranger, composer, or performer. More often he has a business-administrative background, coming out of sales, promotion, law, or accounting. The way in which presidents of large record companies operate will vary as widely as do their backgrounds. Clive Davis, the CEO of Arista Records, likes to become involved with the artists and their records. He advises the artists on directions, tries to match them with appropriate producers, signs artists after actually seeing them perform or auditioning them, and likes to participate in production decisions. The heads of RCA Records have generally tended to be somewhat anonymous—and to stay out of the creative areas.

It is important to know what kind of company you are recording for because it may have a strong influence on your career. It is a cliché in the business that RCA has in the past been run by committees and that it often took an endless amount of time to get a decision from them on a specific artist. On the other hand, RCA has also demonstrated more patience with the development of an artist's career than many of the other companies have. John Denver, for example, didn't really start to become popular until his fourth or fifth solo LP for RCA. Many companies would have given up on him after his first or perhaps second record.

Below the president of a record company are positioned the various departments of the company. Many of the department heads have titles such as vice president of something or other—A&R, marketing, etc. The titles in themselves don't necessarily have any significance and may or may not reflect the importance of a particular job. On page 44 is a chart that will convey some idea of how a major record company might be organized.

In addition to the people shown on the chart, there may be others working at subsidiary labels, such as Epic in the case of Columbia. Some of the same people, such as lawyers, might do work for both companies, but the subsidiary may have its own creative and marketing staff, at least to some extent. The reason behind subsidiary labels is to get different creative input and to develop a different company image. It also enables the company to get more product played on the radio, because no station is going to play an endless amount of product from the same company, for fear that the FCC will accuse it of favoritism.

Columbia and RCA have record clubs with a separate staff. Production work at a record club is largely a matter of thinking up intelligent reissue projects, and deals must be made with various companies to lease

RECORD COMPANY STRUCTURE

RECORD DIVISION SUPERVISOR ON BOARD OF DIRECTORS OF PARENT COMPANY
PRESIDENT OF RECORD COMPANY

A&R (ARTIST AND REPERTOIRE)	MARKETING DIVISION	CREATIVE SERVICES	BUSINESS STAFF	PUBLISHING
Chief	Sales and Promotion each may have a national director	May have national director	Legal, accounting dept., cost analysts, personnel specializing in foreign rights	Head of company
Staff and A&R coordinator	Staff	Staff of various sizes in advertising, publicity, graphics–album covers, or free-lance people may be hired for specific projects	Secretarial staff	Staff
Independent producers hired for specific projects	May be broken down into specific kinds of music (national director of promotion for soul-disco music, etc.)			Professional managers, staff writers
Secretarial staff includes executive secretaries and people who have specific functions, such as dealing with unions, studios, publishing licenses, etc.	May be a national director for singles promotion	Product manager—follows an album project from its inception to its completion		If there is a print division, it includes extensive personnel, such as staff arrangers, a sales division, and an art staff
	Product managers and artist-relations staff	Secretarial staff		Secretarial staff
	Secretarial staff			

Miscellaneous

May include people working on special projects, premium records, or whatever. Record clubs would be a separate division. Subsidiary labels would have their own creative staffs and smaller business and marketing staffs.

their material. A number of the large record companies used to own their own recording studios, but for the most part they found it easier to deal with independent studios and not have to be concerned with contracts with their engineers or studio overhead. The multinationals own their own manufacturing facilities and also do custom work for the smaller record companies.

Currently several major companies are involved in direct mail selling and they are beginning to use the Internet to publicize and promote records. By the twenty-first century records will probably be available by down-loading information from your cable TV directly onto your personal computer.

The major record companies all have publishing divisions. Most of these operations are there simply to pick up the publishing of some of the artists who record for the company, although a few of them, like Warner Brothers Music, are large operations in their own right. Warner Brothers Music also has a print division that publishes sheet music and folios of their own and other artists. They also print music for high school and college bands and choral groups, and instruction materials for various instruments.

Occasionally a record company will have a talent management division to handle its own artists. Motown had such a corporate wing at one time. None of the giant companies do this.

Some companies have people in the A&R department who do not produce records but who are involved in the process of talent acquisition. Epic Records has no producers in its West Coast office, but the coordinator's job is to help choose independent producers as well as to find talent. Companies go back and forth on the question of staff versus independent producers. Independents tend to be "closer to the street" in terms of finding new groups or sounds, but they don't like fulfilling the corporate functions of A&R reps and don't have much loyalty to any one company, since they are hired guns.

Warner Brothers has typically had A&R people who are also hot producers, like Russ Titelman, who produces Stevie Winwood, and veteran producer Ted Templeman.

At the bottom of the corporate hierarchy, working in a cubbyhole in the A&R department, is the office person who listens to unsolicited tapes that are received in the mail.

CLASSICAL RECORDS

The merchandising of classical music is a very different matter from the selling of a pop record. The market tends to be concentrated in an older age group, and the audience is quite particular about the sound quality of records. Liner notes often contain detailed information about the music and a particular performance. In classical music there are certain staples of the repertoire, such as Beethoven's Fifth Symphony, that are recorded over and over again, so the quality of a particular performance is important to the buyer. Compared to popular music or jazz, a very small amount of new repertoire is recorded.

Favorable reviews by important critics are an important means of influencing a record company to place a new artist under contract. Other factors are well-qualified management and any victories in international competitions. Many record producers in classical music are themselves trained musicians, knowledgeable about repertoire and performance.

Certain orchestras, performers, and conductors, such as the Philadelphia Orchestra, Itzhak Perlman, and Yo Yo Ma, to give an example of each, have the same magical appeal to the classical music buff as do pop stars in their field. In recent years some companies have begun to market classical music in a style similar to the way they sell pop music. Columbia has taken this approach with its composers' greatest hits albums and by featuring eye-catching album covers.

Large-scale orchestral works and operas are often recorded in Europe because the union scales for musicians are one-third to two-thirds less than in the United States, depending on the country where the record is produced. Because classical music constitutes a very small share of the record market in the United States,* many companies don't bother with it at all, or they simply distribute records produced abroad. On the other hand, some small record companies, such as CRI, produce recordings of serious contemporary works for a small, select audience.

SPECIALTY RECORDS

Specialty record companies exist in every conceivable style of music, ranging from polka bands to free jazz. These companies must have a

---

* The share usually varies from 3 to 5 percent of the market.

very accurate concept of their audience because when a record is pressed in small quantities there is virtually no promotion budget available. Often the company will have just one or two people working there, including the owner, so it is possible to go right to the top level of management for decisions.

Some specialty companies sell records by mail, advertising in appropriate magazines. The artists may also sell the records whenever they perform. Some companies operate regionally, attempting to concentrate their sales in a specific area. This is particularly true of foreign language music. The interest in Cajun music, for example, is clearly centered in Louisiana.

Many specialty companies offer little or no advance money to the artist and they may operate outside the rules of the AFM or AFTRA. Production costs of these records are usually kept very low, especially if the company owns its own studio or uses portable recording equipment.

The audience for specialty music is very particular, and innovative sounds may result in controversy. This may reduce or increase record sales, depending on the ultimate judge, the consumer. The introduction of contemporary songs and electric instruments into bluegrass music, creating a style called "newgrass," has created this kind of furor.

The owners of these small companies often have a true love for the music and do not really expect to make much money from their records. There are always exceptions, of course. Some of these record people are ambitious and greedy, and some may make money without seeking to do so.

As the A-DAT recording format has become popular, many artists are self-producing CDs and cassettes, because the cost of recording tape and the availability of professional home gear is so much lower than it was in the 1980s. Since the artist commands the full retail selling price, some artists have actually been able to make a considerable amount of money by becoming their own record company.

For example, an artist who sells 2,000 CDs at $15 receives $30,000. For a relatively simple recording project, say one budgeted at $10,000, this represents a handsome profit. Should the artist wish to place her albums in stores, the picture becomes more complicated, because the store owner must receive his share of the profit and the artist must become a bill collector.

Artists have also developed home pages on the Internet, and have promoted their records through this medium to the growing number of "surfers."

Since the largest record companies consider an album sale of 250,000 barely adequate, we can anticipate that more artists will seek to sell and manufacture their own product. Without the pressures of selling multi-platinum, the artist is also free to control the music, artwork, or liner notes. For more information on manufacturing your own records, see Diane Sward Rapaport's excellent book, *How to Make and Sell Your Own Record*, 5th edition.

6

THE RECORD PRODUCER

*I*n the forties and early fifties record producers were called A&R men (they were virtually all males) and they were the kingpins of the industry. They found the artists, usually through the efforts of personal managers and agents, and they also found the songs for the artists to record. In those days artists did not generally write their own songs. The songs were brought in by music publishers, who constantly solicited record producers with future "hits." The songs were brought in on records that became known as *demos*. These demos are a peculiar part of the business because up until recent years the unions did not consider demos legal, yet hundreds of them were recorded by union musicians in New York. There were and are certain studios that specialize in this sort of recording and will even hire the musicians for their clients. Generally, in the making of a demo, a small orchestra was used, most often a rhythm section with the piano or guitar playing lead lines or fills. Occasionally, a publisher might add strings or background voices to help convince the producer and his artist that this particular song was especially suitable for the artist. Usually the singer on the demo was told to imitate the style of the artist for whom the demo was intended, without doing too precise a copy. Many singers who record commercials are capable of doing an exact imitation of a current artist, should the client desire, and some of these people developed these skills while making demos. Similarly, quite a few good studio musicians broke into the recording field by playing on demos. It was a good way to break in because, although the session was usually completed in an hour, there was relatively little pressure, and the session involved a combination of reading and improvisation. Both of these abilities are important in studio work, as you will see.

The publisher would make a lead sheet of the song, with the melody line, lyrics, and chords written out. This would then be submitted, usually in person, to the A&R man. Often the ceremony would include a free lunch at a good restaurant, which is a perfectly legal business device that is practiced in most businesses, when a salesperson entertains a prospective customer.

A key part of the producer's job, in that era, was to be able to recognize a hit song. A producer might listen to hundreds of songs to find that hit single and to fill up the resulting album. Then the producer would hire an arranger or on occasion write the musical arrangement himself. Before the actual arrangement was written the arranger would find the correct key for the artist and, in writing the arrangement, would usually attempt to include some sort of musical catchphrase or gimmick that would be repeated several times in the song. This is called a *hook*. These arrangers were often well-trained musicians with music careers and even careers as soloists or bandleaders behind them. Some arrangers, especially the more jazz-oriented ones, were essentially self-taught but were equally capable.

The producer would then take the artist and the arrangement into the studio. Since recording was done on one or two tracks at that time, the singer and the band recorded at the same time. The producer or the arranger generally used a contractor to hire the musicians. When I talk about studio work you will see how that works. The arrangement was usually fairly preset, and most of the music was written out with an occasionally improvised solo. If background singers were used, still another contractor hired them.

Since there was no multitrack recording at the time, special electronic effects were usually minimal and done at the time of recording rather than in the mix. All that remained by the end of the session was a bit of editing, and the record was ready to go.

The ultimate A&R man at that time was probably Mitch Miller. He was an excellent oboe player before he started his career as a producer. As a producer at Columbia in the early fifties he recorded such artists as Doris Day, Frankie Laine, Johnnie Ray, and Jo Stafford. The popular songs of the day were generally saccharine love songs directed at teenagers. Love was presented in dull and romanticized terms and had little to do with life. The titles alone—"Cry," "Be My Love," "Secret Love," and others of that ilk—convey the subject matter. Most of these songs were written by professional songwriters, who sat in their little offices in the Brill Building at 1619 Broadway and turned out dozens of slushy love songs, together with an occasional novelty tune. In the period of 1950–56 Miller-produced records sold more than 80 million copies, according to sociologist R. Serge Denisoff, writing in his survey of the industry entitled *Solid Gold; The Popular Record Industry*.

At the peak of Mitch Miller's career a new, comparatively crude, and energetic music called rock 'n' roll appeared. The early rock 'n' roll records were mostly "cover" records. These were recordings by white artists of black music of the day, prettified and simplified for the white teenager. The first big hit was Bill Haley's "Shake, Rattle and Roll," a sort of countrified rock version of the original rhythm and blues hit by Joe Turner.* In the next few years a number of white artists, such as Pat Boone and Georgia Gibbs, had hit after hit in this fashion, covering songs that were popular in the rhythm and blues field.

There were several reasons why it was the cover records that became national hits rather than the original versions of the songs. Generally the average white teenager had some trouble understanding the lyrics in the original records, as did the average white disc jockey. Many of the large radio stations did not want to play records by black artists, and in some cases the small record labels that recorded the original records lacked good national distribution and promotion. When the cover

---

* In the twenties and thirties black music was called race music; later it was referred to as rhythm and blues; today it is called soul.

records were put out by the major labels, the small companies were shut out of the major markets.

Bill Haley and the Comets was an important group for another reason as well. It was a self-contained band that could make its own recordings and didn't require the services of a musical arranger to add strings or horns. It didn't need the production services of a sophisticated musician like Mitch Miller. As a self-contained group the Comets foreshadowed the revolution that came full force to the industry with the rise of the Beatles.

Most of the Mitch Miller–era producers or arrangers were older, trained musicians. These people did not like or understand rock 'n' roll and considered it an unpleasant form of musical primitivism. It is amusing to look back on comments that people like Miller, who was producing some of the corniest drivel ever recorded, made about rock 'n' roll. The traditional producers were also beginning to experience the generation gap. They were too old for the kids who were now buying the records. They didn't understand the dances, the black influences on the music, the rebellious nature of the whole experience, or much else about it.

The independent record producers who came to the fore in the middle and late fifties were a different breed of cat from the staff producers for the big companies. Foremost among them were Jerry Leiber and Mike Stoller, who worked as a team, and Phil Spector. These men were songwriters themselves, and they spent a great deal of time rehearsing groups that did not read music before taking the groups into the studio. Spector worked on many of the musical arrangements in the studio itself instead of relying on written music. Besides being younger than the staff producers for the big companies, these independents had a great deal of sympathy for black music, particularly blues and gospel music. If the earlier producers had any interest in black music at all, that interest was usually limited to jazz.

As independent producers developed, a new mode of business operation appeared with them. Sometimes the independents were hired by record companies to produce acts that were in their artist roster but that none of the staff producers felt capable of producing. Soon the independents started to sign acts to contracts, produce the records, and then sell the records to the record companies. In many instances the producers were also songwriters, and they kept control of the music publishing rights when they signed their deals with the record companies. In some cases the producers managed or shared in the personal management of the acts as well. The independent producer replaced the staff A&R person as the glamour boy of the business, and Phil Spector even started his own record company. Spector was a flamboyant example of a style of production that is still practiced today. His productions showcased his production abilities as much as or more than the talent of the artists.

Leiber and Stoller worked in a different way with the studio. They wrote and rehearsed their songs with groups like the Drifters or the Coasters, and then they relied on written arrangements by such arrangers as Gary Sherman for the instrumental tracks. It is also important to mention the work of Ahmet Ertegun, one of the founders of Atlantic Records. Although he was not a musician, he was a great fan of black music. Ahmet wrote songs based on black colloquialisms and went into the studio and cut hit records. Most of the Atlantic Records of the fifties and early sixties were too black-oriented to be hits in the white market, but later Jerry Wexler, another brilliant nonmusician producer, was able to come up with all-market hits by black artists, especially Aretha Franklin.

The rise of the independent producer highlighted a basic change in the music business, which is still having its effects at the present time. The producer now fulfills a great variety of functions, whether working on staff or independently. The producer may find the artist through a network of personal contacts that includes personal managers, booking agents, lawyers, friends, concert promoters, musicians, or accidental contacts. When I worked as a staff producer for ABC-Command-Probe Records I found acts through a music store owner in Denver, a local booking agent in Washington, D.C., and one walked in off the street by chance. Other artists were assigned by the president of the company. In looking for talent, I made several trips to such towns as Albany, Boston, Washington, D.C., and Philadelphia, and normally saw some acts perform in clubs in New York, which was the company's headquarters.

Once the producer finds an act, she goes to the head of the A&R department, who is often not a record producer but is primarily an administrator, and discusses the situation. What sort of deal is necessary, is the act working, do they have a manager, should the deal include an album or just be for a single release, where can the group promote the record effectively? All of these are questions that the administrator might ask, and if the producer and her boss agree, the legal department (if it is a large company) will prepare a contract. The contractual details will be discussed later, but assuming the contract is signed, rehearsal begins and the producer may prepare a budget, which she and her boss will discuss. If the group is a local group, rehearsal is no problem; the producer will attend some rehearsals, help pick tunes, make suggestions about the musical arrangements, and develop rapport with the group. If the group is from a distant city, the producer will probably want to hear tapes of the songs they expect to record. If possible the producer will want to meet with the group. This can be arranged by the producer's going to visit the group or by the group arriving for the sessions several days early and meeting with the producer. It is advantageous for everyone to get to know one another before the sessions start and to work on some of the musical arrangements together.

The producer will usually choose what studio the group will be working in and also the particular engineer who will do the recording. Some record companies like to use their own studios, for obvious economic reasons and also for reasons of convenience. It is most important that the producer and engineer complement each other's abilities because they will be working very closely on this project. Some engineers hate specific kinds of music, and this can create unpleasantness in the studio. If a producer is in a strong bargaining position at a particular record company, she will insist on working with an engineer with whom she is compatible.

Some producers, such as Jimmy Jam and Terry Lewis in Minneapolis, are also excellent songwriters, and they may actually write a song specifically for the group to record. They also may make suggestions to an artist about recording songs by other songwriters to broaden the appeal of an album. Sometimes these suggestions are motivated by a producer owning part or all of the publishing rights to a song, but a good producer should be motivated primarily by making the best possible album for your group.

There is no one style of producing records, and producers usually come from one of three different kinds of backgrounds. Some are trained or untrained musicians or arrangers who may be particularly skilled at putting together musical sounds. Such a producer is especially valuable when working with a young musical group that really hasn't quite settled on its musical directions yet. Richard Perry and Bob James are contemporary producers who possess this sort of background. Generally this kind of producer will concentrate on the music and let the engineer take care of the equipment. This will vary according to how much background the musician-producer has in engineering, and how comfortable she is with the engineer. Other producers are basically engineers, with little or no formal musical background. Bones Howe and Bill Szymsyck are examples of this kind of producer. An engineer-producer is perfect for a group like the Eagles, which Bill in fact produced. An experienced group has a musical groove that is well worked out, and they don't need much advice about musical arrangements. In such a case the engineer-producer concentrates on getting exactly the right sound out of the equipment. Sometimes the producer will also do the engineering. Or she may simply tell the engineer exactly what to do. The third kind of producer is not formally trained in either music or engineering but has a great feel for what constitutes a good record, together with a good natural ear. Jerry Wexler is a prime example of this style of producer. A few producers have both a music and an engineering background, as does Phil Ramone. This is probably the ideal situation, in terms of being able to translate musical conceptions into actual engineering practice.

It is now possible to hook up recording studios through telephone lines, so that a recording session can actually take place simultaneously in two cities. The A-DAT format is so cheap that sessions are sometimes remixed on an A DAT, and the tape is shipped to another city where a particular musician or singer adds his part and then sends it back.

TECHNO POP AND REGIONAL MUSIC SCENES

In the mid- and late eighties Jimmy Jam and Terry Lewis emerged as two of the hottest record producers around. Winners of the 1987 Grammy award for Producers of the Year, they work together in Minneapolis. Using drum machines and synthesizers, and their tremendous ability to find the right groove, these two top producers emerged out of nowhere. Their success highlights the dispersal of the music scene into a larger number of secondary recording centers. Austin, Texas, and Seattle in particular have emerged as recording hotbeds alongside Minneapolis. I recently completed a book just on regional music markets called *How to Make a Living in Your Local Music Market*. Sony Records employs regional A&R personnel in San Francisco, Seattle, and Dallas.

OTHER PRODUCTION SKILLS

The skills required to successfully produce jazz and classical music recordings are somewhat different from those of the pop producer. A classical music producer needs to be able to follow a musical score in order to guide the engineer in making difficult tape splices and to be able to make decisions as to which parts are important in complex orchestral writing. Similarly, a good jazz engineer will have to be able to balance a horn or saxophone section. Often sections of instruments are recorded on a single track. Does the second saxophone have the melody in a specific part of the piece, is one violin playing a countermelody while the others all play the same part? In recording jazz and classical music there is relatively little overdubbing, and the emphasis has to be on getting the correct instrumental balances and then going after a quality performance rather than putting the parts in later. Solo classical pieces are a different matter and may result in a series of splices in order to get a difficult performance to come out well.

The qualities of a record producer can be summarized as follows:

Business Skills. Ability to pick hits, coordinate sessions, do company paperwork, make good deals for oneself (if an independent) or for a record company (if on staff). Attention to detail—booking time, hiring musicians, arrangers, engineers, etc. Working within a budget.

Musical Skills. Having the ability to hear what is in tune or out of tune. Writing charts of supervising "head" arrangements in the studio. Combining sounds in an unusual and pleasing way.

Psychological Skills. Knowing how to handle talent. Judgment—knowing when to take a break, quit, or go on. Knowing how to get the best performance out of the artist and other singers or musicians. Ability to work long hours under stress. Projecting energy and enthusiasm, whatever one's true feelings.

Technical Skills. Knowledge of multitrack recording and the recording console to get maximum desirable effects. Willingness to experiment with sounds, microphones, and outboard gear until the best sound is achieved. Ability to hear what will sound good in the mix in order to highlight the most important parts of a performance on tape.

After the recording session is over, the producer usually goes home and waits for several days or even weeks before mixing the tape down to the 2-track stereo master. This waiting period enables her to take a fresh and more objective view of the project. In the mix, as we have already mentioned, each track is equalized, echo or special effects may be added, and decisions may be made to rerecord certain parts of the song. The producer must decide where to place each track in the stereo spectrum. A track may be heard in the left or right speaker alone, it may be in the center, which makes it equally audible on both speakers, or it may be positioned slightly to the left or right. The way the tracks are placed will influence the total sound, and the producer will listen carefully to the effects of each decision, trying to decide when and how the desired result is achieved. To mix a 24- or 32-track tape down to 2 tracks can take many, many hours. It depends on how complicated the original recording was and what the producer is trying to do in the mix. Often after a whole day of mixing, she will be unhappy with the results and will come back another day and start over again. In many high-grade studios today computerized mixing boards are available. They can quickly re-create a previous mix, which the producer may then wish to modify in some minor respect. When such boards are not available, the producer or engineer must then write down the setting of each dial or take a Polaroid picture of the dials in order to re-create a mix.

Mixing can be very frustrating because people hear differently on different days, so coming back to a studio and using the same settings still may not appear to recapture a specific mix. The equipment itself can be affected by variations in temperature, wearing out of tape heads, replacement or exchange of tape records, or other seemingly intangible phenomena.

After the mix is completed, a master must be prepared in a special studio for manufacturing on disc, CD, or tape. It is wise for the producer to attend the mastering, if it is at all possible. After the mastering is done the producer gets test pressings or a sample tape from the factory or duplicator. The producer must then sit down and listen carefully for balances, hisses, pops, or other distortions. This is a tedious but essential part of production. Many studios now have the ability to cut a CDR master, as described on page 39. This eliminates the need for a mastering studio.

Some producers involve themselves in such matters as the cover, liner notes, credits, and back-cover graphics. Staff producers or coordinators must supervise all of the paperwork that is a standard part of record company procedures. It is necessary to apply for mechanical licenses from the various music publishers that own the songs on the tape or disc; the release of the record must be scheduled within the company; and the staff producer must play the record for sales and promotion people to build excitement in the company even before the record is released to the public. Those producers who have contacts in the promotion area, especially at radio stations, will often try to assist in the promotion of the record as well.

The work of the record producer is at the heart of the creative part of the record business. It is because this work is so important that they can earn fabulous wages. Their royalties can be from 3 to 5 percent of the retail selling price of the record, and they can often negotiate large advances, as much as $50,000 or more for an album. This is an advance against royalties, and negotiations are similar to artist deals in terms of packaging deductions and the like. Producers who work on staff at a record company are paid healthy salaries, have expense accounts, and may or may not earn percentages, or points, as they are called, on their productions. In some cases the company may pay bonuses to the whole production staff or to particularly productive producers. Other sources of income for producers include songwriting, publishing, or even personal management of their artists.

One of the reasons producers are so well paid is that the creative life span of a successful producer is usually short. Styles of music go in and out of fashion and younger artists may feel uncomfortable working with a middle-aged producer. Producing records requires endless patience and dedication, and a producer may burn out. She may be tired of the endless repetition of listening to tracks day after day, or the constant pressure from the artist or record company to come up with hits. A number of producers have said that when they finish producing a record they never want to have to listen to that record again. Chet Atkins, Phil Ramone, and Jerry Wexler are examples of producers who have been able to sustain their careers over long periods of time, but even these fabulous producers have had their ups and downs. Few producers have a successful production career of more than five years. They may then go on to jobs as record company executives, music publishers, radio or television station executives, go into the business of making commercials, work for industry trade organizations, or they may leave the business entirely.

7

RECORD COMPANY CONTRACTS

*R*ecord company contracts with artists are long and fairly complex documents. If you want to see what one looks like, consult page 662 of *This Business of Music* by Sidney Shemel and M. William Krasilovsky.*

The initial contract that a record company offers is not necessarily the contract that you should sign. Dealing with record companies is a chess-style negotiation process, and you should work with a competent lawyer on any aspects of the contract that you consider undesirable. Some of these areas of contention might involve money, whether in terms of royalty percentages or advances. Others might involve artistic control of the product—who will chose the producer, the album cover, or a number of other possible controversies.

In general, you should never sign a deal with a record company without consulting a competent music business attorney. Avoid lawyers who

---

* Be sure to get the 1995 edition, which states on the cover that it is the revised and enlarged 7th edition.

are friends, or friends of friends, or who handle divorces or real estate closings in their practice. It is difficult to find an experienced show business lawyer outside the music industry centers. You may have to use a local lawyer and have him consult with a music industry lawyer in New York, Los Angeles, or Nashville. Recording contracts specify in what state a contract will be mediated if there is a dispute. For this reason it is a good idea to use a lawyer who is licensed to practice in that state, or at the very least be sure that your local lawyer has a colleague who is licensed in the state specified in the contract. I cannot emphasize enough that a lawyer in general practice will not be adequate for your needs. Music industry lawyers charge fees of $100 to $300 an hour. Sometimes they are hired for a monthly retainer or even for a percentage of the artist's earnings.

The royalty offered to you should start at a minimum of 10 percent of the retail price of the record. Some record companies express royalty percentages in terms of the wholesale selling price. If this is the case in your contract, make sure that the royalty on this price is at least double the retail royalty, or even slightly higher. Make sure that the royalties are expressed as percentages and not flat sums of money. I signed several contracts a number of years ago that expressed the royalties in terms of a precise amount of money. As the retail price climbed from $3.98 to $9.98, I realized this was a poor decision.

Two other factors may affect artists' royalties. The medium-size record companies pay a percentage of their income from records to the major labels for pressing and distribution services. Consequently the royalties that they are willing to pay to artists may be somewhat smaller than the percentages paid by the multinational companies.

If the artist uses a superstar record producer, that person may receive as much as 5 percent in royalties and the record company may consequently offer the artists a smaller share of the pie.

The royalty figure I have given is a good royalty for a starting artist. Superstars may get royalties of as much as 18 to 20 percent of retail. Agreements can also be negotiated where royalties increase over certain sales plateaus. Record companies may seek to pay a lesser royalty on CDs and foreign sales, often 75 percent of the normal rate. This is a negotiable item. Generally record companies will design the contract in terms of a one-year time span, with four additional options of one year each held by the record company. In order to exercise "pick up" of these options, the record company must notify the artists or their personal manager thirty days before the end of the first year. This notification must be in writing and is usually sent by registered mail. You may be able to get a provision written into the contract that if the record company picks up the option your royalty rate will go up. Some record companies are now writing their contracts in terms of a number of albums rather than a number of years. This enables the record company to keep the artist under contract until the requisite number of albums is delivered. Since some artists may take several years to deliver an album, this in effect extends the life of the contract.

Advances beyond the minimum union-scale payments are part of negotiating a record deal. The extent of such advances depends on who is doing the negotiating and how badly the record company wants to sign the act. Your lawyer and your personal manager should work as a team to get the maximum amount of money for your group. It is not unusual for artists to receive advances from a major record company upon signing a contract. If several record companies are bidding for your services it is possible you will be able to get a better deal. Getting an advance doesn't mean that you personally must pay the money back if your records don't sell, but it does mean that you will not receive any royalties until all of these costs are paid back in terms of record sales. When a record company is very eager to sign a particular act, it may be possible for all or some of the advance to be regarded as a nonreturnable cash bonus that will not be charged against future earnings. This is an unlikely event at the start of a recording career, but is the type of stipulation that artists like the Rolling Stones or Janet Jackson can insist upon in renegotiating their contracts after the initial contract expires.

Some understanding must be reached with the company as to where your recording will occur. Who will pay your living expenses while you are making the record, who will pay transportation from your hometown? Sometimes the record company will set a budget for the album and let the artist retain whatever is left over after all expenses are paid. These expenses might include such matters as the producer's fee, studio rental, hiring of other musicians or singers, the services of a music arranger, etc. These contractual questions are of considerable importance early in your career; hopefully at a later date your group will be in better financial condition. Often these details can be worked out between your manager and the record company.

Sometimes the advance is not payable until completion of the album. Similarly, your union payments for playing or singing on the sessions are not payable for two or three weeks after each recording session. Since your first recording sessions are extremely vital, and you will probably be fairly keyed up, worrying about hotel bills and food is the last kind of problem you will need at this point.

For a young group the initial advance can be a very important item. With that money you may be able to pay off instruments that were bought on the installment plan, purchase a van or truck, or get new outfits or a sound system. In the United States (European contracts work differently) all the costs of recording your records will be charged against your royalties. These charges include renting the recording studio, fees to musicians or arrangers, your own fees, instrument rentals, and so-called breakage and packaging fees. Breakage is a quaint reflection of the days of 78 rpm records, which were indeed breakable. Record companies also will slap you with a 10 to 15 percent packaging fee, which means you are paying for the manufacturing of your album covers. The breakage and packaging fees are somewhat negotiable, especially if you happen to be Michael Jackson! By the way, the record company may try to negotiate a higher percentage packaging fee for CDs. In many artists' contracts the producer's fees are also recoupable out of the artists' royalties. Record club royalties are usually 50 percent of ordinary record sales. Often no royalties will be paid on free records given away by the record club. If your lawyer can do so, it is advantageous to place some sort of limitation upon the number of records that can be given away. Records given to radio stations, record stores, or music critics will not be computed in your royalties, and this is a necessary concession. If your records don't get played, they probably won't get sold either.

A commonsense approach to understanding royalties is that your actual royalties are going to be about a third less than the percentages indicated in your contract. In other words, a 10 percent royalty really comes out to less than 7 percent after the various deductions are taken.

An important protection for artists in dealing with record companies is one called the *key man clause*. In a key man clause the artist has a right to terminate the contract if a specific person in the company, often the person who signed the artist, leaves the company. This provision protects the artist from getting into a situation in which there is no one in the company who knows the artist well enough to go to bat for him. A large record company may have dozens of acts under contract, and it is important that the artist have some advocates to shepherd his or her projects through a potential bureaucratic morass.

The number of sides or albums that the record company must record will be stated in your contract. If the record company is unsure about an act, they may only commit to recording two or three cuts. You should try to get a deal that commits the company to recording an album a year.

Foreign royalties are usually computed at a lesser rate, often 50 percent of domestic royalties. Companies that own their own foreign affiliates will often pay as much as 75 percent. Some American records may not be issued abroad by the company's foreign affiliate, because they may feel that the record will not sell in their country. In such cases the American company may try to lease the record to another foreign company. The reverse of this situation occurred when Capitol initially turned down the Beatles and EMI leased their product to Swan and Vee Jay Records.

Record company contracts may spell out a company's commitment to record an artist, but may not include any commitment on the part of the company to actually release the recordings to the public. Some artists try to insert a guaranteed-release clause in the contract, which specifies that the record must be released as well as recorded. This is a useful device, but not quite as useful as it appears. The release of a record without any promotion or advertising is not worth much to the artist. To guard against such a situation a powerful artist may insert into the contract some provisions guaranteeing a specific amount of money to be spent on promoting the album.

The record company often wants to publish its artists' songs. The nature of publishing revenues will be discussed in the section on publishing, but it is advantageous for you to control your own publishing rights or to own half of them. This is another provision for negotiation.

Usually the number of recording sessions for which the artist will receive union payments will be determined by a verbal agreement between the manager and the record company. If you spend thirty-eight hours in the studio doing vocal and instrumental overdubs to your songs, it is unlikely that the record company is going to pay you union scale for this time. Instrumental scale is set by the American Federation of Musicians and was $271.72 in 1996, 279.87 in 1997, and is slated to be 285.47 in 1998 per three-hour recording session. Singers are paid through AFTRA, and their scale is a bit more complicated, but scale for royalty artists is $132.50 per person per hour or per side, whichever is greater. AFTRA actually limits the amount of scale payments for a record, and this limit is a maximum of three times the scale no matter what the length of the recording sessions may be. Generally singers must join AFTRA and instrumentalists AFM, but in some instances, when a musician sings and plays, he may end up having to join both unions in order to do television performances or sing in commercials.

Union payments for recording sessions can get to be a sticky matter when it is the performer's own record. It is impossible for the union to monitor all recording sessions, and so much overdubbing takes place in popular recording today that union payments should be a matter of good faith and mutual understanding on both sides. Make sure that you know just how many recording sessions you are going to be paid for before you start to work to avoid disputes later.

In return for advances and union payments the record company makes certain demands on the artist. Generally the individual or group will not be allowed to record for any other record company without permission. Often the company will grant such permission in return for a credit on the back of the album, such as "Jane Bridger appears courtesy of Austerity Records." The record company will demand free access to your photograph or any promotional materials for use in advertising. Some record companies try to reserve additional promotional rights, such as the use of your name or group logo on T-shirts, candy bars, and so on. Naturally it is best to retain such commercial rights for your own use. Record companies will usually put a group and all individuals in it under contract both individually and severally, which means that if you should leave the group, or if the group breaks up, all members are still under contract to the company. The company can then determine whether it wishes to continue recording you. Sometimes complex trade-offs occur when a group consisting of superstars forms. The group may be under contract to one company, and each of the individual group members may have separate recording contracts for individual records with different companies. This may reflect some past obligations, such as an artist recording as a group member for Company A. The group breaks up and this artist continues to do solo albums for Company A, but joins a new group, which has a deal with Company B. Company A may approve that deal if the artist continues to record as a soloist for them, and if Company B gives Company A some financial compensation, or does the same thing with some other artist who has just joined a group that records for Company B. When Buffalo Springfield broke up, this sort of musical chairs game was played. David Crosby got a release from CBS (he had been a member of the Byrds); Richie Furay went to CBS from the Springfield's home label, Atlantic, to join Pogo; Neil Young ended up as a solo artist on Reprise; and Graham Nash went from CBS to Atlantic, which was the new home label for Crosby, Stills, and Nash. Such negotiations with high-priced superstars can be complex.

Sometimes an artist is contracted to an independent record producer, who in turn makes her own deal with the record company. If you have such a deal with an independent producer, make sure there is some sort of time limitation on selling the completed product. The producer should have to sell the product in a reasonable amount of time—say, six months after completion. Remember it does take time to negotiate with a record company and reach a final agreement. A sample independent production deal appears on page 672 of *This Business of Music*.

Whether you are under contract to a record company or an independent producer, you will want to have some provision for auditing upon receipt of your royalty statements. There is usually a specified time period during which the artist must notify the company or producer as to his intention of auditing the books. It is sometimes specified in the contract that if a certain dollar amount of royalties is uncovered that has been unjustifiably withheld from the artist, the company must pay the costs of the audit. Certain accountants specialize in such audits and are able to smoke out false costs that a record company or producer may be charging to the artist. Most record companies pay royalties every six months, so a reasonable notice of audit might be within thirty days of receiving the statement. In record company audits that cover long periods of time accountants have recovered as much as several million dollars. This is not necessarily money that has been stolen from the artist but may involve disagreements in defining such matters as packaging allowances, free goods, or other terms of the contract.

CONTROLLED COMPOSITION CLAUSES

Under a controlled composition clause the record company publishes the songs that are written by the recording artist. It then arbitrarily sets a reduced rate to be paid on these songs, usually at three-quarters the normal 6.95 cents per song to the publisher and songwriter. The record company may even seek to limit the royalties paid out on noncontrolled compositions, which in effect requires an artist to seek reduced rates on the tunes that she records that come from various outside publishers. This puts a particularly severe burden on the artist who writes a few songs on each album. If that artist cannot get other writers and publishers to agree to accept reduced rates, the artist-writer may be virtually waiving her own writer's income from an album.

CROSS-COLLATERALIZATION

Cross-collateralization exists in two ways. The most common form is that in which one album is charged against the royalties of the next recording. In other words, if the artist makes an album that costs $100,000 to produce, but earns only $65,000 back, the artist starts the next project at $35,000 in debt. No royalties will be paid to the artist until the expenses of the new album plus the debt on the first album are paid off.

Over the years I have come to realize that many readers have trouble comprehending the nature of cross-collateralization. Think of the record company as a bank that sells you a mortgage on your house. If you don't make the payments, the bank simply takes over the house. They don't attempt to take your car away, as, for example, the IRS will do if you don't pay your taxes. Your debt to the record company is a paper debt, not one they can collect on until such time as you earn royalties.

A worse form of cross-collateralization occurs when the record company pools the artist royalties plus songwriting royalties that would normally be paid to the artist in one pot. This is only possible when the record company owns the artist-songwriter's publishing. The record company will then charge the costs of an album not only against the artist's royalties but against her royalties as a songwriter.

It is also "normal" for record companies to cross-collateralize the cost of an artist's videos against her record royalties. Since very few videos ever break even, this practice really impacts an artist's record royalties. Try to limit the extent of this charge. Under no circumstances should an artist have more than 50 percent of her video charges cross-collateralized.

The justification that record companies offer for cross-collateralization or controlled composition clauses is that the expenses of making records are so high, and so few albums actually make money, that it is necessary for the companies to endeavor to reduce their expenses and increase their profits. Although some of this logic may contain elements of truth, it is difficult to feel sorry for a business that grossed over $33 billion in world record sales in 1994.

Recently I encountered yet another strange variety of cross-collateralization. In this instance the record company co-published the artist's music with the artist. They then got the artist to sign an agreement stating that the artist's publishing performance rights (income from radio and television airplay) would be paid directly to the record company. They then cross-collateralized these performance publishing royalties against the artist's mechanical (record) royalties. Since the song had earned considerable television airplay income because it was used as the theme for a major sports event, the artist suffered a serious loss in his royalties.

OTHER WAYS TO GET RECORD DEALS

Sometimes a music publishing company finances recording sessions, in return for which the artist relinquishes his publishing rights to them. Hall and Oates had a deal of this sort with Chappell Music, and it worked out well for both parties. Some of the larger music publishers own their own 24-track studios and have the ability to produce excellent product in their own facilities. The publishing company may or may not be involved in the actual production of the recording, but their main motive is to own the publishing rights. Since so many artists write their own songs, the traditional role of the publisher is no longer to find artists to record songs written by professional songwriters who are not recording artists.

When you surrender your publishing rights in this way, you should try to get a time limitation on this deal. Otherwise you may find out that your publishing rights are tied up but you still don't have a record deal. Some record companies refuse to sign acts if they can't own all or part of their publishing. Another factor in publishing-production deals is whether the publishing company has good contacts with record people and whether they are active in contemporary music and will assist in promoting the record.

Another way to get a recording contract is by using a record company to help you make a demo on a first-refusal basis. The record company pays for your studio time in return for which they have the right to sign your group if they like you. If not, you can walk away with a free professional-quality demo. Once again it is best to place a time limitation in order to keep the company from delaying the progress of your recording career for no more than a specified time after your demo is completed. If you don't want to record for a particular company to begin with, it is best to avoid this sort of deal.

Contests

Some recording deals can be obtained by entering national contests sponsored by such products as Wrangler Jeans. The winner of such a contest usually receives a cash prize and a recording contract. By all means take the cash, but don't expect a great deal from the record company. Generally they will release a 45 rpm single and not make any great attempts to promote it. It is simply a way for them to get favorable publicity from the media.

To sum up, negotiating with a record company necessitates that you have a good lawyer and manager, and lots of patience. Many major artists have been turned down by dozens of record companies and were on the verge of despair before they finally made a deal. With luck more than one company will be bidding for your services. If this is the case for you, you may come out with an excellent contract, with a high royalty rate, a lot of artistic control, and few options on the part of the record company. If you are a beginning artist, do the best you can, but don't sign a contract if you don't feel you can live with it.

If a record company really likes an artist, and the artist has no personal manager or lawyer, the record company may recommend someone with whom they have a good working relationship. However, don't accept a lawyer or a manager simply because a record company has recommended him. Find out what clients he represents and make sure that he will be representing your interests in any possible conflict with the record company.

8

How Records Are Sold and Distributed

When you buy a record at a retail store it is the last step in a rather complicated distribution process that starts with the record company and ends with the consumer. The giant record companies have their own sales and promotion offices in all major cities. These offices service retail stores and radio stations with sales and promotion personnel. Promotion is a key part of the marketing of records. As Top 40 radio has become Top 15 or 20 in some markets, it becomes harder actually to get records played on the radio. Top 40 is a radio format where forty records a week are played in a rotation system. Many stations play the top four or five records every hour. Even the so-called progressive rock stations often have playlists for their albums. Disc jockeys today have only a limited amount of control over their own programming. The extent of that control depends upon the station format and the way the program director enforces the use of that format.

Sales personnel from the record company now give away promotion copies of records to retail stores, many of which play records in the store. In some of the giant record stores considerable sales can be generated through the playing of records in the store itself. Retail stores have sixty to ninety days in which to pay the bills to the record company branches. If they don't pay the bills they are placed on what is called *credit hold*. At that point new merchandise is withheld from the store, or the branch may insist that the store pay cash for all new records on delivery.

Some retail stores, especially small ones, don't like dealing with a number of different companies to get records. Starting in the sixties there arose a middleman called a *one-stop*. A one-stop is a place that stocks records from all record companies, especially the major labels. For a very slight markup the retailer can get all of his records from one place, simplifying bookkeeping, traveling, and the time it takes to respond to a customer's orders. Jukebox operators also buy their records from one-stops.

When retailers are in financial trouble, they will often juggle buying records from one source against another. While they are on credit hold in one place they will get records from the other source. As they clear up their credit situation in the first place, they then do the same thing to the other. Since operating a small record store is a hand-to-mouth existence, especially with the competition of the large discount stores and chains, this situation is not unusual. Sometimes branches of different companies stay in touch with one another to cooperate in pressuring retailers to pay their bills, but few companies can resist a large order. It is worth mentioning that when the record company gets paid late, artists and music publishers will also experience delays in getting their royalties.

By the middle 1980s the medium-size record companies all used the six multinational record companies to distribute their product. In return for these distribution deals the major labels received a percentage of the sales. The advantage of this setup for the medium-size labels was that it offered extensive national or even worldwide distribution.

There is another kind of record distributor, called an *independent distributor*. This type of wholesaler carries records from a large number of minor labels. Independent distributors may also do record promotion for the smaller labels. Generally these distributors carry specialized product such as bluegrass, country, progressive jazz, ethnic music, or whatever. When an independent distributor does promotion, it is usually fairly simple—for example, getting new Greek records to the one radio station in town that has a Greek program. By the nineties, all of the medium-size companies of any size had been purchased by the six multinationals. A few companies that operated in specialized product areas continued to use independent distributors, but most were folded into the distribution wings of the major labels.

By the mid-nineties, a few independent distributors, including Koch and Rykodisc, were operating on a national level, albeit without the muscle of the major labels' distribution wings. Some small labels used these distributors, but continued to service some of their own specialized accounts.

In 1952 another form of record distribution began. This distributor is known as the *rack jobber*. Rack jobbers service supermarkets, variety stores, drugstores, and department stores. The rack jobber actually chooses the records that are sold in these locations and offers 100 percent return privileges. The rack jobber may actually own or lease the record department of the store; in any case, the owner of the store itself doesn't have to worry about servicing his records or tapes. Rack jobbers generally operate from the top albums on the music trade paper charts. Occasionally they will bow to local tastes by including a German record in a store in a German neighborhood, for instance. According to the RIAA (Recording Industry Association of America) publication *Statistical Overview*, in 1995 rack jobbers controlled 28 percent of the record business in the United States. Nashville lawyer-manager Bill Carter, at a student seminar in Nashville in 1988, estimated that one racker, Handleman, controlled 27 percent of the record business in the United States. Rack jobber domination tends to limit the sales of recorded products to hits, and for the specialty artist this is frightening.*

Another way that records get to the consumer is by direct-mail sales. Record clubs, such as CBS's Columbia House, the RCA Record Club, or the Musical Heritage Society, advertise in newspapers and maga-

---

* Because the RIAA doesn't break down rack jobbers as a separate category, the 28 percent figure is larger than the actual percentage.

zines, or occasionally on radio or television. There are also TV packages, records that are assembled from older recordings and reissued as "Greatest Hits" or memorial tributes. They are usually leased from the record companies and are sold through television advertising. Other active mail-order record outlets include the Franklin Mint, Smithsonian Institution, Reader's Digest, and numerous mail-order catalogs of jazz, folk, and New Age records and tapes. The latter have also been sold with great success at alternative health food stores, bookstores, and boutiques.

A few small record companies, like Rounder and County, have gone into the record distribution business themselves. Some of their artists also sell their own product at live performances. In certain kinds of music, such as bluegrass or polka music, the audience expects the artist to sell his records before and after the show, or during intermission. Since a good performance is probably the single most effective way to create an immediate demand for a record, this can be a highly successful move. It also may antagonize local record store owners, who may regard it as unfair competition.

The sale of T-shirts and other accessories has become a lucrative sideline for record stores. In terms of giveaways, the sales department of a record company can provide a number of promotional aids to the record store that are attractive to the store owner and help promote the company's artist. Some of these tools include giant window displays, posters, special sales displays, browser bins with the record company name printed on them, mobiles, and other store decorations and giveaways.

PROMOTING RECORDS

Promotion has always been a significant part of the business, and it is crucial to the introduction of new artists. The larger record companies deliver thousands of free records to radio stations. These records are usually marked PROMOTION RECORDS, NOT FOR SALE, or they may have extra holes punched in them or a small part of the cover torn off. Nonetheless it seems as though every major city in the country has at least one record store that sells promotion copies at huge discounts. These promotion records may be extra radio station copies or records that the stations never played, or they may come from record reviewers for newspapers or magazines.

How does a record get played on the radio? It is important for a promotion person to have a good relationship with the radio stations that she services. Most stations have certain days or hours when promotion people can contact the station manager or program director (sometimes the same person) and deliver the company's new releases. Large companies may release as many as fifteen or twenty albums in a month, especially in September and October. Those months are generally regarded as the best time to release records because of the return of students to schools.

Your manager needs to have convinced the record company that your group is going to make it, and he should have gotten your booking agency to arrange a tour of major cities coordinated with the release of your record.

If the local promotion person knows that you will appear in her market and that the record company is spending money on various promotional devices, then she will walk into the station with your record on top. This requires good communication between the company and its local branches. The program director or music director is unlikely to program all of a label's new releases. Some will get priority because they are already well-known artists. If your group is high on the record company list of new products that he feels can sell (not an actual list but a feeling passed down to local promotion people in the form of suggestions or even commands), it may well be your record that gets played at the station. Without record company support based on an enthusiasm for your product together with the work of your manager and booking agency, your record may well end up in some obscure spot in the station's record library, at a local used-record store, or will be given away to some station employee's family.*

Albums may be advertised on the radio, in print ads, or even on television. It is harder to promote singles, but there are a few things that can be done to stimulate sales. T-shirts, bumper stickers, and radio station giveaways have been used many times, but if they are handled in an

---

* Record companies recently have been promoting records by setting up listening stations in the larger record stores. The record company actually leases that space and pays the record store for it.

imaginative way can still work. The record company may also sponsor a contest within the company itself. The promotion person who gets the record on the first Top 40 chart wins money, or a free trip to Bermuda, or whatever the company thinks will stimulate interest. In certain cases the record company will give away extra records to the distributors, or will establish a special discount structure. When the Kingston Trio reformed with John Steward replacing Dave Guard, Capitol gave away free records when copies of the new single "Where Have All the Flowers Gone" were bought by stores. This helped stimulate the success of the record and started a whole new cycle of success for the group, a big seller for Capitol at the time.

A record promotion person today must be fairly flexible. Major cities have so many radio stations with so many formats, and there are also the college radio stations. A few record companies even hire college-age promotion people to concentrate on college radio promotion and on helping promote the artists who are appearing in concert at the colleges.

When a promotion person cannot get a major market station to play a new record, she will try what is called a *secondary market*, a station in a comparatively small city that beams into the major market. Milwaukee radio, for example, can be heard in Chicago, and if a record hits in Milwaukee the promotion person will try to spread its success to Chicago. The trouble is that many of the secondary markets and even the small-town markets may have their own tight playlists. Breaking a record by a new artist takes a lot of work and a great deal of communication with the home office to find out where the record is being played.

It is most important for record companies to have strong staff liaison with the music industry trade papers, which include *Billboard*, *Cash Box*, *Radio and Records*, and *Hits*. These liaison people will report any radio or sales action on records to the trade papers in hopes of getting the record on the trade paper charts. There are also a number of radio station tip sheets, such as the *Bill Gavin Report*, which have detailed weekly reports on what stations are playing what records, together with the records that these people feel have potential.

No matter what a record company may do, promotion and advertising are not guarantees of success. At the height of the San Francisco sound, Moby Grape, a group from the Bay Area, was promoted to the tune of $100,000 by Columbia Records, and five singles were released simultaneously. It was a great idea that didn't quite work; in fact the built-in hip audience for the group in San Francisco was alienated by this approach. Other disastrous promotions were the MGM "Boss-town Sound" of Boston and the mysterious David Soul teaser ads in *Billboard*. Although Soul achieved success as a television actor, overhyping his record career probably hurt him.

When a record company believes strongly in a group, it may finance a series of promotional parties or performances in key cities. The act will usually do a brief performance and then meet the local disc jockeys, music critics, and record store owners or buyers. This sort of tour can be useful in introducing a new act, provided that the right people show up at the party. Some record companies have curtailed tour support, choosing to spend their money on videos of a group. Videos can be a very important selling tool, but they are geared more to selling to the consumer than to publicizing a group within the business.

Another way to promote records is to have the artists perform in the store itself. The performance is usually an informal way for consumers to meet new and promising artists, buy records, and have the artists autograph their CDs. In return the store will usually advertise the artists' appearance and set up a store or window display featuring them.

Promotion people are superb at coming up with crazy promotional schemes or contests for promoting records. Some of these amusing schemes are detailed in a long, rambling, and amusing book by Shad O'Shea called *Just for the Record*. He invaded radio stations with stale hamburgers and other colorful items. Of course, if the radio station personnel are annoyed by such tactics, they may refuse to play a record.

Contests can provide effective promotional tools. The Bill Halsey Agency in Nashville promoted a record by the Bellamy Brothers called "Santa Fe" by arranging for the winner to get a free trip there. It is unusual for a booking agency to become involved in record promotion, and this in itself probably made this promotion effective.

There is another tool used in promoting records. It is called *payola* and is illegal under federal law, but can also operate in a variety of ways that are legal. Free lunches or dinners and Christmas gifts are standard practices in many businesses besides the entertainment industry. Less legal are such goodies as free drugs, payments of money, cars, trips, illicit sex, or other such favors. It is difficult to tell just how widespread

WAYS TO PROMOTE RECORDINGS

In Record Stores

- *Free goods.* Give stores twelve CDs for every one sold.
- *Reduced prices.* A way of introducing a new artist, or reviving the career of an artist who has not had success for some time.
- *Extra copies.* Play them or use them in listening stations.
- *Promotional goods.* T-shirts, posters, bumper stickers, mobiles, window displays, Frisbees, guitar picks, etc.
- *Performances.* The artist performs in the store and signs autographs. Concert ticket giveaways are another tool.
- *Mall tours.* Used by teen star Tiffany. Meet the fans at a shopping mall.
- *Advertising.* Record company shares ad costs with retailers.

Radio Promotion

- *Inside information.* Special bios, artist visits station, artist does radio station announcements.
- *Bizarre or teaser promotions.* A lucky fan gets to meet the artist. Free ski weekends or trips to concerts. Humorous giveaways—vary according to the imagination of the record company and radio station.
- *Freebies.* Record company takes radio people to lunch or dinner, gives albums to the stations for listener giveaways.
- *Special awards.* Plaques or certificates for breaking an album in a market. Special records for radio play only, not available to consumers.
- *Payola* (illegal).

Promotion to the Consumer

- *Extra songs on a record.* A variation is a 45 with interviews or unreleased songs.
- *Advertising.* Radio, TV, print.
- *Samplers.* Collections of more than one artist.
- *Product endorsements.* Especially if music related—guitars, drums, amplifiers, microphones. Clothing endorsements.

At the Record Company, Through the Efforts of the Artist's Manager

- *Tour support.* Purchase of equipment, pay transportation expenses for an important tour, help purchase equipment. Billboards, trade paper ads.

Fan Clubs

- *Merchandise.* Limited-edition recordings, newsletters, photos, posters, merchandise.

Et Cetera

Music clinics, commercials, appearances in a movie or on dramatic or comedic TV shows, charity appearances (fund-raisers for worthy causes).

these practices are, but they are certainly not limited to the music business. You may recall local scandals in your hometown, or the Iran-contra hearings, or similar episodes. Payola scandals come and go, and it is probably impossible to totally eliminate them.

Record companies used to allow 100 percent returns. By the mid-1980s companies started charging percentages against returned merchandise that stores retained for long periods of time. Returns further complicate the royalty situation of artists, publishers, and songwriters. Many record companies withhold a certain percentage of royalties for what they call "reasonable returns." Under the current copyright law passed in 1976 the register of copyrights is directed to come up with a time period after which a record is regarded as being sold and after which royalties must be paid.

After records are returned, they may be scrapped so the vinyl can be reused, or often they are sold again at reduced prices. They are removed from the catalog and called *cutouts*. When cutouts are sold, not only does the price get reduced but there will be smaller royalty payments or no royalty payments at all to the artist. In effect, the record is being re-distributed.

Similarly, many of the record companies reissue old product at greatly reduced prices. In some cases, as with the great delta bluesman

Robert Johnson, no royalties were ever paid to the artist in the first place, and of course there are no new recording costs to speak of. On many reissue projects there are also no publishing royalties, because the artists signed away their rights at the time of the actual recording. The CD market has created a new demand for reissued product, not necessarily at lower prices, but with allegedly improved sound. Some CDs are simply reissues of unaltered product; some have been remixed and remastered and are superior to the original issues.

Another division of record company operations is the creative services department. Most record companies have some sort of publicity apparatus that sends out biographies of the artists to radio stations, newspapers, and magazines. It may also be involved in writing advertisements for recorded product. Another part of this department is artist relations. These people help to coordinate tours with visits to radio stations and key record stores, and arrange for the artists to do radio station IDs.

Another group of people, called product managers, see each specific product through the company apparatus, scheduling album releases, double-checking budgets, arranging for graphics (which can be done in-house or by free-lance firms), checking on the progress of liner notes, label notes, and anything else necessary. Some of the larger record chains, especially Tower, publish monthly magazines that help record companies promote product. Local music papers also afford an opportunity for interviews with new or established artists to be published.

We will discuss record company music publishing companies in our section on music publishing. There is often an international vice president, who arranges for foreign releases by affiliates or other companies and does the same for their releases in this country. Details such as foreign royalties, subpublishing agreements, and other matters have to be worked out. This executive is often an administrator and not a creative staff person.

The legal staff, which in the larger record companies is an in-house operation, handles contracts with artists, any business problems relating to contracts on mergers or acquisitions, and lawsuits. The legal staff must make sure that artist options are picked up before expiration, and they handle negotiation or renegotiation of contracts. Usually the president of the company will set the general policies that the lawyers who do the actual legal work must follow. When an artist is negotiating with a record company the process may be quite lengthy, going in an endless chain from artist to artist's lawyer, to record company administrative head of A&R, to record producer, and back again.

There is a business division of the large companies that includes an accounting and payroll department. It is their responsibility to make sure that all bills and royalty statements are paid on time, delinquent accounts are placed on credit hold, and the like. Company policies on such matters may be set by administrators, but the business department will follow through on these decisions.

Most major record companies operate their own pressing plants, and they can totally control the entire process from initial recording to the finished product. In such operations the company has employees working in its pressing plants, in packing and shipping functions, and in company warehouses around the country.

AGENTS AND PERSONAL MANAGERS

*M*any artists don't understand the differences between an agent and a personal manager. An agent is someone who finds work for performers. Think of an agent in the sense of an employment agency. A personal manager is someone who performs an entirely different function. A personal manager represents the artist as the negotiator in any kind of business deal that involves the artist. The deal may be with a booking agency, a record company, an advertising agency that wants to sign the artist to do commercials, a clothes manufacturer that wants to name a line of clothing after the artist—in short, any activities that will result in revenue and publicity for the artist. In the larger cities a booking agency can be a large office employing quite a few agents. Agencies such as the William Morris Agency have offices in Paris, London, and Rome, in addition to offices in the major cities of North America.

Most agents will seek to sign the artist exclusively. This means that they will represent the artist in all phases of activity in the entertainment world. Sometimes an artist will seek to limit the authority of an agent. This could happen in the case of a good rock artist who has movie ambitions and has one agency for booking rock shows and another for movie representation. The agent will always seek exclusivity but may be willing to settle for representation in a specific area. Below is a chart that illustrates some of the differences between the agent and the personal manager.

AGENT	MANAGER
Finds employment.	Doesn't find work for an act, except occasionally during initial stages of career.
Large agencies always operate under union contracts.	There is a union agreement for personal managers, but most managers don't use it.
Many agents in an office, may have many offices and a large organization.	Relatively small staff, usually 1 or 2 principals and a handful of assistants. Usually one office, occasionally one on each coast.
Pays own overhead.	Part of overhead, such as trips on the artist's behalf, are payable by the artist.
Standard fees, 10–20% of the gross wages, depending on which union covers the contract. Occasionally fees are lower, if a strong manager and a superstar artist are involved.	Considerable variation in commissions. Usually 15–25%. Percentage may be based on artist's income. In unusual cases as low as 10% or as high as 50%.
Possible conflicting obligations to artist, club owner, or promoter.	Primary commitment always to the artist.
Comparatively little personal involvement with the artist.	Considerable personal contact with the artist, may assume counseling role.

AGENT	MANAGER
Not deeply involved with image or long-range career plan.	Helps formulate image, deeply concerned with long-term career plan.
Rarely has power of attorney.	Often has power of attorney.
Three-year contract or less, under union rules.	Like a record company, 1–2 years, with options often extending to a total of 5 years. Generally not governed by the union.
Often books artists who are competitive to one another. Worldwide.	Usually does not manage artists who compete with one another. Usually based in New York, Los Angeles, or Nashville.
Not much dealing with record companies.	Frequent dealings with record companies.
May have limited functions (limited to TV, movies, etc.).	Unlimited functions, except for occasional foreign representation. For example, a British act may have separate British and American managers.
Little involvement with promotion of a specific artist.	One-person hype operation. Plants stories in newspapers; constant word-of-mouth publicity fed to others in the music business.
No financial investment in an artist's career.	May lend an artist money, may defer or even excuse commissions during the formative part of an artist's career.
Not involved in artist's music publishing.	May copublish artist's material with her, supervise the operation of a music publishing company.

AGENT	MANAGER
Little direct involvement with the act.	May help supervise artist's songs, musical arrangements, lighting, the act itself, choreography, selection of publicist, road manager, hairstylist, and stage costumes.
Little business involvement.	May invest artist's money or help in finding a financial manager to do so.

Let's review some of the material in this chart in a bit more detail. The agent is responsible for finding employment for the artist. This is generally done by telephone, although in the case of local employment it may involve visits to clubs and concert promoters or colleges. She generally tries to ascertain what the budget of a particular location is, then proceeds to sell the employer an act from a large list of acts that the agent books. She usually has photos and recordings, which she gives to the buyer. An agent is a salesperson and naturally will build up the act verbally so that the buyer thinks he is getting something unusual. This is always easier to do if the act has already had some success. It is difficult for an agent to do much until an artist has a recording on the market. However, it may be possible to find a young artist work as an opening act at a local nightclub or as an opening act for an established concert performer. The manager needs to stay on top of this action. He is continually working to convince an agency that the record company is behind the act and that the act is going to make it. Meanwhile, he is doing the same thing at the record company—keeping them informed about any important bookings, telling them about a great new song that the act is working on, and so on. He must spend a great deal of time with the record company people, getting to know the people in the various departments of the company. The album cover needs to reflect the correct image of the group, the release date of the record should coincide with a tour, the promotion people at the company need to know about the tour, and the salespeople should be preparing some special displays with which to introduce the group to the public. A good manager can deal with record people in an effective and confident way without alienating them by being an obnoxious pest.

An agent works repeatedly with some club owners and promoters and may be caught in the middle of an argument, not wishing to alienate the employer or the employee. A manager should always look after the interests of his meal ticket, the artist.

One of the main functions of a good manager is to make sure that the agency is representing the artist properly. Agents are paid commissions on a percentage of the gross, so they really are not overly concerned about the amount of traveling that a group must do between jobs. Traveling can be mentally and physically exhausting, and it can also eat up all of the profits of the job itself.

The manager often has power of attorney, which means that he is allowed to sign contracts. This is important because the artist may be traveling at the time an important job offer comes through. Often the agent will require an immediate answer, and the manager should be qualified to give one. A good manager makes sure that the bookings are in reasonable geographic proximity and that if the job is a return engagement (replay) the price of the artist goes up with each booking. Setting a price for a group is a complicated procedure, and it requires cooperation between the manager and the agent. The price for the artist should not be so high as to discourage job offers, but not so low that the group doesn't make a decent living.

Building an image involves such matters as stage costumes, lighting, performance techniques, choreography, programming of the music, and media interviews. Agents usually don't have the time to devote to an individual act in order to deal with such matters. The manager needs to attend some rehearsals and performances in order to gauge how successful the group is in getting the effects for which they are striving. Sometimes specialists may be hired to write special comedy material, stage an act, design costumes, help with choreography and lighting, or do whatever else is necessary. The manager should be an objective judge of whether a group's performance is coming off successfully. Some managers fancy themselves as musicians and may try to intervene in the actual musical arrangements. It should be a matter of judgment by the artist as to whether he feels the manager is qualified to deal in such questions.

It is not unusual for a new act to go on tour with a well-established act, thereby playing to an audience that they themselves are not yet capable of drawing. The manager and agency need to work together to create such a situation. The manager may have such an act in his own roster, or the agent may come up with one. Great care must be exercised so that the acts can share the stage successfully. A soft-folk duo might be a very poor choice as the opening act for a hard-rock group. The audience for the rock group will not want to listen to an unknown group playing such a different style of music.

It is necessary for agents to have acts that are competitive to one another because the agency gets hundreds of calls from different parts of the country and one act couldn't possibly take all of these jobs. It is best for a manager not to work with competing groups because one group will inevitably feel that it is receiving less time and attention than the other group gets.

Any large agency works under standard union contracts. The American Federation of Musicians allows agents to charge 15 percent commission on jobs of two days or longer and 20 percent on one-night engagements.* This commission is charged on the gross wages, with no expenses being deductible. The agency often asks for an advance deposit of 50 percent from the promoter or club owner, which protects the artist and the agency against nonpayment of the agreed wages. Usually an agency is knowledgeable about a particular promoter or club owner. They will warn the artist to demand the rest of the payment immediately after the engagement, or even before going on stage, if there is some doubt about payment. It is often specified in the contract when the additional monies are to be paid and in what form—cash, certified check, or whatever. In three years of working with the same booking agency, the group in which I performed had only three incidents of nonpayment. One was settled by lawyers, one concert promoter in Miami disappeared into the great American night with the remaining 50 percent of our money, and one club in Phoenix eventually went bankrupt. Without the services of an agent the artist must turn into a bill collector, and often in a strange town with people whom the artist does not know.

Under the rules of the musicians' union, if the agency does not get any

---

* Superstars are sometimes able to negotiate deals with agents for far lower percentages.

work for the artist for four consecutive weeks or doesn't provide twenty weeks' work in the first year of the agreement and forty weeks' work in the second year of the agreement, then the contract is invalidated. A week is defined as four or more days of work in a seven-day period. AFTRA allows the agents only a 10 percent commission on bookings.

Some of the larger booking agencies today are the William Morris Agency, International Creative Management (ICM), the Agency for the Performing Arts (APA), and in rock Premier Talent Associates and the Bill Halsey Agency for country music.

In classical music the agent and personal manager are often the same person. This agent-manager takes a 20 percent commission. Classical recitalists operate under the rules of the American Guild of Musical Artists (AGMA). Some of the large classical booking agents are Columbia Artists Management Inc., Shaw Concerts, ICM, and Hurok Concerts Inc.

There is considerable variation in the commissions paid to personal managers. In some cases a sliding scale is used and the manager gets more money as the income of the artist goes up. Such a deal might provide for 15 percent commissions on weekly earnings of $1,500, 20 percent for up to $2,500, and 25 percent for over $2,500. In the case of sliding scales, royalty payments, such as record royalties, are usually paid at a flat commission and are not included in the weekly earning schedule. Record royalties are usually paid every six months.

Managers often wish to publish the songs written by an artist. Few managers would own a really active music publishing company. Often a manager will co-own a publishing company with the artist. In such instances his share of the income should be restricted to publishing, and he should not collect additional commissions on the artist's songwriting (songwriter-publisher income is usually split fifty-fifty). Some managers do try to collect this double income.

It is difficult for a young artist to know exactly what constitutes a good personal manager. Most managers are glib and have great plans for the artist, at least verbally. The artist should try to institute a trial period during which he will have an opportunity to see if the manager can justify his words. A good trial period might be six months, or even a year, with a mutual option. Sometimes an earnings limitation may be placed in the contract. The group must earn a certain amount during the first year of the contract or they can get out of the agreement. The second year of the contract might include a higher figure. In the early part of an artist's career, a manager may waive or defer payment of commissions, knowing that the artist is really pressed for money.

When a manager undertakes trips to represent an artist in a business negotiation, this money is payable by the artist. In some cases the manager may be able to represent other clients in separate business negotiations during the same trip. If this happens the costs should be divided. There is a great deal of mutual trust involved in an artist-manager relationship, and that trust can easily be abused by either side. It is more important that the manager understand the artist as a person, and that there be a mutually agreeable career plan, than that the manager be all that knowledgeable about the artist's music or pursue a life-style similar to that of the artist. Because many managers are years older than the clients whom they represent, their life-styles and values may differ.

Occasionally an artist will act as her own manager, or an act may hire people to run an office for a flat fee. Whether this kind of business activity will interfere with the artist's creative impetus is a decision for the artist to make. Certainly most performers are ill-equipped by temperament and a lack of business training to pursue the business end of things.

Some acts hire spouses or relatives to manage their careers. Often the personal and business relationships both break up after a series of disastrous disputes. One example is the dispute between the father of the Jackson family and most of his children over his handling of their career. The Helen Reddy–Jeff Wald split-up is another sad example of this phenomenon. A career is best managed by a professional manager and not by a friend, lover, or relative. Even if the spouse is a professional manager the twin stresses of marriage and business don't go well together.

There is a sort of managers' guild called the Conference of Personal Managers, with offices in Los Angeles and New York. You might check out a prospective manager with them. A good manager is likely to be a member of the organization, although not necessarily.

Some artists have separate business managers who handle their investments and taxes. These advisers usually work for commissions of 2 to 6 percent of the artist's earnings. Some personal managers fulfill that role as well, depending on their training and interests.

CONSIDERATIONS IN A MANAGEMENT CONTRACT

1. Limitations on Commissions from a Recording Fund. Many artists have deals whereby the record company sets aside a specific amount for the making of an album. If anything is left over after the expenses of renting a studio, paying other musicians, etc., the artist gets to keep it. The manager should not take commission on the recording budget, because it will reduce the amount of money used for recording. At a 20 percent commission rate, the budget for a $150,000 album would become $120,000. It is reasonable for the manager to receive a commission on nondeductible recording advances, or what money is left over after expenses are paid.

2. Trial Period. If an act is already working and enjoying a reasonable income, it is possible to create a "trial marriage" period wherein the income during the tenure of the new manager must exceed earnings before the new manager enters the picture. This deal should be structured so that if these earnings do not rise to a mutually agreeable point, the act is able to bow out of the deal. This will enable the act to protect themselves from a manager who does not really do anything for them.

3. Limitations on Expenses. When a manager needs to travel to represent an act, these expenses are often charged entirely or partially to the act. It is advantageous to avoid excessive charges, such as flying first class. On the other hand, if the manager is doing business in a major city, it is reasonable for her to stay at a prestigious hotel. Whenever possible, the act should try to split these expenses with the manager's other clients. Often a manager will be representing the interests of several groups simultaneously, and it is fair to all parties that they share in the expenses.

4. Songwriting and Publishing Royalties. It is not unusual for a manager to own or co-own a music publishing company with one of her acts. If this is the case, the manager should not take commissions on songwriting royalties earned by the artist. If the manager sets up a deal with a major music publisher, the manager is entitled to a percentage of any income derived from that agreement, just as she would receive a percentage of record royalties.

5. The Key-Man Clause. The concept of the key-man clause appears on page 63 of this book in regard to record company contracts. It is particularly important if you are signed to a managerial partnership and the person who signed you retires, dies, or leaves the company. If you have a key-man clause in your management contract, you can then legally terminate the contract.

A personal manager may also help an act by hiring various personnel to work with them. These might include a road manager and an equipment crew as a group does more traveling and earns more money. Other people may be hired to help with the group's stage act, appearance, etc. A manager will also work with the record company press and advertising people, and at some point may assist the artist in hiring independent press agents. He should oversee any promotional material or photos of the artist.

If possible, have a trial relationship with your prospective personal manager. As with other situations, contractual obligations are negotiable. It is a matter of how badly an artist wants a manager and how much the manager wants to represent that artist.

When an act and a manager sever their relationship, one of the most controversial aspects of the settlement is the question of whether the manager will continue to collect her percentage of income on sales of existing records or on jobs that the manager already had some role in obtaining. The manager will argue that she is entitled to this income because she was responsible for creating it. On the other hand, the new manager whom the artist employs will want his share of the pie as well, arguing that he is devoting time, energy, and overhead to the artist's current and future career. It is important that the artist reach an agreement with both managers so that he is not paying double commissions for the same jobs. Such settlements can include paying a set amount of money to the original manager or splitting the commissions between both managers. Otherwise the artist may very well receive no net income from her own work. It is essential that a competent attorney negotiate such a settlement and that the attorney represent only the artist and neither manager.

10

MUSIC PUBLISHING

*M*usic publishing has three primary aspects—mechanical use fees for recordings, performing rights for radio and television, and the actual printing of music. When most people use the word *publishing*, they are referring to music in print, whether it is the sheet music of a song, artist collections such as a Garth Brooks collection or a greatest hits album, an instrumental method such as *How to Play the Bassoon*, or music for school bands or choral groups. In the early days of the record business sheet music was actually a bigger seller than records themselves. Piano players demonstrated songs in five-and-dime stores and music store windows and people flocked in and bought the music.

Today the biggest part of the publishing business is in mechanicals and performing rights fees. *Mechanicals* are the royalties that are paid by record companies to the music publishers. *Performing rights* are the rights paid by the radio and television stations, and some other users of music, for permission to use the music.

There are now fewer than a dozen publishers who are active in the actual printing and selling of written music. These publishers license the songs from the original publishers, paying a royalty fee for print rights. There are thousands of music publishing companies in the United States that dream of publishing a song that will become a hit. They vary in size from the publisher with an office in his living room to large companies like EMI Music, a publishing division of the highly successful Capitol Records–EMI Records.

Most of the monies that such publishers as EMI (the nonprint publishers) get come from record sales, as we will see in our discussion of the copyright law.

The publisher has the right to control the first recording of the song. Thereafter anyone may record it, provided their record company applies for a mechanical license and pays royalties to the publisher. This right to control the first recording may assume some importance because it enables the artist-songwriter to make sure that his version of the song is the first one that is commercially released. In the forties and fifties there were often many versions of a song, called *cover records*.* Today the cover record is mostly a thing of the past. When it does occur, the new recording is often done some months after the original record and in a totally different style. Such a modern cover record was Aretha Franklin's version of "Bridge Over Troubled Water," recognizably the Paul Simon song, but not sounding a bit like the Simon and Garfunkel version. The 1990s saw a vogue for tribute albums where current artists covered hits by artists ranging from the Carpenters to Curtis Mayfield and Merle Haggard. In the old days a cover record might even be a close copy of the original. Kay Starr's cover record of "The Wheel of Fortune" used an arrangement identical to the original by Sunny Gale and had a similar vocal treatment. Musical arrangements, by the way, cannot be copyrighted.

Most publishers utilize the services of the Harry Fox office to collect their mechanical royalties. The Fox office charges the publisher 3½ percent of the collections, based on the gross of the publisher. There are other offices that perform similar services, but the Fox office represents more than 3,500 music publishers and is the undisputed leader in the field.

---

* A cover record is a recording of a song that has already been recorded. The word *cover* indicates an attempt to compete with the original record.

Another form of publishing rights is called *synchronization rights*. They are granted to television and movie producers for the rights to use music with a film. These rights are negotiated by the music publisher, except that the Fox office may negotiate the rights for previously published music that is reused in a new film.

MUSIC PUBLISHING CONTRACTS

In order to make contact with a music publisher, you pursue the same basic strategy that was described for getting a record deal. The difference is that there are many more companies, and they are more accessible to a new artist. The bulk of the large publishers are headquartered in New York, Nashville, and Los Angeles. ASCAP, BMI, and SESAC can provide you with a list of their affiliates. For their addresses, see the Appendix. You might also try a publisher who publishes material in the vein that you feel is similar to your work. You may want to write an initial letter before sending your tape, asking if the publisher will listen to unsolicited material. Lead sheets should be included, if you can write them. If not, at least include typed lyric sheets.

When you make a demo for a publisher, the primary idea is to expose the song. It is not necessary that the performance or arrangement be great, only that they be in the correct general context in which you want to place the song. The lyrics should be enunciated clearly, with or without a typed lyric sheet. If you have a number of songs on the tape, remember to place leader between the songs.

If possible, try to convince the publisher to let you be there when she listens to your songs. If you are there, the chances are that she will listen more carefully, and there will be fewer interruptions. Even more important is the possibility that she may have some constructive criticisms to make of your songs, and the two of you will get some feeling as to whether the chemistry exists between you to establish a good working relationship. This kind of contact cannot be established by mail.

If a publisher is interested in your work, you will get a contract. The contract may be for one song only, for a group of songs, or it may provide that the publisher will own and publish all of your material. It would be foolish to tie up all of your songs with one publisher unless she is willing to offer you a cash advance or a salary. If you receive a contract from the publisher, there are a number of provisions you will want to place in the contract. If the publisher is unable to get a recording of the song within a specified time (six months to a year is fair), she should either return ownership of the song to you* or pay you some sort of fee to show good faith in keeping the song. As a writer you should receive 50 percent of all monies that the publisher gets, including foreign or any other rights. For sheet music sales you should get a royalty of 6 to 8 cents a copy, and a proportional share of 10 percent of the retail selling price of any songbooks that include your song. Some publishers try to charge the writer up to 50 percent of the cost of any demonstration records or dubs the publisher makes. Sometimes these dubs might be made directly from your tapes, while other times the songs may be rerecorded with professional singers and musicians. It is better, of course, to have the publisher pay all such costs. You should have the right to audit the books of your publisher within a specified time after receiving royalty statements. No assignments of publishing rights to other companies should be made without your permission, nor should the publisher be allowed to make any changes in your words and/or music without your permission.

Do not pay any publisher money to make tapes or records of your songs. No legitimate publisher will ever ask this of you. Publishers who operate in this way are known as "song sharks." They advertise in popular magazines, hoping to dupe inexperienced writers who have a dream of getting their songs recorded. These sharks may even offer to sell you 500 or 1,000 copies of the recording of your song. I have met people who have been bilked out of as much as $1,000. They end up with some bad records of their songs, a few lead sheets, and an empty wallet. Similarly, you should never have to pay anyone to collaborate on words or music with you. Their payment should be in a share of the song's royalties, when the song is recorded.

If you are worried about your inability to recognize a good writer's agreement, check out an organization called the Songwriters Guild. They will provide you with fair songwriting contracts and will collect your writing royalties for a fee of 5 percent of your earnings on the first $20,000 annually, then 5 percent up to a maximum of $1,400 a year. They will audit questionable publishers and expand your knowledge of

---

* This provision is called a *reversion clause*.

the music business through seminars, classes, and newsletters. Their address is in the Appendix.

A proven songwriter is sometimes able to attain the position of a staff songwriter for a major publishing company. Such a company may pay the writer anywhere from $300 to $500 a week. This is an advance against the writer's royalties.

Look out for cross-collateralization in contracts.* This is a technique whereby the publisher will charge the royalties made by one song against the expenses of another song. Of course, if you are a staff writer, this is inevitable. If you are recording for a record company that also is publishing your music, make sure that the two contracts are separate and that your recording costs as a recording artist will not be charged against your songwriting royalties.

THE COPYRIGHT LAW

If you are worried that publishers or other artists may steal your songs, you may want to copyright your songs. You must remit $20 to the Copyright Office in Washington (see Annotated Bibliography for further information). If you have written a number of songs, this can mount up to a good deal of money. You can copyright all of your current songs as a body, calling it "The Collected Songs of Jane Doe." As each song is recorded or printed, you will have to recopyright it individually and pay the proper fee, but it is one way to protect your songs without having to pay so much money. There are also services that will register your songs with the Bureau of Copyrights, but the cheapest way to do it is to register all of the songs under one title. Lyrics without music or music without lyrics can be protected in the same way.

There are two ways to register a copyright. One way is to send lead sheets of your song or songs with the proper fee. A lead sheet contains the title, words and/or music, the name of the publisher, and a correct copyright notice. (See a sample lead sheet appearing in the Appendix.) The other method of copyrighting a song is to send a tape recording or phonograph record with the copyright form. The actual performance will be protected and so will all of your original words and music. Since

---

* See Chapter 7, "Record Company Contracts."

many musicians have trouble writing music in manuscript form, this protection can be important. The actual copyrighting of a tape or phonograph record is one of the features of the current copyright law.

The current copyright law, which was passed by Congress in 1976 and went into effect January 1, 1978, represents a considerable advance for songwriters and publishers over the old law. Besides the increase in mechanicals from 2 to $5\frac{1}{4}$* cents per song and additional monies for longer songs (1.3 cents a minute or 6.95 cents, whichever is greater), jukeboxes pay a $50 fee and cable television companies pay a fee based on their gross income. These are all new sources of income, as in public television, which pays a fee set by the copyright tribunal. This tribunal is appointed by the President of the United States and approved by the Senate. The members serve staggered seven-year terms and review royalty rates and other provisions of the law during their sessions.

Under the old copyright law, if a mistake was made in the copyright notice, the song lost its copyright protection and went into the public domain. Under the new law reasonable time is given to correct any mistakes in the notice of use. The new longevity of copyrights is the death of the last living collaborator plus fifty years. In cases where anonymous works or works for hire are created the term will be seventy-five years from the first publication or one hundred years from the creation of the work, whichever is shorter.

Under the current copyright law, the writer can reclaim a copyright from the publisher after thirty-five years. Under the old law the publisher could copyright work for twenty-eight years and then renew it for an additional twenty-eight years. This represents a considerable advantage to the writer or her estate.

LICENSING AGREEMENTS

The compulsory license works like this. Within thirty days of recording the record company must apply for a license from the music publisher. Because compulsory licenses require compulsory payment of royalties every thirty days, the procedure usually followed is that the Harry Fox office grants a negotiated license to the record company. This is neces-

---

* The tribunal has the right to increase this amount.

sary because most record companies pay royalties only every six months. In fact sometimes the record company tries to get a lower rate on the song than 6.95 cents. This would often be granted if the song is a new work by an unknown writer or if the record contains a number of songs by the same writer. Record clubs usually pay only 75 percent of the ordinary licensing rate, and they negotiate directly with the publishing company instead of with the Fox office. Sometimes this lower rate is granted because the record club agrees to pay on a large minimum order of records. This can be done with a record that the club is confident will sell well. Smaller fees are also negotiated for budget records and premium records.

The structure of music publishing companies is relatively simple. The company may be owned independently, by a record company, or by a number of partners. Below the chief officer of the company or president is a general professional manager. The manager is responsible for signing writers and for placing songs with recording artists and record producers. In the larger company the professional manager may also have a number of assistants who spend much of their time contacting artists and producers. Larger companies have offices in the various music centers and may even have foreign branch offices.

When a music publishing company also has a print division, as Warner Brothers Music does, the print division is run separately from the rest of the publishing company. It is considered a different business.

SONGWRITING CONTESTS

There are numerous local, regional, and national contests for songwriters. Some of them pay fairly lucrative prizes and award publishing contracts to the winners. There is no harm in entering such contests, especially if you have some way of making sure they are reputable, but I have heard about some contests that did not pay the prizes that they advertised. There are going to be hundreds of your fellow writers entering the large, national contests, so be aware that you are entering what amounts to a lottery. Despite what the contests claim, a good demo will get your song a closer listen than will a mediocre one.

11

PERFORMING RIGHTS
SOCIETIES

*P*erforming rights are
the rights granted for performances of songs in public. This includes radio, television, concerts, nightclubs, and other performance places. The
money that a writer makes from these sources is not paid by the music
publishing companies. Both writers and publishers receive performance
money from one of three performing rights societies. They are ASCAP
(American Society of Composers, Authors, and Publishers), BMI
(Broadcast Music Inc.), and SESAC (Society of European Stage Authors
and Composers). To join one of these societies, a writer needs to have
had at least one song published or recorded.

ASCAP is the oldest of the performing rights groups. It was founded
in 1914 and is owned by the membership, who pay annual dues of $10.
BMI was founded by the broadcasters in 1940 when they objected to an
increase in rates that ASCAP was attempting to negotiate. Historically

ASCAP was uninterested in country music and blues, and BMI started with an aggressive open-door policy, welcoming writers of any kind of music. ASCAP now pursues a similar policy, although some of the Nashville publishers still refuse to join ASCAP because of its attitude toward country music in the old days. BMI claims to log more smaller stations in the country and soul fields than does ASCAP, and if you write many songs in these fields, you might wish to check comparable hit songs in these areas with BMI and ASCAP and with your lawyer to see which organization will earn more money for you. Although the broadcasters still are the stockholders of BMI, the stock has never paid a dividend, nor was it expected to do so. SESAC is a private company founded in 1931, and it is the only profit-making organization of the three societies.

On the next page is a chart reflecting some of the differences in the three performing rights organizations.

In order to determine the amount of airplay a song is getting, ASCAP tape-records radio station programs for six-hour periods and brings the tapes back to New York for analysis. While this procedure ensures a lack of favoritism since no one at the station knows that the taping is going on, it also relies on the ability of the listener to identify the song if the disc jockey does not identify it clearly. If the song is a current hit, there is little question that the listener will spot it. ASCAP has song files containing all sorts of melodies, and the listeners are musicians, but one may still wonder how much time can possibly be spent on identifying any one song. BMI logs radio stations every twelve to fourteen months. The radio station sends BMI a list of all songs played during a one-week period, with the names of the writer and publisher written on the log. Both ASCAP and BMI have complex formulas for converting airplay from a single station into a mathematical factor and multiplying it to produce an index of national play during the time surveyed. Neither system is foolproof; if you have a local hit in a particular place that is being logged, you will get more national credits than you deserve; on the other hand, if it is not logged at all, you are being cheated. With ASCAP you must rely on the ability of their listeners, and with BMI you need to hope that the disc jockeys have not played records by friends or associates during the logging week. If this is too obvious

ASCAP	BMI	SESAC
$10 dues for writers.	No dues for writers.	No dues for writers.
To be a member must have one song recorded or published.	Same.	Same.<None>
More than 40,000 writers.*	More than 111,000 writers.	1,000 writers.
More than 18,000 publishers.	More than 56,000 publishers.	1,000 publishers.
Collected over $422 million.†	Collected about $340 million.	Collection figures not available.
Airplay is determined through taping radio stations.	Radio stations are logged every 12–14 months.	The basis of the SESAC payments is from chart activity in music trade papers. Further explanation in text.
Bonuses for songs with 20,000 feature performances, classical music, religious music.	Special credits for local FM airplay of classical music, songs with 1,000,000 performance credits.	Bonuses for longevity on trade paper charts and crossover from one chart to another—for example, soul to pop.
50% income TV. 30% radio. Balance of income from miscellaneous sources.	45 % TV. 30% radio.	Television 32%. Radio 55%.
Educational functions include classes for songwriters, speakers furnished for educational purposes.	Musical theater writing workshops, Songwriters' Showcase in Los Angeles, sponsors seminars with speakers on the music business.	Provides speakers for educational workshops.
Pays reduced credits to composers of commercials.	Same as ASCAP.	Same as ASCAP.

Continued next page

Continued from preceding page

| Performing rights only. | Performing rights only. | Also issues mechanical licenses for records and synchronization rights for movies and television. |

---

* Figures from Shemel and Krasilovsky, *This Business of Music*, 7th edition.
† 1983 figures for ASCAP and SESAC, 1984 for BMI.

the computer will throw out the results, but there is no question that some favoritism can be shown when the station knows it is being logged.

SESAC does only spot checking on airplay and devises its writer payments mostly from trade paper activity. Credit is also given for growth of the publisher's catalog within SESAC, seniority, diversity of the catalog, and so forth. SESAC pays the writer and publisher $240 each on release of a pop single, and $100 each for any song recorded on a pop album. The SESAC system is probably the quickest way for a popular music writer to receive payment.

Television payments differ according to the hour of the day; they are the highest during the evening prime-time periods. The networks are easy to monitor; for local programs the societies rely on local TV magazines and occasional sampling procedures.

All three organizations license radio and television stations for performing rights. The rate for ASCAP and BMI is just under 2 percent of the station's gross receipts. According to Shemel and Krasilovsky, due to "certain adjustments" the BMI rate is less than what ASCAP charges, but BMI has asserted that its goal is for the two organizations to charge the same fees. SESAC fees are much less, ranging from $330 to $7,200 a year for AM radio stations.

At the present time neither of the major societies is giving advances. They will provide information to banks that can aid a writer in getting loans, however. The BMI bonus system gives publishers credits on their entire catalog, so it is easier for a publisher to receive bonuses than for an individual songwriter to get them.

ASCAP has two systems for paying writers. If the writer prefers to defer normal regular payments, the Four Funds System can defer payments, which can be useful to a writer in a temporary high-tax situation. It can also help the writer with no assured income who needs to take time off in order to write a show. ASCAP also offers special annual payments to legitimate writers in specialized forms of music who do not tend to get logged for radio play.

No matter which society you join, it is most important that you report any recordings or performances of your songs to the society. Some writers rely on their publisher to do this for them, but you should fill out a clearance form yourself to ensure that you will get credit. If you do not report the songs, the societies are not obligated to pay you.

In my opinion your choice of society should be determined by discerning which one is most responsive to you. All of them are capable of opening doors to publishers or record companies, doors that are frequently closed to young writers. Each group is staffed by different people, and I feel you should go to the one where you have the best rapport. Personally, I would like to see all of the societies place less emphasis on performance bonuses and give more help to young writers. They are really the ones who need the money. It is true that both ASCAP and BMI make some special grants to young composers of classical music and offer educational seminars on various subjects.

When the 1976 copyright law was being written, there was some heavy lobbying by performers who felt that they should receive money when their performances were aired in the same way that songwriters receive payment. They argued that the success of radio stations was largely dependent upon playing records by successful performers. The radio stations took the opposite view, saying that without the radio stations the artist would not become popular. Part of the problem involved in such a performance royalty is the question of how it would be divided. What percentage would the artist get, and would the record company, studio singers, and musicians be entitled to payment as well? In a number of countries, especially in Western Europe, performance royalties are paid to artists for play on radio or TV. Radio station and television station owners are totally opposed to such a royalty because it would cut into their profits. Frank Sinatra is currently spearheading efforts by performers to receive this money.

SOURCE LICENSING

Following several defeats in court proceedings, local television stations have introduced bills into Congress that would take away the blanket licenses granted by performing rights societies and make the producer of local or syndicated television shows responsible for paying performance rights. The initial bill carried only a one-time payment to composers. Since most of the money for composers and songwriters comes from reruns and repayments, composers strenuously opposed this bill. It was reintroduced in the 1987 Congress with provision for possible repayment, but once again died in committee.

This is a complex subject that could easily fill up an entire book, but the passing of this bill or anything similar could endanger the future of intellectual property in this country. Because of this, writers, dramatists, actors, songwriters, and composers are generally opposed to it. Television is a lucrative business, and it is hard to shed crocodile tears for the poor station owners. At the present time the broadcasters seem to have abandoned their efforts to obtain source licensing legislation.

12

COMMERCIALS

*C*ommercials are an amazing phenomenon in American society. Radio and television commercials include technically superb and highly artistic levels of work in such areas as songwriting, filming, editing, music writing, acting, singing, and special effects. It would be virtually impossible to put as much care into a complete film or play as is lavished on a thirty-second TV spot for a major product. The cost of buying time on network television for a top-rated show eclipses the cost of filming, editing, music performance, acting, etc. A thirty-second spot on the Super Bowl costs over a million dollars. If the cost of filming a jingle is $750,000, this amount of money pales to insignificance when one realizes this amount of money might buy 15 seconds of Super Bowl advertising.

The number of people who actually are employed in the commercials industry is small. It is estimated that some 500 people write, direct, and produce the majority of national television commercials. With the introduction and spread of cable TV this number has undoubtedly increased. The majority of the commercials are actually filmed in Los Angeles because of the easy availability of color labs, experienced crews, and lighting and film technicians. When a major commercial is shot in Boston or Atlanta the chances are that most of the film crew has flown in from Los Angeles. The music is cut into the picture after the film has been edited. Since most of the advertising agencies have their headquarters in New York, the agencies usually record the music there. Some filming is done in New York, and Los Angeles and Chicago are the next largest music centers for commercials. There is a smaller but thriving jingle business in Dallas, particularly for what are called *drop-ins*. Drop-ins are commercials that use the same instrumental tracks but different copy. A radio commercial for Frontier Chevrolet that I have heard in Denver has the identical music track as one for another product that is aired in Cheyenne, Wyoming. The singers are also clearly the same, but in each case they sing the name of the client in the specific market. A drop-in can be used in several dozen different markets.

A good commercial is one that the viewer or listener remembers and one that helps sell the product. The manufacturer takes great pains to make packages attractive and recognizable, and similarly the advertiser wants you to have their jingle in your head when you see the package. Many manufacturers spend more money on the packaging than they do on the actual contents of the package.

Commercials start with the client, which is the company that makes the product. The client representative goes to an advertising agency. The agency formulates a campaign, with or without extensive consultation with the client. At this point an independent film house is generally assigned to do the actual filming. The commercial is then cast by the agency, with some possible input from the film house. An account executive from the advertising agency who is assigned to the particular product will attend the actual filming. The film is then edited and the agency hires another independent creative group to work on the music. This "music house" will then write the music for the spot. They may also write the lyrics, or the agency people may supply the music house with the lyrics. Some agencies have their own music departments, and the actual jingle may be written by agency people, or these people may act as supervisors over the work of the music house. There is considerable discussion between the agency and the music house about the type of campaign that the client wishes. It may be an aggressive hard-rock jingle for a youth-oriented client, or a friendly down-home country fried chicken commercial, or the music may be written in some other style. The music house will do the musical arrangement or hire a free-lance arranger to do so.

The agency, and even the client, often hears a rough skeleton of the actual jingle. This demo may actually be sung live, or it may be taped with a modest accompaniment, such as a piano, a guitar, or a rhythm section. For the music house this is the most troublesome time in the entire process. Most clients and many agency people are not particularly musical, and making a sketchy demo may not be enough to convince them that the finished commercial will sound good. It is difficult to do a big band arrangement, for example, without a big band. If the demo is approved, then a final recording session will take place. The best singers and musicians are hired to do these sessions. They are readily available because the pay scale for commercials is higher than for any other type of recording. The singers can make fabulous sums of money based on exactly what use is made of the commercial. Many commercials don't actually get on the air, and some are test-marketed in one area and then abandoned, but if a campaign is used nationally the singers will make thousands of dollars from a single product. The best jingle singers in New York earn six-figure incomes, but there are scarcely more than a dozen of them who do the bulk of the work. Payments for singers are graded for different-size population markets and for national network use, and reuse payments must be made for commercials that are used on both radio and television. Commercials are generally bought for thirteen weeks at a time, and if they are used for another time cycle the singers get additional payments, called *residuals*. Residuals are the heart of the singers' income; by comparison session fees are insignificant. Session fees vary according to the size of the singing group; for a soloist the pay would be $333.30 for two hours.

Musicians who play on commercials get $90 an hour, plus a $22 payment for the first thirteen weeks of use. In December 1997 the minimum wage will go to $94. There is an extra 30 percent added for playing more than one instrument. This is called *doubling*. Musicians also get residuals based on thirteen-week cycles, but they are not paid nearly as well as the singers. Both musicians and singers receive additional payments for their pension and welfare funds.

In recording television commercials a device called a *click track* is often used. This is a click that sounds like the beat of a metronome, and it is heard in the musicians' headphones. This click establishes exactly the right tempo, and that tempo can be varied as different frames of the picture show different things. On some sessions all of the musicians will have the click track in their headphones, while on others only the drummer hears it, and the other musicians must follow the drummer. Commercials must be timed exactly or the client will be charged additional money by the networks. A thirty-second commercial usually runs twenty-nine seconds, and a sixty-second jingle might be fifty-eight or fifty-nine seconds long.

Sometimes more than one music house competes for the same commercial. Each of them may make a demo, from which the agency and client will choose the winner. In the past many of these demos were made at the expense of the music house rather than the advertising agency. Through an organization called SAMPAC (Society of Advertising Musicians, Producers, Arrangers, and Composers) the music houses have banded together and tried to formulate some ground rules for working with the advertising agencies. They now generally get a small creative fee and budget for such demos, usually in the area of $200 to $500. If musicians are hired on the demos they must be paid union scale as if they were doing a finished commercial. Technically the same rule holds for the singers, but because the rewards of singing on a national commercial are so great, singers will sometimes waive the session fees.

Commercials are written in different sections. There is usually some kind of musical introduction, a basic tune, a sort of musical bridge, sometimes with spoken copy,* and a tag at the end. This tag is the product signature and may be used in a number of different campaigns by the same product. It is really the equivalent of what we have called the hook in songwriting. Sometimes a product will run a number of different jingles during the same overall campaign, using the same tag at the end of each one. Usually the product name is mentioned early in the commercial, almost always by the end of fifteen seconds. When an announcer is used the agency generally selects the announcer. Some disc jockeys make quite a bit of extra income doing these announcements, called

---

* The tune used with spoken copy is called a *doughnut.*

voice-overs. When a commercial is sung with a videotape the singers are paid through AFTRA, and when the commercial is sung with a film the singers are paid through SAG. The AFM sets different scales when a musician is shown on camera playing an instrument.*

I have mentioned that some agencies test-market commercials in one or two markets before airing the commercial nationally. They may also test commercials on theater audiences, or they may use the Gallup Organization to make phone calls checking on whether people like or remember commercials shown during a particular television show. Sometimes these sampling techniques are also used with records. The theory behind test-marketing is that it is better to fail in a single market than to go immediately to the huge expense of national marketing and promotion.

A good jingle singer must be very flexible and also possess a certain degree of anonymity. Although actors or models on television are often identified with a product, the singers prefer to remain free of this identification. This enables them to work for many competing products. One friend of mine had ten beer commercials playing simultaneously all over the United States, some network and some local campaigns. Such singers are incredibly versatile. The qualities that make for success in the jingle business are often opposite to what makes an artist successful on records. One can generally identify a popular singer on a record almost immediately. It would be hard to confuse the sound of Mick Jagger with the sound of Randy Travis. In doing commercials a singer imitates dozens of styles and voices. A male singer might do a Johnny Cash–style commercial in the morning for a beer company, he might sing in a six-person jazz group in the early afternoon for an auto manufacturer, and go back and do a rock solo late in the day for a skin cream company. Basically it is the product that must be sold, not the personality of the singer.

Because of this contrast between record and jingle styles, it is difficult for recording artists to succeed in the jingle business and equally difficult for jingle singers to succeed in the record business. Self-expression is an important part of the artist's work on records, but on jingles this

---

* SAG is the Screen Actors Guild; AFTRA is the American Federation of Television and Radio Artists; AFM is the American Federation of Musicians.

expression must always be filtered through such primary selling points as the name of the product and its image. If the singer gives too much personality to the performance, the agency may feel that the product image is being shortchanged. Sometimes an agency will hire a specific artist because the artist image and product image coincide. Andre Agassi promoting tennis shoes is such a successful marriage of product image and artist image. A famous recording artist has usually become successful through developing a particular recognizable style, and that artist cannot reasonably be expected to change this style for a product image. This is exactly what a good jingle singer can do. A good jingle singer is equally capable of doing solos or group singing, can read music quickly and accurately, and can also improvise in a variety of styles. Through developing stamina and good microphone techniques such singers can sing many hours without losing the proper vocal qualities.

People who write jingles demand creative fees that may vary from $500 to $25,000 or more. Additional fees of up to $1,500 are received by the musical arranger. This creative fee is a one-time fee with no residuals, although sometimes a deal can be negotiated whereby the composer gets an additional payment if the same tune is used with a new set of lyrics.

Because singers get handsome repayments for their work on commercials, many composers seek to sing on any spot that they write. On a complete set of national spots for a major product, if the campaign runs constantly, as some do, a singer can make $100,000 from that product alone. Consequently I have witnessed sessions where composers who couldn't carry a tune in a basket could be seen singing their lungs out. I have witnessed other commercials where the composer actually lip-synced the words, as though he were doing Dick Clark's "American Bandstand" show. Some composers don't go to all this trouble, but simply do their demos for little or no money and make an agreement with the advertising agency that if the campaign is bought by the client, the composer will be added to the AFTRA or SAG contract as a singer.

A few commercials have also become hit records. This is an extra bonanza for the product because most listeners will mentally fill in the product name when they hear the song, even though that name has been removed from the record.

To break into singing on commercials singers usually make demo tapes consisting of a group of jingles they have recorded. If they are young singers they may simply include twenty- to thirty-second snatches of songs. Any jingle where the singer has sung multiple parts is useful because it indicates the singer's range and versatility. If the singer wishes to do both solos and group work, then examples of both should be on the tape. If a singer wishes to do on-camera work, then pictures or a video should be included with the tape. Singers in the jingle field do not generally use agents—work is gained through word of mouth in the industry and by contacting vocal contractors, independent music houses, or even the agencies themselves.

Besides drop-ins, discussed earlier, there is also considerable work available recording radio station ID packages. These are jingle versions of a station's call letters. Many drop-ins and station ID packages are recorded in Dallas and San Diego. These packages may pay union session fees to the singers and musicians, but many people in the industry believe that the producers of these packages do not pay reuse fees.

Unfortunately in local markets many singers and musicians are willing to do commercials for less than union scale. Such performers are cheating themselves out of a great deal of money. Unlike recordings, commercials represent more of a craft than a form of emotional expression, and it is difficult for me to understand why anyone but a rank beginner would want to do such work without receiving proper payment.

There are a number of production libraries available where generic music can be bought for $50 to $75 per selection of music used. This is called "needle drop" music and provides cheap if uninspired background music.

In 1989 Bette Midler won a suit restricting Ford from using a look-alike and sound-alike version of her doing a commercial. It remains to be seen what ramifications this will have for the industry. After all, a great part of the commercials industry has been built on specific or general imitations of sounds or performers.

I spent about ten years in the New York area working as a studio musician. During this time I worked on many commercials. One of the people I worked for was Mitch Leigh, who wrote the music for *Man of La Mancha* and also operated a successful jingle house called Music Makers. One day I played on a Gleem commercial that Mitch had written. I was playing twelve-string guitar, and there was an orchestra of some ten or twelve pieces. Mitch had written a beautiful melody, with a soprano sax and an oboe playing in a sort of rhythmic counterpoint against the rhythm section. We recorded a few takes of the song, and then Mitch disappeared into the control room for about forty minutes. Just before the hour ended and we would have had to go into overtime, the contractor appeared and told us that the session was over, but that he'd be calling us again soon.

None of us could figure exactly what had gone wrong. The tune and the orchestration were excellent; they were even enjoyable for the musicians to play. About a week later the same basic crew of people went back and recorded four of the most unimaginative commercials I have ever heard for Gleem. Apparently the agency liked them, because a couple of them were used for over a year. The conclusion that I drew from this experience was that when one works on commercials artistic validity may not be synonymous with the way a client or an advertising agency conceives the image of a product.

13

MUSIC TRADE PAPERS

$\mathcal{T}$he lifeline of communication in the music industry is the music trade paper. Almost everyone active in the music business reads some or all of these papers. The most popular trade papers are *Billboard*, *Cash Box*, and *Radio and Records*. All of the trades come out weekly. Each of them has certain special features but all contain stories on industry trends, executive job changes, the formation of new companies, the sales, manufacturing, and distribution of records, and, most important of all, the charts. Charts are listings of the current top recordings, placed in different categories. The single most important chart is the chart of current pop records, which includes the top 100 singles and the top 200 albums. The *Billboard* chart of top albums and singles is the one that is most universally studied by record people. Rack jobbers and various distributors govern a great deal of their buying by the chart position of a record. Trade paper charts reflect the records that are selling best and getting the most national airplay. In addition to the pop chart the trades publish listings for the top records in jazz, soul, rap, classical, easy listening, and gospel music. There are also surveys of the records selling abroad, especially in Western Europe.

Sometimes a record may be fairly high on the charts, but the sales are not commensurate with the amount of airplay the record receives. Such a song is called a *turntable hit*. On the other hand, strong regional sales may cause the trades to place a record in a higher position on the chart than it may actually deserve. Sometimes a record sells very well over a long period of time, but it never hits the charts or it stays near the bottom because the sales are never that heavy during any particular week. Longevity is as important a factor in ultimate sales as sheer chart position.

Each trade paper has a different way of compiling its own charts, but they all rely on sales reported by the various record distributors and rack jobbers, radio station chart activity, and sales reports from retail stores. There is usually little difference in the chart positions of the top ten singles or albums in the various trade papers, but as you get lower in the charts you will notice more variation. Included with the charts is the name of the artist, the record label, and whether the record is available on LP, cassette, or CD. With its hot 100 singles chart *Billboard* also includes the name of the producer, the songwriter, and the publisher of the songs. Strong sales activity on the charts is reflected by stars or bullets, which represent particularly hot records.

The record companies all have people whose job it is to be liaisons to the trade papers. Naturally they spend a good deal of time hyping the trades on the wonderful sales and airplay that the companies' records are showing. Chart position is very important to the record companies in order to help convince rack jobbers to stock their records. It is also the key factor in the way that many individual stores or chains order their records and tapes.

The trades also review new records, and of course the record companies seek to have their product reviewed favorably. This accounts for the numerous full-page ads in the trades from record companies. The record company assumes that by virtue of its advertising in the trade paper magazines will treat a new recording more seriously and perhaps more favorably than if no advertising takes place. Other ads celebrate gold records, anniversaries in recording, and other special events or promotions.

The main differences between the trade papers are more matters of style than substance. *Billboard* tends to be the most conservative paper, while *Hits* is written in a sort of breathless high school style. *Cash Box* seems to have declined in size and influence, and *Radio and Records* is full of want ads, radio station profiles, features, and interviews. All of the trades have gossip columns of a sort, outlining executive job changes, the formation of new companies, and the sale of others.

Variety is somewhat different from the other papers in that it focuses on movies, theater, radio, television, and nightclub acts. It offers only minimal coverage of the music industry. It is vital reading for movie and TV people because it reports grosses of films and ratings of TV shows. A daily version is published in Hollywood, as is a similar daily called *The Hollywood Reporter*.

Any chart activity or favorable trade paper reviews are used by record people in their ads in the other trades and during their visits to radio stations. Trades are sold on the newsstands in the major cities of the music industry and usually at one or two locations in other cities. They are rather expensive, costing roughly $5 for each weekly issue.

Pollstar and *Performance* are trade publications that specialize in covering live performances. They are weekly publications, and list gross receipts for artists' performances. Both magazines publish various directories that list performing venues and provide a source for accessing artists through their managers and agents.

Other specialized trade publications deal with music retailing, advertising, specific musical instruments, performances, and every imaginable sort of music. *Rolling Stone*, *Musician*, *The Music Connection*, and *BAM* are consumer magazines that are often read by people in the industry. Any favorable reviews in these papers provide more ad copy for the record companies.

THE AMERICAN FEDERATION OF MUSICIANS

*T*his chapter will deal with unions in a general sense but will focus on the musicians' union, the American Federation of Musicians (AFM). Toward the end of the chapter I will discuss some of the other music-related unions—AFTRA, SAG, AGVA (American Guild of Variety Artists), and AGMA (American Guild of Musical Artists).

Why do we have unions in the music business? Basically for the same reasons that the auto workers or garbage collectors or teachers have them—to regulate wages and working conditions and provide some degree of job security. The typical American union worker works in one job at a single location, but a musician may play a wedding, a funeral, a record date, a television commercial, and a dance all during the same week. If the musician had to negotiate the wage scales for all of these separate jobs, there wouldn't be much time left for practicing, not to mention the legal fees that might accompany the preparation of various necessary contracts and the bill-collecting chores that would follow each job.

Many young musicians ask if they have to join the union. In other words, what does the union do for them other than collect dues and initiation fees? The union regulates wages and working conditions at two different levels—nationally and locally. The national union sets up wage scales and working conditions for recordings, television, commercials, and film work. These scales can be fairly complex or fairly simple to understand, varying with the circumstances of the work and the use that will be made of it. As of February 1996 the minimum wage scale set by the AFM for nonsymphonic recording was $271.72 per three-hour session for each sideman and double for the leader or contractor. A contractor is required on any sessions that use twelve or more musicians. The contractor may be a playing musician—one of the twelve or more on the date. For symphonic recording* the scale is higher, about $16 more per three-hour session, with a higher scale for four-hour sessions. These figures are the minimums that an employer can pay whether the musician is employed for the full three-hour session or plays a thirty-second solo and leaves the studio after ten minutes of recording. This may actually happen on certain occasions. All of the major recording companies are signatories to the AFM code, which stipulates these wages and also specifies when and how the money is to be paid. No more than four songs or fifteen minutes of music may be recorded at any single recording session, or else more money must be paid to the musicians. Provisions are made for additional payments for recordings of reuses in other media such as a movie album sound track or other multiple-use situations.

All of this may be complicated by overtime payments of time and a half after the first three hours; by the playing of additional instruments (called *doubling*), which requires additional payments of differing amounts for the various media; and by premium time spent for recording on holidays or late-night recording. It would be literally impossible for each musician to negotiate all of these payments individually. The current AFM phonograph labor agreement is over fifty pages long, and there are separate agreements for movies and commercials. We have al-

---

* *Symphonic recording* means recordings by a symphony orchestra.

ready discussed the problem of reuse fees for commercials. These would be virtually impossible for the individual musician to monitor.

There are some 350 locals in the AFM in the United States and Canada. Each local has its own specific territory. For example, Local 802 in New York City is a large and powerful local, but there are other locals in New Jersey, Westchester County (north of the city), and in Connecticut. Each has its own circumscribed territory. Each local union sets minimum wage scales at clubs and theaters in its own jurisdiction. The theory is that people who live in the area know the operating conditions better than the national union would. The scale for a million-dollar nightclub is quite a bit higher than the scale for a local piano bar. For the last ten years the union has been consolidating locals into larger units in order to limit costs and provide members with more efficient services. The dues and initiation fee of each local are subject to the approval of the national federation.

The initiation fees for the AFM range from as little as $10 to as much as $150. This is the initial amount required to get into the union. In addition to this, members pay quarterly dues. In the larger locals these dues may run as high as $20 a quarter. The smaller locals are invariably cheaper to join, but once you have a card in a specific local, if you work in another jurisdiction you must pay traveling tax, and you are not allowed to work a steady job in another territory unless you join that local or transfer to it. Since you may spend a year or two at a steady job in a new territory and then go back home, you may end up with several membership cards, sets of initiation fees, and sets of dues to pay. If you plan to make a permanent move from one jurisdiction to another, you may transfer your membership. Unfortunately, this usually requires that you wait six months before you are permitted to work a steady job. If you are a nightclub musician this procedure makes it difficult to survive. The system of local jurisdiction is rather antiquated. It was designed to protect the local musician from excessive competition, but it is probably more of a nuisance than a help to anyone.

All musicians must pay work dues when they work a union job. These work dues are a small percentage of scale wages, usually 1.5 to 3 percent. This applies to symphony players and barroom pianists alike. Some locals set a maximum amount of work dues, such as $25 a year, and collect it in a lump sum in advance.

The union does more on a job than regulate scale wages. You are free to negotiate wages above scale; you simply may not work for less money than scale. On the job the union specifies rest periods between sets in a nightclub or after each hour of a recording session. This is important for your health and well-being, particularly if you play a brass instrument. Some instruments cannot be played indefinitely without rest periods. The union also has an unfair list and a national defaulter's list, which are designed to protect members against employers who have not fulfilled contracts. It is illegal for a union member to work for an employer on these lists. You also may not work for employers who have not signed union contracts. The union contract not only protects the musician, but it can protect the employer against musicians who do not show up or are capriciously unable to perform. Each local has a trial board, which deals with disputed contracts.

If enough pension credits are built up over the years, a musician receives a pension from the local to which he or she belongs. In the case of studio musicians this can mount up to quite a bit of money.

Under the Music Performance Trust Fund (MPTF) record companies that are signatories to the AFM agreements must pay less than ½ of 1 percent of their gross annual profits to the MPTF and a slightly higher amount to the Special Payments Fund. The money collected by the Special Payments Fund goes back to the musicians who make recordings, based on their earnings from recording. The other half goes to the MPTF. Each local union receives an allocation of some of this money and hires musicians to do school concerts, hospital performances, and other live music jobs. Some concerts are funded by the MPTF alone and some include matching funds from local schools or charities. These concerts are always free to the public and constitute one of the most intelligent and progressive activities of the musicians' union.

Unions do not usually get jobs for their members, but they do function on behalf of the working membership. Many locals of the union do assist their members in getting jobs through an availability list. This list states the type of music the musician plays, whether the musician reads music, and whether the musician is free to travel. If you join the union, you should be sure to ask the secretary of your local about this list. The qualities of one union local may be quite different from those of another local. Some of the larger locals are quite impersonal; others are informal. In twelve years of membership in the New York local I never worked an MPTF job, nor did I ever get a job directly through the union. In the numerous years I have been a member of the Denver local I have gotten quite a few jobs through the union, including some MPTF concerts. It is up to you to make it clear to the secretary of the local what you can do. If your union officers are not responsive to your needs, then you should vote against them in the local elections. Many locals publish a directory of members, stating what instruments they play and including addresses and phone numbers. Make sure that your listing in the directory is correct.

Other benefits of union membership include special discounts, group health insurance, credit unions, life insurance plans, instrument insurance, and educational workshops. Some locals guarantee that a contract will be paid if the job is played and will help members take legal action against an offending client. Other unions offer free videos for their members. The union has an excellent pension plan that covers all national recording work and also includes disability protection. Unfortunately, only about forty locals of the union include local work in the pension program.

If you are planning to pursue a successful career as a professional musician, you will eventually have to join the musicians' union. When should you join? It is difficult to answer this question, but here are some guidelines. Most people start out by playing occasional professional jobs while going to school or working in another field. In most cases this is not the right time to join the union. Many small clubs or coffeehouses don't hire union musicians because they cannot afford to pay the union minimums. Once you are a member of the union there are a number of regulations that you are expected to follow or you may be fined or expelled from the union. You may not play professionally with nonunion musicians or work without a union contract. Even such a seemingly innocent activity as playing a benefit for another musician or cause without pay requires the permission of the union.

In my judgment the time to join the union is when you have decided to be a full-time professional and when you have some reasonable basis to assume that you are going to be able to support yourself as a musician. If you get an opportunity for a regular symphony job, a recording date, or a job offer from a working band, then the decision will be made for you. Don't join in your hometown if you know you are going to move to Nashville next month. It is best to hold off and join in your new location rather than put up with the complexities of transferring your membership. There may be a minimum residency requirement in your new local, although this can sometimes be overcome with the help of a manager or record company, or a friend who is a member of the local that you wish to join.

The union is really making an effort to deal with the 1990s, but some outmoded rules remain. For example, the commission rate for personal managers is limited to 10 percent. Maybe this made sense in the big band era, but no competent manager would work for this fee today.

The union has set up an 800 phone number—800-ROAD-GIG. It is staffed twenty-four hours a day, seven days a week, by a human being, not a machine. Its purpose is to provide emergency assistance to musicians in trouble. Its intent is to prove to traveling musicians that the union is prepared to help them with financial or legal assistance in times of emergency.

Another move is the establishment of a reduced scale for pressings produced in quantities of under 5,000. Before the adoption of this scale, all musicians who played on recordings were paid the same minimum fee, unless they demanded extra money, as do some of the key Nashville, Los Angeles, or New York side musicians. In 1996 another scale was established for records budgeted at under $85,000. This scale is a recognition of records that fall between superstar-status albums and esoteric musical projects. This new scale pays musicians just over 60 percent of the higher budgeted projects.

OTHER UNIONS

AFTRA represents singers and radio and TV talent. It has forty-three locals in the United States. In many of the smaller towns, the media are nonunion. Dues are based on annual earnings, ranging from $24 to several hundred dollars a year. The initiation fee varies from local to local—in Los Angeles it is $800. AFTRA has a bonus agreement with the record companies that provides for bonuses for background singers at various sales plateaus. This is an intelligent concept reflecting an appreciation of the value of studio singers to the finished record.

LA SAG has an initiation fee of $1,122.50. In order to join you must have been a working member of AFTRA, Actors' Equity, AGMA, or AGVA for at least a year, or you must have a promise of employment as a player (not an extra) in a film or a commercial on film. Dues are based on earnings.

AGMA is the union for performers in opera, ballet, concerts, recitals, and oratorios. AGMA negotiates for Metropolitan Opera singers and for touring opera companies. Dues are based on income, and the initiation fee depends upon the fee received in your initial contract.

AGVA (American Guild of Variety Artists) represents comics, jugglers, magicians, variety acts, and nightclub singers. In recent years it has not been a significant voice in the music industry.

It is unfortunate that many performers have to join three or four different unions in the entertainment field. AFTRA, Actors' Equity, AGMA, and AGVA have a loose affiliation agreement. Members of these unions pay reduced dues and initiation fees when they join the other unions. The AFM does not participate in this agreement.

All of these unions hire numerous full-time employees on a national and local level. This is particularly true of the AFM. On a national level there are attorneys, recording representatives, and a variety of officials who are elected at the national conventions of the various unions. The larger locals also have their own attorneys and specialists in such areas as Broadway show scales, recording scales, commercials, and other media. The AFM employs many business agents at the local level who enforce union rules and recruit new members. As a union member of the various unions you are required to carry your membership card at all times. Nonpayment of dues eventually leads to expulsion from any of the music unions.

15

RADIO

*T*he owner of a radio station may set policy in a general way, but the general manager of the station is responsible for the day-to-day operation and management of the station. Below the general manager is the operations manager. She must have a good general concept of both the business and creative ends of radio. The operations manager hires the program director, who may also be the music director on a music-format station, or the music director may be another person.

There are several departments in a radio station. The programming director is responsible for the on-the-air operation of the station. The traffic department handles the time that is available for commercials and attempts to keep commercials for competing products at least ten minutes apart. The sales department sells commercial time in the community, and the continuity department writes script and public service announcements. The people in continuity may rewrite commercials to conform with the station's image and standards, and they also write public service announcements and make sure that the radio station log is kept. The log is a minute-by-minute description of what goes on the air and is required by the FCC (Federal Communications Commission). The FCC licenses radio stations, and these licenses must be renewed every three years. The station is required to devote 10 percent of its airtime to public service programming. This programming may include news and public service announcements (PSAs).

The air personnel in radio include news and announcing personnel and disc jockeys. In larger markets the disc jockeys work with engineers, whose job is to cue the records, monitor the sound, punch in the correct commercials (usually on cartridges), and make sure that the station signal is operating correctly. In smaller stations one person may be a disc jockey, an announcer, and an engineer. Similarly the program director and the music director of a small station may be the same person and may also have a shift on the air as a disc jockey. Many stations do some sort of production for local commercials. This production may include voice-overs, announcements by disc jockeys, and sound collages. In the larger markets disc jockeys make a good percentage of their income from voice-overs. Sales departments at radio stations get paid on a commission basis. In some stations they make more than anyone at the station.

Disc jockeys in the largest cities may make upwards of $2,000 a week. They can also make additional money by doing record hops, assuming the role of master of ceremony at social functions, and doing commercials. In New York and Los Angeles the top jockeys earn more from commercials than from their radio jobs. FM radio now dominates the airwaves, so all of the top radio people are now working on FM.

Radio station offices are often in the downtown section of a city, but the transmitter and antennae are usually located in the suburbs. The signal is transmitted from the offices to the transmitter on specially leased telephone lines or radio circuit cables running from the studio to the transmitter. In 1995, according to the Statistical Abstract of the United States, there were 5109 AM commercial radio stations, and 4413 commercial FM outlets. The same book reports an additional 400 Corporation for Public Broadcasting noncommercial FM outlets in 1993. NBC was the first radio network. It was founded in 1926 and is now owned by Westwood One. CBS started in 1927, and ABC was formed when the government broke up the two separate divisions of NBC in the late thirties.

Radio today operates under a number of formats, which cover virtually every type of music—from heavy metal to New Age to Country & Western—and news. Top 40 radio used to dominate AM radio. It began as a result of an incident in a bar in Omaha, Nebraska, in 1955. Todd Storz and Bill Stewart were sitting in a bar for several hours, and they noticed that one record kept getting played. Just before closing time they saw a waitress take a quarter of her own money and play the same song three more times. From this experience Storz developed the concept that people liked to hear the same records over and over. In a Top 40 format a station has a playlist of forty songs, which are played in rotation throughout the day and night. On some stations four to seventeen records are rotated every one or two hours; on others there is somewhat less repetition. Occasional golden oldies are played, and sometimes a new record is added as an extra. If there is a good listener reaction to the extra, and if the stores start to report sales, the record then gets charted for the next week and is played on a regular rotation basis.

Top 40 radio was an ideal medium for singles, because the continual exposure would make or break a record in short order. Disc jockeys on Top 40 tended to be fast-talking and enthusiastic, talking over the intros and endings of the songs.

By the mid-1980s Top 40 no longer dominated radio, but had given way to AOR—album-oriented rock—and CHR—contemporary hit radio. AOR radio plays various cuts from a hit album, thereby giving the appearance of having a looser format than top 40. CHR is a blend of Top 40 together with selected oldies. Today's oldies are not necessarily fifties or sixties hits, but are also records that may have been popular as recently as six months ago.

Radio is increasingly inclined to program material that will keep the listener tuned to the station without changing the dial. Older hits provide that sort of security to the stations, and because of this, in addition to CHR and AOR, there are many stations that limit their programming to golden oldies.

When FM radio was young, it was a much more experimental

medium than it is today. KMPX in San Francisco pioneered free-form radio in the sixties. Disc jockeys programmed their own music and approached a radio set like a performer doing a set in a club. They mixed many sorts of music and improvised some of their programming and comments on the air, much the way a jazz musician plays. The free-form format itself became somewhat self-indulgent and stagnant, and today can be found in part only on some public radio stations or an occasional late-night FM show on commercial radio.

Even classical and jazz stations tend to use formats and to stay away from more adventurous music. It is the rare station that will program avant-garde jazz or classical music, for fear of losing the audience.

Other formats today include news radio, business radio, and various Country & Western, rap, soul, and disco formats. In the 1990s the AAA, or soft-rock, format became important, and even more recently an Americana format has emerged that combines elements of country and folk music.

Heavy metal music is programmed from Dallas on a satellite feed. Some stations use automated or satellite formats. The programming is provided on tape from one of a number of automation services, such as TM in Dallas or Drake-Chennault in Los Angeles. A local announcer usually adds the local news and weather live on the air. Automation saves quite a bit of money in station salaries, and once the format is decided, all programming is done by the service. Many stations that are not automated use certain syndicated shows, such as a weekly Top 40 countdown. The reason for buying a syndicated show is that a local station could not provide the expertise or production slickness that is evident in syndicated shows. Some of the syndicated shows also feature interviews with celebrities, who would not be available to a local station.

Before Top 40 took over the air waves many disc jockeys used to do a great deal of their own programming. In 1960 the FCC discovered the existence of payola. Some disc jockeys were receiving money and expensive gifts, and sometimes a cut of the publishing on a record, in return for playing records on the radio. Several jocks, notably Alan Freed, were indicted and in effect driven off the radio. Stations began to take programming out of the hands of the jocks, and the music director decided on what records were to be played. In some cases the jocks are allowed to choose which records they play from a group of several records, classified by category. For example, there may be a list of six golden oldies from which the jock's third record is selected. The next record may be a novelty record from another list. Industry gossip accepts the existence of some payola, but it is presumed to be less common than during the early rock days. It is common knowledge that stations catering to the black audience ("soul stations") pay less money to their employees than the Top 40 stations do, and it is often hinted in the trade papers that such stations are more vulnerable to payoffs. Sometimes disc jockeys take odd measures in reaction to current records or programming practices. Al "Jazzbo" Collins once programmed Art Mooney's "I'm Looking Over a Four-Leaf Clover" for three and a half hours on a radio station in Salt Lake City. The interest that he created turned a record that Collins played as a joke into a national hit.

The FCC regulates station policies by insisting upon a number of standards in hiring, programming, and free use of the air. When a station editorializes it must offer free time to people with opposing ideas. There must be someone working at the station who is a licensed engineer or a disc jockey with a first-class FCC license. In order for a disc jockey to run his own equipment, he must have a third-class FCC license. Licenses are granted to those who pass the FCC examination, and some schools specialize in preparing students for these examinations. Many disc jockeys are able to pass the examinations through studying the manuals without outside assistance.

The monetary heart of radio beats to the sale of commercials. The rates for these spots are set largely through the Arbitron ratings. There are four rating periods a year. These ratings pinpoint the station's share of the market and the age group that listens to the station. During rating periods stations often hold contests, but the FCC rules specify that the contests must start before the beginning of the rating period. The prizes include money, trips, cars, records, or concert tickets. Many of the stations get the prizes through trade-outs. The station trades free commercials in return for the prizes. This is supposed to benefit the listener, the advertiser, and, of course, the station. The Arbitron ratings are done by fifteen-minute periods, and any five-minute section within a fifteen-minute period is considered to be a separate segment. The station tries to get people to listen from 4:10 to 4:20, for example. This ranks as two segments. Arbitron relies on diaries to get its results. These diaries are kept by a small population sample chosen by the rating service from the general population. Arbitron ranks radio markets according to the population of a metropolitan area. The survey targets consumers who are twelve years old or older. The diary is filled out for seven consecutive days. Diaries are now scanned on an optical disk, then entered and edited on a computer. By using the ratings, an advertiser can target specific age, ethnic, or gender groups. When the ratings go up, so do the prices of a station's one-minute spots. In several cases program directors have been caught buying the diaries and filling in fake listening data.

There are seven FCC commissioners, appointed by the President of the United States and approved by the Senate. No more than four of them may be from one political party. The FCC has a staff of nearly 2,000 people and an annual budget of $20 million. It regulates price fixing; monitors inequality in rate cards (no special rates for preferred customers), kickbacks to advertising agencies, and obscenity on the air; prohibits trading in radio station licenses; and acts in the community interest. In some instances people have petitioned the FCC to prevent a format change in a market where the old format was unique in serving the community but the new format was already represented by the programming of another station. This has been quite effective, because few stations want to undergo an extensive FCC investigation. In forty years the FCC has lifted only one radio station license for something said on the air, but on a number of occasions the FCC has provisionally approved a license renewal, contingent upon the performance of a station within a specified time period. The FCC grants some stations authority to broadcast twenty-four hours a day, and others receive authority to broadcast from sunrise to sundown. The commission ruled that FM and AM radio could use only 25 percent duplicate format in 1979. This aided the development of FM radio.

Under the Reagan administration many rules were eased, in terms of public service programming or compelling an owner to keep a station for three years before selling it. As a result of this, many more radio stations were brokered on a profit basis and formats were changed even more rapidly than before.

Radio and Records is probably the leading radio trade paper. There are numerous weekly tip sheets for radio stations, notably the *Bill Gavin Re-*

port. It surveys a number of stations, which are called Gavin reporters. They report additions of new records to their playlist and unusual listener response to new records. Record company people avidly follow Gavin and take any favorable information about their records to other stations in hopes of getting more airplay. There are numerous other station tip sheets, like the *Monday Morning Quarterback* or the *Brenneman Report*, that circulate to stations and record companies.

Today the last outpost of Top 40 radio in its pure form is the weekly rock and country countdown shows pioneered by Casey Kasem. They play the Top 40 of the week, along with oldies, interviews, and special features. A few AM radio stations broadcast in stereo, but most are in monaural. FM radio uses stereo and generally has a superior sound to AM.

Perhaps AM radio will become more experimental, since FM has displaced it in general popularity. It would be refreshing to hear more daring programming on some sort of commercial radio. Since there is a market for all kinds of music in this country, advertisers should realize that that potential market must include consumers whom they are not currently reaching.

16

MUSIC VIDEO AND CABLE TELEVISION

$\mathcal{T}$he original edition of this book avoided the subject of television, but recommended Bob Shank's fine book *The Cool Fire* as a good vehicle for understanding television. With the worldwide existence of MTV, the success of the Nashville Network, and the start of other cable channels that hope to compete with MTV and VH1, it is time to take a quick look at video as an outlet for music.

First of all, music video is definitely a powerful tool for the promotion of records. It has also created a sort of new music genre, in the sense that many of the older stars of rock and country music are not comfortable with the medium itself. A major record company expects to invest $50,000 or more in a music video. According to Ann E. Kaplan, in her book *Rocking Around the Clock: Music Television, Post-Modernism and Consumer Culture*, written in 1987, there are some 228 videos shown every twenty-four hours on MTV. Because of the high cost of videos, the channel initially was flooded with European videos, simply because European producers were able to come up with quality product at less cost.

As music video is currently presented, there are a rather limited number of forms being utilized. There are clips that could just as easily be movies of live concerts; there are abstract and often pretentious art videos that owe a great deal to the medium of art films; there are a certain number of videos that are visual feasts, presenting a series of camera shots that highlight a song; and there are humorous videos, notably those of ZZ Top that present the group in a fantasy-filled way that makes them human.

So far the video always seems the captive of the song itself. Why shouldn't a video be ten or fifteen minutes long? Why couldn't the song be a sort of departure point, with sections of a song repeated and combined with, God forbid, acting, dancing, or some sort of visual feast?

Some feature videos try to cover an entire album, like Michael Jackson's *Thriller*. I still feel that this is missing the potential of the medium. In the future, video and music video could become just as experimental as, say, the music of the Beatles was in the late sixties. This is not likely to happen on MTV, where Kaplan points out that it is difficult to tell the music videos from the commercials, because they all blend into the same visual, auditory, and kind of temporary look.

One of the advantages of cable over radio is that eventually the viewer will be able to dial dozens of different stations. I would hope that this will inevitably lead to some experimental channels and some that will dare to program experimental videos, just as public radio at its best dares to program new, experimental music. Most cities have cable access agreements with their suppliers that obligate the stations to teach local residents how to use the equipment and to develop shows. This program may ultimately lead to some very interesting possibilities, just as many artists today are releasing their own music on self-produced cassettes in limited quantities.

From a consumer standpoint, by 1986, according to Marjorie Costello and Cynthia Katz in their book *Breaking into Video*, there were some 20,000 stores specializing in videocassettes and more than 10,000 other outlets that carried them. They are appearing in supermarkets and all sorts of convenience stores now.

So far cable television, outside of MTV and its competitors and the

Nashville Network, hasn't made all that much use of live music. There are movies of various festivals available and an occasional live concert video or a special program about a particular group. Nickelodeon features some Canadian children's shows that have music as an important part of the format.

By the mid-nineties MTV had introduced more and more non-music programming on its American programs. It has also expanded its influence throughout most of the world. MTV Latino is seen in most Central and South American countries. It uses local video jockeys, but the music is a blend of English- and Spanish-language songs. MTV also has European programs, and has even started broadcasting in India.

I look forward to the time when cable will have live and prerecorded music shows emanating from different parts of the world. In the meantime, mastering the art of performing on videos is increasingly important for the artist who wants a music business career in the twenty-first century. Opportunities abound to apprentice with local cable companies and perhaps get their help in preparing a video demo.

The future of technology certainly will include the production of interactive disc or videocassettes, where the consumer can see an act perform, hear the sound on some sort of compact disc or DAT format, and dial up biographical information on members of the group. By the year 2000, computers, television sets, and CD or video disc players will probably be aligned in a single machine. Record stores and radio stations as we currently know them will probably be unrecognizable to the twenty-first-century consumer.

part 2

CAREERS
IN
MUSIC

17

STUDIO WORK AND ENGINEERING

One of the most lucrative professions in the music industry is free-lance studio work. A free-lance player is one who works for a number of people in the recording of movies, television shows, commercials, or records. Most studio musicians do relatively little public performing, spending the majority of their working life in recording studios. Although all kinds of recording sessions take place in all the music industry centers, New York does the bulk of radio and television commercials, Hollywood does the great majority of film scores and television shows, and Nashville and Los Angeles do the most records. Lesser amounts of studio work are available in such cities as Toronto, Chicago, Montreal, and Miami.

Breaking into studio work is difficult because studio musicians guard their jobs very carefully and because the people who hire studio musicians have a very low tolerance for musical mistakes. Generally the vehicle for breaking in is sponsorship by an older musician or singer. This sponsorship is a delicate thing. Technically a new person is brought in only when he possesses a skill that does not replace one of the working players or singers. Usually this is not literally possible. What happens is that a musician is brought in who has a particular kind of expertise that is undeniable. A young keyboard player might break in on synthesizer or a guitar player might enter the circle through playing special effects for rock records. While these skills might be competitive to the talents of existing players, employing them is less abrasive than, say, bringing in a young high-note trumpet player to replace an older musician whose skills are declining.

A studio person needs to be a completely reliable person. Sessions are very tightly scheduled because of the high pay scales and the expensive studio rentals. The player is usually expected to be a good sight reader, to be able to pick up a piece of music and perform it almost perfectly without any rehearsal. The union does not permit rehearsals for studio jobs unless they are paid at the same rate as the actual job. The player is also expected to be able to improvise freely in any style required. He should also have an even temperament and not get upset at any changes made in the music, whether they are cuts or additions. Too much concern about one's own abilities can be harmful because the decisions made on whether to use a particular piece of music or a solo may not be at all relevant to the work of an individual player. These decisions may relate to a future cut in a commercial or film, a change of mind by the producer, or some other factor not apparent at the time of recording. The player must have the ability to shift gears rapidly without apparent effort. The key of a song may be changed to accommodate a singer, an improvised section may be thrown in to fill in for a solo that is thought to be inappropriate—any number of things may result in a modification of the music.

The player is also expected to be able to double on various instruments. A guitar player should be able to play mandolin or banjo; sax players should also play flute, clarinet, the recorder family, and even the oboe; and brass and string players should have some doubling facility as well. Players receive extra fees for doubling, but it is still cheaper to hire a doubler than to pay an additional player for some slight passage. Singers are often expected to sing in styles or vocal ranges that are unfamiliar to the average singer.

The bulk of the hiring for studio work is done by contractors. They are paid double scale for this service and also usually play on the session. They are responsible for calling rest periods, for making sure that the sessions are reported to the union, and for seeing that proper payments are made. In Hollywood there are some fifteen or twenty major film contractors, according to Robert T. Faulkner in his fascinating book *Hollywood Studio Musicians*. Each contractor has a first-call list. These are the people the contractor prefers to work with. If they are unavailable the contractor resorts to a second- or third-call person. One of the ways that people break into studio work is when no one whom a contractor knows is available and he takes a chance and calls an unfamiliar person. This is a nervous situation for both the contractor and the musician. If the musician flubs the job, the particular composer or arranger may not use that contractor again, and you can be sure that the contractor will never hire that musician again. Sometimes people get the opportunity to do studio work too early in their careers; they blow the chance and are in effect forever blacklisted, even though at a later date they might well have played the same part perfectly.

I have a good friend, Dan Fox, who is an arranger and composer and also a jazz guitarist. While he was a student at the Manhattan School of Music he got a call to play six-string bass guitar. This is a rather awkward instrument (it was used in the early James Bond movies), and music for it is written in the bass clef. Dan went to the date and sight-read the part without a mistake. It was a fairly difficult part, written in the key of G flat (6 flats) in the bass clef. Most guitar players have trouble reading in the bass clef, so this was a reasonably difficult reading assignment for a young guitarist. During the next few days Dan got four or five calls for studio dates, although he had done scarcely any studio work at the time. On one of these dates he had to play a style of rhythm guitar that used a rhythm pattern called a shuffle beat. Dan had never done anything like that, and he flubbed the part. He did not receive any further calls for several months, and never again on a regular basis.

Let me review what happened to Dan in the light of my previous observations about studio work. He was probably called as a sub for some unavailable player on the first date. When he did an exceptional job with a difficult part, it was assumed that he was as good and as versatile as any of the leading studio players. Therefore he got the other calls. When he betrayed his lack of experience, the same grapevine that had worked for him turned against him—and contractors don't like to take chances. There is nothing especially unique about this situation. What is peculiar is that the whole process takes place without the musician's really understanding what is going on and without anyone trying to explain it.

The market for studio singers, particularly in regard to the performance of radio and television commercials, is even more restricted because the financial rewards are so great and the competition is so fierce. Nevertheless the business must hire new people in order to continue to grow. It is important to be honest with the people who hire you. Some kinds of studio work are available to people who do not read music, for example. Glen Campbell was making $100,000 a year, supposedly, as a studio guitarist in Los Angeles before he became a successful singer. He did not read music, but he could play country music and some other things better than the studio guitarists who were available in Hollywood. Similarly, soloists are hired to sing on commercials and specialists are hired to do guitar solos on rock records who read little or no music. Generally, doing studio work gives the musician some incentive to learn how to read better, and he ends up studying music. In Nashville most basic sessions are done without any written music at all. Sometimes there are chord charts using the number system. In this system a chord number is written with slashes for beats. A C-chord would be I in the key of C, or IV in the key of G. The players follow the numbers and improvise the solos based on these chord patterns. Some of the Nashville studio players also read music, but reading isn't required in order to work.

In order to make a good living in studio work it is necessary to work for a number of contractors. This can be awkward if you get several calls for the same time period. Often a musician is not told what is being recorded. Occasionally a contractor will ask a musician to try to get out of a previous commitment. Whether a musician will do this depends upon how much work the contractor gives the musician and what the relationship is between the musician and the other contractor. If you ask favors too many times, the contractor will probably stop calling you. Similarly, many studio players and singers do not take any real vacations, or they take vacations for very brief periods of time. There is a certain paranoia in studio work. If you are away and the contractor calls someone else, he may stop using you. In the major recording centers many musicians and singers use answering services. When one of these services makes a mistake on a time or date of a session the contractor will not always believe the musician's explanation and may not hire him again.

In Faulkner's study of studio musicians he found that most string players were frustrated recitalists. They never had any desire to play in the symphony but wanted to do solo recitals. Since the market for such recitalists is small, they drifted into studio work as a remunerative alternative to the symphony. For these string players anything less than a solo career was musically insignificant, and studio work paid better and was more varied than symphonic work, so they went that way. Brass and woodwind players usually find studio work more challenging. Their parts are usually more interesting and more demanding than the string parts on today's rock records or in most of the current movies. Some ex–jazz players became arrangers and composers through diligent study. A few of them, such as Quincy Jones and Lalo Schifrin, are now successful film composers.

Some studio players continue to play music in their spare time that is closer to their own personal preferences. They play in chamber groups, community orchestras, jazz bands, or compose and conduct. Except for some record dates, the bulk of recording sessions are done during the day, so it is possible to perform other music at night. As musicians get older it becomes a question of how much energy and love they have for playing music. After working all day do they really want to play at night? One excellent studio percussion player in New York once told me that he doesn't have a musical instrument in his house and hasn't practiced in twenty years.

Studio work pays quite well. Faulkner found that the income of the musicians he surveyed in 1965 ranged from $7,000 to $62,000, with the median point at $27,800. I suspect that the current range would be more like $20,000 to $100,000. A few musicians do better, but the use of samplers and synthesizers has reduced the volume of work for many players. Singers command even higher wages. Whether you should go after a career in studio work depends upon whether you have the right personality, talent, and contacts. For the first time musicians are beginning to work in the studios who have actually sought such a career in their college programs. Most of the people in studio work today got there by accident rather than intention.

There really is no way for musicians to break into the studio scene. Singers can make tapes and give them to contractors, but musicians do not get hired this way. A positive approach is to use any opportunity to get into any recording situation. When you are starting out, do local commercials, demos for songwriters, work in a studio at your college if you can. Once you get to one of the recording centers try to meet as many musicians as possible. Some of the musicians will become arrangers and composers, and they will tend to hire people that they know. Take any opportunity to play that will bring you to the attention of composers, arrangers, and contractors. If you continue to study your instrument to perfect your skills, study with someone who has been or is a studio player. He may be able to help you meet some of the people who do the hiring. Think in terms of developing versatility. Take up other instruments if you can, and in your practice sessions work on your weaknesses rather than your strengths. Have patience and keep practicing so that when the work comes you are ready for it.

THE DECLINE OF STUDIO WORK

The late 1980s saw a decline in work opportunities for studio musicians. Synthesizers, drum machines, and advanced sampling devices together with the use of MIDI (musical instrument digital interface) to program multiple keyboards have enabled a single composer working out of a sophisticated home studio to write and produce commercials and even film scores. Although there are still quite a few film scores that utilize large orchestras, more and more composers are turning to electronic musical instruments to replace musicians.

The good news is that this is the era of the composer, and if you write music you can make use of this same technology to experiment with a whole new world of sounds. No one can accurately predict future trends in music, and optimists feel that the electronic sounds will be integrated with acoustic instruments to form a whole new world of music. Pessimists feel that we are witnessing the death of orchestral instruments as we have known them. Regardless of who turns out to be correct, it behooves the young musician to master the technology and to orient herself in a more compositional direction than might have been appropriate ten years ago.

ENGINEERING

In the last few decades the technical aspects of recording have become increasingly complex. A multitrack studio looks like something out of a science fiction film. Often two engineers sit at the giant control panel. One operates the tape machine and the other does the actual recording. The tape machine operator, or second engineer, may be an apprentice engineer.

Currently there are two contradictory trends in recording. One is the superstar projects, which often combine analog and digital multitrack machines, together with a very lengthy mixing process that involves all sorts of expensive outboard gear.

On the other hand, the A-DAT format has enabled competent musicians and engineers to record at relatively low cost. The cost of this equipment and the tape that it uses is much lower than that required for the analog format.

More and more records are partly or largely recorded in home studios using MIDI, sequencers, computers, and sampling. These tapes are often made in the home studio but mixed in the high-end studios of the major recording centers.

Many of the best engineers in the business have started out as apprentices. Gradually they worked their way up to doing small sessions and eventually larger ones. A good engineer has an almost unlimited reserve of patience and tact. Many hours must be spent in the studio. Much time is wasted on following the whims of producers or musicians, but there is a great deal of gratification, too. Larger studios also employ maintenance engineers because many recording engineers don't have a great deal of technical knowledge of the equipment. Maintenance engineers are responsible for maintaining and repairing the equipment, and they usually do little recording work. Mastering engineers work in mastering studios and spend their time converting tapes to disc or making cassette masters. There are many such studios in the leading music centers.

A number of colleges and one- to two-year vocational programs have their own recording studios. Studying at such a school is one way to learn how to operate the equipment. The annual school directory of *Mix* magazine, published each June, lists dozens of such schools all over

North America. Another way to get into engineering is to apprentice yourself to a studio for little or no pay. Over a period of time you will become familiar with the equipment and end up doing some recording sessions. It is increasingly difficult to get this kind of training in New York or Los Angeles because there are too many people who want it. You might be better off starting in your own hometown or the town where you are going to school. When you do come to a music center you will then have a basic grasp of the equipment and have a better chance of getting a job. If you study engineering in college, you should also take some basic music courses. This will help you to work with musicians and arrangers. Some business courses can help if you harbor any thoughts of owning and operating your own studio someday.

There are studios all over North America now that have reasonably contemporary equipment, although they may not have three and four 32-track digital machines. Hit records have been cut in Miami; Omaha; Muscle Shoals, Alabama; Aspen, Colorado; and Sacramento. Local commercials and industrial films and music videos are recorded anywhere that studio facilities and a reasonable-size market exist. A few engineers are even beginning to free-lance in the same way that producers do, not working for one studio but working for specific clients. For a successful engineer this is one way out of the exhausting routine of recording hour after hour. For a few lucky engineers it is also the road to riches, because the superstar engineers get a small royalty for each record sold, as do most good producers.

If you elect to study engineering at a college or vocational school, be sure to check out:

1. The quality of the equipment. It should be at least 24-track. An automated mixing console is also a desirable teacher.

2. How much hands-on time you will actually get with the equipment.

3. What sort of experience the teachers have. What have they done, how many markets have they worked in, and have they recorded a variety of musical styles?

18

CAREERS IN RECORDS
AND RADIO

$\mathcal{S}$ ince I have covered the scope of the record business in some detail you should have a good overview of what jobs are available at record companies. How does one prepare for these jobs? There are quite a few colleges offering degree programs, or at least courses, in the music industry.* If your orientation is toward the creative side of the business, such as producing records, it is helpful to have a fairly comprehensive music background, some knowledge of engineering, and a business background. If the college of your choice does not offer all of these options, take some courses at another college and arrange for the credits to be transferred. Any work in a studio will build familiarity with the equipment and give you a chance to experiment with various sounds and instruments.

If your direction is in the business area of records, including promo-

---

* See chapter 23 and the list of colleges offering music business programs in the Appendix.

tion, sales, or accounting work, you will probably want to get a degree in business administration. Take as many music courses as you can, particularly a few basic theory courses and a history of popular music and jazz. Try to take some courses in copywriting and advertising, if they are available. Show business law is another business area that is available to the law student. Vanderbilt University has a course in show business law, and some other schools offer seminars in it from time to time. The most practical way to get started in show business law is to get your degree and find a law firm in one of the music capitals that specializes in entertainment law. Books like *This Business of Music* will give you a general introduction to music industry procedures, but it is necessary to get some practical experience with a firm that handles many industry clients.

Because so many of today's record companies are active in other forms of media, it is useful to take courses in radio, television, and film even though you may not plan to work in these areas. Foreign language courses are also useful as the population of the United States starts to include more and more Spanish-speaking people, and as more and more record companies are owned by Japanese or European transnational conglomerates.

Do you have to go to college to pursue a career in the record business? Not necessarily. Particularly in the creative area, it is possible for musicians to develop production skills through extensive work in recording studios. In my opinion at least a couple of years of college will definitely be helpful in developing your skills and expanding your general knowledge. As the business expands, degrees will probably become more of a prerequisite to getting good jobs and advancing up the corporate ladder, particularly with the larger companies. Be sure if you are going to school that there is some relationship between what you are studying and what you want to do after graduation.

RADIO

Program directors and air personalities should choose a communications major in college. Histories of popular music, jazz, folk, and country music are useful to an air personality in order to build a broad understanding of the roots of American music. Unfortunately, most colleges offer limited surveys of American popular music, if they offer any such courses at all. Sometimes it is possible to take such classes through the extension departments of a local college or university. Local schools that advertise on the radio and in the newspaper promising you careers in radio or television should be carefully investigated. Who is doing the teaching, and what has happened to graduates of the programs? Be skeptical about any extravagant promises offered by such schools. They may be able to help you pass the FCC engineering license examinations, however.

In their day-to-day work disc jockeys may have to cue their own records, operate a control board, do live commercials from prewritten copy, prepare copy for commercials, do some production work for commercials, set up microphones, answer the telephones, do public service announcements, weather, and sports, and offer occasional or frequent bits of humor. The morning disc jockeys tend to talk more than those on the air later in the day. In the larger markets the engineering work may be done by an engineer, but on a small radio station the disc jockey is a one-person team. Many disc jockeys get their start on college radio. The vehicle for progressing is an audition tape called an *air check*. An air check is a tape of the jockey, featuring disc jockey patter, introductions to records, weather, and other talk, interspersed with only fragments of the actual records.

There is a great deal of turnover in on-the-air personalities because of changes in station ownership or format. Formats may change because of poor ratings, sale of the radio station, a revamping of station policy, or arbitrary decisions on the part of the station management. Personality is a key factor in getting a job as a disc jockey, and it is important that the personality of the jock be compatible with the format of the station. Disc jockeys are expected to do their homework. They should read the music trade papers and be able to provide some background on the records they air. Some jocks keep a notebook in which they write down thoughts or bits of humor. Some do quite a bit of home preparation before they come to the station and some are masters of improvisation. They are often involved in public service community activities, such as fund-raising events for charities.

A salesperson for a radio station is more apt to come from a business background, with a college degree in business or no degree at all. Salespeople need to develop an intimate knowledge of a community's structure and its business life. They need to be able to match a station's ratings and demographics to the needs of a particular business, and they must have the type of personality that enjoys selling. Sometimes they may prepare sample copy for commercials for prospective clients.

The operations department of the station must referee any disputes between sales and programming. Sometimes these departments have opposing orientations. A commercial should not be at odds with the music format of the station. Certain disc jockeys may do particularly good commercials for products that go along with their own image. The operations manager must know what the station does and where it is going.

Station managers come out of a sales or programming background, as do many general managers. Some radio station people have turned to syndication as a more lucrative source of income, and some program directors have turned to consultation services or are involved in the production of station jingle packages or comedy packages for radio stations.

19

COMPOSING, ARRANGING, AND FILM MUSIC

A composer writes original music. An arranger is someone who orchestrates music by himself or by other writers. Some composers are also arrangers, but the two skills are somewhat different. Irving Berlin was a composer; he wrote melodies and lyrics. He had little formal knowledge of music and did not arrange his own songs. Nelson Riddle has arranged quite a few songs for recording sessions, songs that were written by other people. Lalo Schifrin is a composer and arranger who writes film scores. Some people would not have considered Berlin to be a composer but would describe him only as a songwriter. This is their attempt to differentiate him from Beethoven or Bartók.

Composers and arrangers usually have music school backgrounds, with years of study in theory, orchestration, and composition. Some successful composer-arrangers have extensive playing backgrounds and pursued their interests in arranging and composing through private studies with a master teacher.

Very few musicians can make a reasonable living composing music for orchestra. Contemporary serious music does not sell well on records, and contemporary music is not widely performed by symphonies, so composer royalties are small. The copying of parts for symphonic works is incredibly expensive because of the large number of pages and parts involved. Many composers survive by teaching at colleges. Their works are performed by college orchestras or chamber groups, and graduate students are enlisted to copy parts. This can be a somewhat frustrating existence because the student orchestras are usually mediocre and because the composer may prefer to spend all her time writing, not teaching beginning music theory courses. Quite a few composers, such as George Crumb at the University of Pennsylvania, seem to be able to compose a considerable body of work while teaching at a college.

Lucrative careers are available to composer-arrangers in the composition and scoring of commercials, television shows, nightclub acts, Broadway shows, and movies. This sort of work requires a broad understanding of jazz and popular music. Most colleges have some sort of jazz or marching band, and writing for such groups is an invaluable experience in the training of a composer-arranger. Certain colleges, such as the Berklee College of Music in Boston or North Texas State University in Denton, Texas, specialize in training their students in the performance and writing of contemporary music. Some schools also offer courses in writing for film.

FILM MUSIC

Composing for film is one of the most challenging possibilities available for the contemporary composer. There are many drawbacks, but also quite a few aesthetic challenges. Generally the composer must work quickly, with little notice and tight deadlines. Often film-editing decisions are delayed, and so the music deadlines get tighter. In writing music to picture, the composer watches a rough cut of the film and is provided with cue sheets, which describe the action on the screen and give timings expressed in terms of feet of film. Using a conversion chart, the composer converts these footages to minutes and seconds. Today's film composers receive video dubs of the film and watch the film repeatedly to come up with creative musical contributions to a film.

In the 1930s many of the film composers were really songwriters, and they could not do their own orchestrations. Today the same person may arrange, compose, and conduct all of the music. If time problems develop, an orchestrator may be hired, but usually the composer will at least sketch out the arrangements. When a rock band "scores" a film they work in a different way. Usually they will write a series of songs around the action of the picture. Someone else may then do background instrumental music as required or the group may do it themselves. Whether a rock group's music will work with a film better or worse than a more formal score depends upon the subject matter of the movie and what the director is trying to achieve. Film music can be quite subtle, expressing unconscious motivations, setting time and place, helping to develop a character, and even expressing contradictions in a characterization. Some serious music composers, such as Aaron Copland, Virgil Thomson, and Irwin Bazelon, have composed quite a bit of film music.

It is usually the director of a film who decides on the person to write a film score and who makes the final decisions on what music will be used and what gets cut from the film. This is a sore point with composers, who often feel that their music is mutilated in the process, just as the cinematographers may well feel that their work has been butchered in the editing room. In the final dubbing process all of the music and other sounds in the film are synched with the picture. These other sounds include dialogue and natural sounds, such as thunderstorms. The director is the one who decides on the final mix, and the composer is usually not even present at this session.

There is a great deal of pressure placed upon the film composer to come up with a hit song to help promote a movie. A hit song is undoubtedly a potent promotional tool in selling the movie to the public, and a hit sound-track album can produce further revenue for the studio and for the composer. Many film companies, among them Warner Brothers and United Artists, have strong music publishing companies. Usually the film company keeps the publishing rights to the music of a

---

THE ROLE OF MUSIC IN A FILM

There are many excellent books on the use of music in films, but here is a rough outline of how music can contribute to the artistic qualities of a film.

1. It can underline the unspoken thoughts of a character.
2. It can convey a sense of time or place.
3. Music can imply a change in the action that will be shown later in the film.
4. Music can underline the qualities of a particular character.
5. It can contribute to the mood of a film. This can be done subtly by writing in opposition to the action on the screen, or obviously, for example by using a large string orchestra playing romantic love themes in a love sequence of a film.

---

film. A particularly hot composer may be able to retain half of the publishing rights for himself.

The fee for composing a major feature film score is usually $50,000 to $200,000 or more, although it may be more or less depending on the total budget of the film and the reputation of the composer. Certain songwriters, such as Sammy Cahn, are brought in to write a hit song for a film.* This is usually the title song, and it will be performed at the beginning and/or end of the film. Such a songwriter will demand as much as $15,000 to $25,000 for this sort of assignment, and of course there is no guarantee that the song will become a hit. Some film composers, such as Henry Mancini, have been quite successful in coming up with hit songs or instrumental themes for films. When film scores are written outside of Los Angeles the composer must often provide his own timing and cue sheets.

Jobs available in the composing and arranging field include composing and arranging for films, music copying, music supervision for a film

---

* Sammy Cahn is recently deceased.

studio, music librarians, vocal arrangers, lyricists, composers and arrangers for Broadway shows, and people to do the cue and timing sheets for movies.

The challenge of doing film music is in the variety of subjects that a film may cover. Each subject may necessitate research and experimentation in the music of another culture or historical period.

20

CONCERT PROMOTION AND CAREERS IN PUBLICITY

To be a good concert promoter one must have the heart of a gambler and the brain of a computer. Concert promotion begins with the choice of an act to promote. The promoter should check on record sales, airplay, and the attendance at any previous concerts that a group has done in the immediate area. If the act has appeared nearby, the promoter will want to know if the group is reliable and whether the concert appearances were a financial success. Most promoters concentrate on a single city or a small area that may include several cities. Occasionally a promoter or even the manager of an act will attempt to promote an entire national tour for her artist. Most local promoters will resent such invasions of their territory, and few promoters try such tactics.

The price of an act is usually set by the act's booking agency. Often that agency will have a strong relationship with certain local promoters and they will discourage a new person from entering the business. Some promoters start their careers while attending college. This gives them the luxury of operating without risking their own money, since most college concerts are financed by student activity fees.

To keep up with the current music scene a promoter must read the trade papers.* She may also read such papers as the *Village Voice*, *Rolling Stone*, the *New York Times*, and the weekend sections of the *San Francisco Chronicle* and the *Los Angeles Times*. These papers will keep her informed on what new acts are appearing in the major cities and what reviewers think of them.

In determining how to promote a particular concert, it is important to know exactly what age group the act will draw. This will govern the type of advertising that a promoter will do. If you are promoting a country music act, it would be natural to advertise on the local country music radio stations and to concentrate on newspapers and magazines that you think country music fans might read. The timing of a concert must be carefully considered. If you are planning to draw from a college age audience and the college is in finals week or out of session, you will be in trouble. Certain holidays may cause people to stay home, while others may draw them out to celebrate. If a concert is held outdoors, attendance will be affected by the weather, and you may also need to arrange an alternate site or a rain date.

Most of the more successful acts today demand a percentage of the gross receipts of the concert. This percentage may vary from 60 to 90 percent of the gross. If an act has been overexposed through frequent concert appearances, you may not be able to create sufficient excitement to sell many tickets. If the act is virtually unknown in your area, it is going to be necessary to do an all-out promotion job so that people will be enticed to the performance. Similarly, these factors should affect the setting of the ticket prices. A relatively unknown act will not sell out if the ticket prices are set too high. In the late fifties and early sixties percentage deals were less common, and a promoter could hire acts by paying a flat fee.

Promotional help may be available from the artist's record company. They may be willing to sponsor newspaper or radio ads advertising the group's current record and also mentioning the concert. These ads may

---

* Especially *Performance* and *Pulstar*.

be bought by the record company or the costs may be shared with the promoter. The record company can also help with posters, giveaways, radio interviews, window displays, and by reservicing the local radio stations and record stores with large quantities of the group's records.

Once a price is agreed upon and a signed contract is received, preparations for the concert should go full speed ahead. The campaign really gets under way some six to eight weeks before the actual concert. Tickets must be printed and ticket distribution outlets arranged. If the group does not provide its own light and sound equipment, arrangements must be made for rentals. Newspapers and magazines should be contacted with press releases, pictures, and other promotional materials. Enough lead time should be given so that the newspapers don't print their stories after the concert is over.

Posters should be printed and distributed in neighboring towns as well as in the city where the concert is to take place. The initial posters should go out well in advance and should be placed in important locations, such as college bookstores, record stores, important intersections, and any retail stores that cater to the age group that you think will attend the concert. The promoter often inserts a rider in the contract stating that the group may not perform within a certain radius of the concert for a number of months before and after this particular concert. This is to protect the promoter from any overexposure of the group in this particular market.

Advertising must be planned with great care. The promoter may set a minimal advertising budget and hold a reserve fund for extra newspaper and radio ads if ticket sales are slow. It is important to advertise in media that match the demographics of the group's audience. Free radio publicity can be obtained through community bulletin board features. College newspaper rates are cheap compared to the rates of commercial newspapers. There may be local entertainment magazines and tourist-oriented weeklies that will be happy to include details of the concert without charge. Sometimes a promoter presents a series of concerts and offers discounts for season tickets. The same brochure may be used for the concerts of an entire season. This requires committing funds and getting signed contracts in advance.

As the actual date of the concert approaches, the promoter should send out mailings to her own mailing list. Press releases should be followed up by phone calls and invitations to the press to attend the performance.

If the concert appears to be in trouble a week or two before the date, certain remedial measures can be taken. More money could be spent on advertising, and discounts can be offered to such groups as hospital patients, handicapped people, charity groups, or others. Any revenue is better than an empty hall. Flyers can be handed out on the street if necessary and even placed on the seats at other concerts that precede yours and might appeal to the same general audience. If an act is planning to arrive several days before the show, it may be possible to arrange interviews with any media people of influence in your city.

The promotion of classical music is somewhat more dignified, but it assumes the same general forms. Critical praise by prestigious reviewers should play a prominent part in any publicity releases. It is also easier to focus on the demographics of a classical or jazz audience. It is fairly obvious where to advertise and what music critics would be especially interested in such an event. The demand for classical artists is more of a long-term demand, so it is possible to book concerts in advance with some measure of security. The demand for an artist like Isaac Stern will change little from year to year. In popular music an artist who has a hot record may no longer be hot by the time of the actual concert. Even in classical music artists occasionally may be in great demand because of winning an international contest or making a best-selling record.

One of the worst features of concert promotion is the riders that appear at the ends of contracts with so many of the contemporary rock acts. These riders may regulate the color of the limousines that chauffeur the act around, or they may contain detailed specifications on what type of food the group and its road crew should be served. The Rolling Stones travel with a road crew of fifty people, and their setup time includes hours of lighting and sound checks. In the contract between the promoter and the group there should be specific information as to what time the group intends to do a sound check and what hours the auditorium will be available.

The promoter must arrange for security and must hire stagehands. If the city owns the auditorium it may specify the type of security that is required. The stagehands are usually union members, and for a large concert the cost of hiring them will run into thousands of dollars.

During the concert the promoter needs to check on the light and sound throughout the show, make sure there are no disturbances at the box office, and make sure that the show runs on time. After it is all over it is time to assess the situation. Did the concert make money, were the reviews good, would the promoter want to do it again? Thank-you notes and personal calls should be made to radio people, music critics, and anyone who helped.

The easiest way to find out how to promote concerts if you are attending college is to get on the concert committee at your college. This will give you the experience of working with booking agencies, talent, and the media. It will also enable you to see what the possible risks and rewards may be before gambling with your own money. After your college career has ended you might consider working for a local promoter or booking agent to give you a better feeling for the actual promotion process. At some point you should leap in with your own promotion, taking care not to risk everything on your first venture.

CAREERS IN PUBLICITY

A publicist or press agent needs to know how to write in an informative and entertaining style and to understand image-making and the promotion of images. Some publicists work on record company staffs. They are involved in the promotion of record acts, and naturally their work centers on the recording career of the artist. The publicist needs to spend as much time with the artist as possible, finding out interesting sidelights of his life and any hobbies or unusual talents that he may possess. Many newspapers will print stories ghosted by publicists if the stories are sufficiently entertaining.

Independent publicists are hired by the artist or his manager. They are paid a monthly fee, and there may be a contract guaranteeing a number of months of work. In selling a pop group through the media the image of the group is as important as the music. A good publicist will have all sorts of ideas for creating or promoting the image of a group. These ideas may relate to costumes, stage gestures, attitude presented to the media, and the type of photographs that the group uses as promotional pictures. Certain photographers might be perfect for a specific kind of action shot, but not as good for another type of pose.

The publicist needs to coordinate the overall campaign of creating an image. It is most important that the act, the record company, the personal manager, and the publicist agree on what the image of the group is. Images can vary from serious artistry (Paul Simon) to macho (Metallica) to playful (Garth Brooks). The goal is to get the attention of the public, and it really isn't necessary that the artist be what the public thinks an artist is. Once the attention of the public is captured, an act is on the way toward building an audience.

21

CAREERS IN MUSIC PERFORMANCE

*T*here are many long roads to travel for a young musician who decides to pursue a career in music performance. Your initial goal should be to get performing experience wherever it may be available. Singers or players should start to participate in school musical activities as soon as they can find such outlets. For most schools this means singing in the choir or playing in the band. Most schools have several scheduled performances by such groups during the school year. These may be in the school itself, in other schools, or for various community organizations. Churches have choral groups that provide good early training for singers, and most communities also have amateur bands and choral groups that are constantly seeking new members.

Pianists and string players generally start to take lessons by the age of five or six, but woodwind and brass players often start between the ages of ten and twelve, depending on their physical development. It is difficult for a young child or his parents to know exactly what musical direction he wishes to go in, but as a child gets older he should be sure that the music that he is studying will be useful in his eventual music career. A jazz pianist, for example, will do quite well taking some lessons from a classical teacher, but after several years the lessons should include some theory and harmony. Many classical teachers simply teach reading and technique because that is the way they were taught. A jazz-oriented player must receive training in chord structure and music theory. The actual playing techniques in the performance of different styles may also differ. If your playing habits are too deeply entrenched in one kind of technique, it may be difficult to master another method of playing. Such questions as what constitutes a good sound on an instrument may have different answers in the context of different musical styles. Anyone who is studying a musical instrument should get some training in music theory and learn how to sight-read music. It is possible that you will not require these skills because you will primarily perform your own music, but reading and writing music are efficient ways of communicating with other musicians.

By the time you enter your teens you need to use some common sense in determining whether to continue with the same teacher or to find another one. If you are headed for a chair in a symphony orchestra, it is advisable to study, if possible, with a first-chair player in the local symphony. Studying with a solo recitalist will not prepare you for a career in symphonic work, which concentrates on ensemble playing rather than solo work. If you are aiming toward a free-lance career doing studio singing in New York, you should not devote all of your attention to operatic vocal production because that is not what will be required of you. If you have any intention of doing studio work, be sure you are studying with a teacher who can improvise as well as read music. The more musical styles you have at your command, the more studio dates you will be eligible to play. The first-chair player in the symphony or an outstanding studio player will also be able to introduce you to people who will offer you opportunities to work, and they will be able to explain the music business to you in a way that someone who has not had these experiences could never understand.

No matter what kind of work you intend to pursue, there are certain jobs that are staples for musicians and singers everywhere. Club dates are available in every large city and in many small towns and resort areas. These are one-night jobs where a band or group is hired to provide dance or background music, depending upon the occasion. In New York such club dates are actually contracted on the floor of the union (Local 802, AFM), and your own union local may be able to help by giving you the names of leaders who contract club dates. Other one-night or one-day jobs are weddings, parties, and meetings of clubs or organizations. If these are small affairs, union membership may not be necessary. If you are not in the union, make sure that there is some sort of written agreement between the leader of the group and the employer stating the wages and hours of the performance. One protective feature that the union offers is that such details appear on the union contract, leaving little room for misunderstanding about when the band is supposed to play.

It is possible to solicit such small club dates by advertising in local newspapers, by putting posters or cards up in music stores, and by contacting local restaurant owners and caterers. Restaurant people are often asked to recommend bands for banquets or private parties. In the club date field versatility of any kind is useful. The larger your repertoire, the more jobs you will be able to play. If you can play more than one instrument, this makes you a more desirable employee for a leader, and it also enables you to play a lengthy job without becoming too bored. If you are weaker on one of your instruments, this will give you a chance to practice in a relatively unpressured situation. Musicians who can sing and singers who can play also do better in the club date field. Multiple skills reduce the necessary size of the band and increase the amount of money for each musician or singer. If you are comfortable fronting a group and selling a band to people, there is no reason why you can't put together a band yourself and earn a bigger share of the take. The leader of a band in union contracts gets double scale, or twice what the "sidemen," or other players, are paid.* The leader of a club date group may not be the best musician in the band, but he is almost always the best salesperson in the group.

Churches provide another source of supplementary income for singers and keyboard players. Pianists and organists often play for

---

* Under certain conditions the leader gets one and one-half times scale.

church services, funerals, or weddings, and singers may also be hired for such occasions. There are full-time opportunities for choral conductors and organists at the larger churches, but for the free-lancer these jobs provide a steady flow of extra income.

To work in a small club it is customary to audition for the owner or manager, sometimes in front of a live audience. The union may control any auditions at larger clubs to eliminate unfair competition, but we are talking now about neighborhood bars. Generally, such clubs provide a forum for performers who are seeking to work out the kinks in their style. It should be a temporary step because the pay is bad and the hours are long—often from 9:00 P.M. to 1:00 or 2:00 A.M. Sometimes these jobs are available six nights a week, sometimes on weekends only. Quite a few clubs hire singer-pianists or singer-guitarists for the cocktail hour, from 4:00 to 6:00 P.M. or thereabouts. These "happy hour" jobs are generally available five days a week and will provide a basic living, leaving the performer free to concentrate on songwriting, rehearsing with a band, or studying music. In resort areas, such as ski resorts, mountain resorts, or beaches, such jobs are readily available during the tourist season.

Some clubs have what are called *showcases* or *open stages*. On these nights performers are invited to come in and sing for fifteen to twenty minutes. Performers are not paid but may be hired in the future by the club owner. In fact artists seldom get work in this way, but sometimes the exposure before a live audience is useful. As mentioned previously, a few select clubs are frequented by a number of industry people, and a few performers actually started successful careers at these showcases. Other opportunities to perform free are available through hospitals, charity groups, mental hospitals, homes for the aged, and other such organizations. Arts organizations, such as state or local arts councils, offer additional possibilities of employment. Check out your local arts council for details, and also ask them if your city has an arts organization that specifically sponsors performances in psychiatric or penal facilities.

In New York and Los Angeles there are so many bands that some clubs have adopted the bizarre custom of having the bands pay in order to work at the club. The band is obligated to publicize its performances and receives credit for the customers who say they have come to see them. This reverses the responsibilities of the club and the musician and is a custom that musicians ought to resist.

If you play or sing and are looking for people to form a group, you might check on the musicians' referral services that advertise in *Rolling Stone*. Other ways of finding musicians are checking the bulletin boards at music schools and music stores, hanging out at showcase nights in clubs, and placing your own ads in newspapers or on school bulletin boards. If you are friendly with the owner of a local music store, he may help you to meet other musicians with the same goals. The musicians' union is another place to find people looking to put together a musical group. If your local is small enough, talk to some of the people who work there and put a notice on their bulletin board or in their newspaper.

Many colleges have performing ensembles that play at school dances, football rallies, or do jazz or symphonic concerts. Such playing experience gives you practice in reading music and following a conductor and is another source of contacts that might lead to your own group. Many college students are able to get part-time work while going to school by playing dances and parties on the weekend. Check with the local college fraternities and student activity boards to find out about such jobs.

Many singers and musicians, particularly if they have moved to a large city from their hometown, are forced to find some other kind of employment until they can build up some contacts to get jobs in music. Try to find a job that is sufficiently flexible so that you can pursue job opportunities in the music business. Office-temporary groups may have jobs that are on a day-to-day or week-to-week basis. Jobs as waitresses or waiters also leave enough free time for practicing and doing auditions, or even playing jobs. Try to find a job that will leave you some free time and is not so exhausting that you can't devote any time to music.

I have not spoken about agents or managers in this chapter because there really is no need for them at this stage of your career. If you have playing experience and you or your group are ready to find a record deal, then it is certainly time to find some representation.

CLASSICAL MUSIC PERFORMANCE

In building a career in classical music the nature of your early training is very important. High-grade teachers will not want to give you lessons unless you have had good early training in technique. If you are trying for a career as a recitalist, you should try to study with a player who is or was a famous soloist. When you and the teacher decide you are ready to take the risk, you then must do some sort of debut concert in New York City. This is usually done at Carnegie Recital Hall or a similar smaller auditorium. The student rents the hall and makes sure that agents and critics are invited to the recital. There are certain managers in New York, like Norman Seaman, who specialize in presenting such recital debuts. The promoter handles such arrangements as the renting of the hall, printing the program, and placing small ads in the newspapers, and will try to urge music critics to attend. A good review of the concert, particularly one in the *New York Times*, will spark some interest from one of the classical agent-manager groups, such as Columbia Artists Management. They may take the young recitalist under their wing and ship her off to community concerts all over the United States. Such concerts do not pay big money but will give the artist a good deal of performing experience and some more reviews. The next level of the artist's career could include appearances with some lesser-known symphony orchestras, higher-level concerts, and perhaps some recordings. The summit of a recital career includes frequent recordings, solo recitals in major halls, and guest appearances with major symphonies throughout the Western world.*

The career of a classical recitalist presents an attractive picture, but it is a vista open to only a handful of musicians in the world. Think of the number of piano and violin soloists who you can name—even worse, think of the number of solo flute or oboe players who come to mind. The odds against a successful solo career are very heavy. There are a number of international competitions, especially for pianists and violinists, that can provide the winners with the entrée to a successful career. Victory in such a contest, especially a European contest, will almost surely bring the opportunity to do recordings and invitations to play with good symphony orchestras. I really can't think of a music career that is harder to achieve than that of the solo recitalist. Alvin Toffler, writing in *The Culture Consumers* in 1973, reported that there were only 500 people making a living in the United States as recitalists.

There are numerous contests for operatic singers. The prizes usually

---

* Sometimes artists do these recitals in other major cities, such as Boston, Chicago, and Washington, D.C.

are a scholarship or a chance to apprentice with an outstanding opera company. There are very few permanent opera companies in the United States, but roles are available for younger performers in the choruses or in bit parts. Some opera singers go abroad and get their experience in one of the many European opera companies. There are some touring companies in the United States and some opportunities for acting roles in musical comedies that may require particularly strong voices. During the past such roles were not uncommon in movies as well, but today there really is no one who corresponds to the light-opera singers of the past like Nelson Eddy or Jeanette MacDonald.

Studying voice with a renowned performer or ex-performer is a valuable calling card, and the contacts that your teacher has developed over the years may help you to meet the proper agents, managers, and promoters. The demand for opera in the United States is still relatively small when compared to that for other kinds of serious music. It is possible that government art subsidies in the future will help to form new opera companies in cities that do not have such companies now. The current trend, however, is for the federal government to cut subsidies or grants to arts organizations.

Jobs for symphonic players are available through playing auditions. These auditions are conducted whenever vacancies occur and are advertised in the American Symphony League's magazine and in the *International Musician*, the monthly publication of the American Federation of Musicians. The prospective player must send a résumé to the personnel manager of the orchestra. Lessons with a distinguished teacher are part of a good résumé that will help you to survive this screening procedure. If you pass the initial application, you will be invited to an audition with a number of other players who are competing for the job. For the first audition the player must always pay his own expenses, a disturbing part of the procedure for a young player since the audition can involve considerable travel expenses. There may be any number of other players at the audition—as many as 120 in some cases. Some orchestras hold their auditions behind a screen to avoid any charges of sex or race discrimination. Usually a personnel committee of the first-chair players of the orchestra will hear the initial auditions, with or without the permanent conductor. Out of this large group a very small number of players are called back to a second audition. In the larger orchestras the expenses will be paid by the orchestra on this second trial. The audition is judged again, and the conductor is almost always the final judge.*

Sight-reading and familiarity with the symphonic repertoire are important in a large orchestra because there are only a limited number of rehearsals set by union regulations. There might be three two-and-one-half-hour rehearsals for a single concert performance of three or four works. This is one reason why conductors are reluctant to program new and difficult music. There simply is not enough rehearsal time available.

Before the auditions are conducted the orchestra has usually informed the contestants that there are certain specific pieces that they will be expected to play. The players are judged on such criteria as tone, sight-reading, expression, technique, concept of style, rhythm, and even general attitude. While ensemble playing and sight-reading may not be important in a solo career, they are essential for a good symphony player. This is why it is necessary to be so careful in selecting a teacher. Teachers who are preparing a student for a career as a soloist often concentrate on taking a few pieces and polishing them over and over. Soloists never really have to be concerned with ensemble playing because the ensemble is usually playing behind them. Because the presence of a screen makes the audition procedure so impersonal, there are some who feel that it is not a good way of judging applicants.

The top five symphony orchestras in the United States are the Boston, Chicago, Cleveland, New York, and Philadelphia symphony orchestras. They all guarantee the musicians a fifty-two-week season, and their minimum pay scales at present are in the neighborhood of $1,500 a week, with extensive fringe benefits and some money from recording sessions guaranteed. At the moment there are some 2,500 full-time symphonic musicians employed in the United States.†

At the present writing many of the smaller and medium-size orchestras are experiencing financial difficulties. Some have actually gone out of business, some have reorganized as cooperative groups, and others have reduced the length of their seasons. The outlook for symphonic music at the present time is not very positive. It is failing to attract younger people in its audience.

---

* Some orchestras now ask for audio or videotapes before the live audition.
† American Music Conference, *Careers in Music*.

Usually a young symphony player starts his career with a local community orchestra and works his way up to a small orchestra with a short season—say, twenty weeks—in a medium-size town. The player then tries to gain a job in a major orchestra as a "back chair" player, meaning the fourth French horn or one of the many violin and viola players who sit in the rear of the orchestra. The ultimate goal is to play first chair in a major orchestra. First-chair players get paid well above union minimums; they get extra fees for recording, do some solo work with the symphony, and are able to teach a small group of select students at very high fees. For a brass or woodwind player the first-chair position is particularly rewarding because the solo opportunities for such players are so limited.

Many of the community or regional orchestras have shorter seasons and lower pay scales. An orchestra member working in a town where there is a twenty-week season must pursue other job opportunities. He will often teach at a local college, give private lessons, or try to get a summer playing job in another town. Some players prefer such diversified careers to full-time work with the same orchestra.

Members of chamber music ensembles must usually teach college as well in order to earn a satisfactory living. They may combine their concertizing and recording with these teaching posts. There is a very small demand for touring chamber music ensembles in this country.

JAZZ PERFORMANCE

Opportunities for jazz players and singers vary according to how much interest there is in jazz at any particular time. At the moment there is something of a flowering of demand for jazz, and quite a few clubs are flourishing in some of the major cities. To pursue a jazz career without making any commercial compromises, a musician has to anticipate a lifetime of playing in bars, interspersed with occasional concerts and recordings. Some jazz musicians end up teaching school or doing studio work. These jobs require versatility and technical ability rather than brilliant individual improvisational style, so a jazz talent is not always compatible with these careers. Players like John Coltrane or Charlie Parker had too identifiable a sound to make them valuable commodities in the anonymous world of the television commercial. The jazz life has also typically encouraged rootlessness and instability, also qualities incompatible with studio work. The newest jazz always seems to be somewhat ahead of its audience, in the same way that modern classical music of the twentieth century has a difficult time holding its audience. Some opportunities are available for jazz players in various cities to back up traveling singers who come into town with a conductor and/or piano player and hire a local band. Reading ability and reliability are the prime requisites for a player seeking such work. Other opportunities for such work include ice shows and circuses. These shows also generally hire sizeable bands in every town, besides traveling with their own rhythm section and one or two soloists.

Some of the younger jazz players have broken through to the market for popular music by recording rock tunes or using heavy studio electronics. Whether a player is comfortable in such a role is a matter of individual choice. The audience for rock music is a different audience from the relatively placid listeners at jazz clubs. They also are usually intent on having the musicians reproduce the sound of their records, something a real jazz player is not excited about doing. George Benson, Chick Corea, Donald Byrd, and Herbie Hancock are some of the jazz musicians who have achieved commercial success in the past. But today there are a number of "smooth jazz" artists who have achieved commercial success. Kenny G. makes multiplatinum albums by simplifying jazz and writing attractive melodies. Many would argue that what he is playing is so watered down that it is not really jazz.

Different kinds of music are popular in different parts of the country and with a variety of audiences. There is still a solid audience for folksingers in coffee houses and small folklore centers in different parts of the United States, and such varieties of music as Cajun music, polka bands, gospel groups, or dozens of other musical styles may be found in different clubs and locations. Performing careers in popular music were badly hurt by the disco craze, but this finally seems to be slowing down. Live musicians have the advantage of being flexible, unpredictable, and versatile.

Many people combine part-time music careers with other full-time jobs. Club dates are the most common jobs for such players. Many cities also are convention centers, and local groups may exist that play conventions and annual meetings. These shows are generally patterned after Las Vegas variety shows. The music is a sprinkling of different styles, with the emphasis on humor and entertainment rather than musical expertise. Some jobs that can take musicians abroad are USO tours and cruise ship jobs. The USO goes wherever the United States Army may be. Cruise ships generally are busiest in the winter months, going to warm climates. Other foreign jobs that are available are tours for the State Department. In these tours a group is selected to represent some particular aspect of American music to people in another culture. The musicians selected for such tours may find themselves performing in almost any part of the world, from Paris to an African village.

The *International Musician*, the journal of the American Federation of Musicians, carries job vacancy listings in foreign orchestras as well as for the United States.

Individual foreign promoters or agencies sponsor concerts of American music all over Europe and Asia. It is important to work out arrangements for work visas, taxes, and payment in minute detail before accepting such engagements.

22

SONGWRITING AS A CAREER

efore Bob Dylan came along, the rules for writing songs were cut-and-dried. There were the good music "standards" of the thirties and forties and the rock songs of the fifties. Standards had an introductory melody followed by a verse and chorus. Sometimes there was a reprise of the verse, but the music was slightly different the second time. Chorus and verse melodies were different from one another. Rock 'n' roll songs often used the same melodies for the verse and chorus, and the form of the song became simply verse-chorus. The chorus was a repeating part and usually contained the title of the song and some sort of musical hook that the listener was supposed to remember. "Poison Ivy," by Leiber and Stoller, is a good example of the fifties rock song. The unusual title is sung in every chorus, and there are lots of choruses. Songs were expected to be under three minutes in length to get more radio play, and many of the songs were under two and a half minutes long.

The hit songs of the thirties were performed by the big stars of the day, such as Al Jolson. Many of the hits came from Broadway shows, written by such sophisticated musicians as Richard Rodgers, Jerome Kern, or George Gershwin. Lyricists like Lorenz Hart were equally clever. There was another kind of songwriter of the day, the Tin Pan Alley songwriter, exemplified by Irving Berlin. He was an untrained musician with a natural talent for writing catchy tunes and simple, direct lyrics that captured the ear of the American public. Most of the popular songs of the thirties and forties were nostalgic love songs. They were miniature fantasies describing a world that didn't exist. Love in the sand, never leave me, I'll love you always, it had to be you. Once in a while a song like "Strange Fruit," about a lynching or "Brother, Can You Spare a Dime?" about the Depression interrupted America's reverie over faraway places and nonexistent times.

The rock composers of the fifties were not suave, but they were smart and they really shook up the apple cart. Many of their songs were based on black slang or teenage colloquialisms. Some of the songs were bizarre epics about people dying in car wrecks and being kissed by their lovers as they expired, but others had a note of reality and the spark of humor. If anything, the composers of the fifties were, of course, more conscious of radio airplay than the earlier writers, and everything seemed to get done in about two minutes. Most of the records had extremely broad hooks, and they were repeated many times in the record. Later the *fade hook* was developed, where the ending of the song was repeated endlessly. "Hey, Jude," by the Beatles, was probably the ultimate example of the fade—the ending was longer than the rest of the song.

Then along came Dylan. His songs were not usually about one thing. Even when they did have a focus, like "Blowin' in the Wind," the songs seemed to fragment out in all directions from the central point. When Dylan added electricity to his sound in 1964 the forms of his songs became even stranger in terms of the existing pop songs. Dylan enjoyed a sort of surrealist blues, as in "Positively 4th Street" and "Highway 61." When there was a hook, as in "Like a Rolling Stone," it was presented in an almost parody form. There were no set times for Dylan's songs; some were three minutes long, some six or seven, and "Sad-Eyed Lady of the Lowlands" took up one whole side of an LP.

There is no question that Dylan changed the course of pop songwriting. Some of the earlier writers tried to match his artistry, but found they really couldn't write outside of the familiar formulas. Younger writ-crs, like Neil Young or Joni Mitchell and later Bruce Springsteen, were free to express themselves as they wished. Often these songs were not performed by other artists. The songs tended to be personal and obscure at the same time. The artist usually recorded the song first, and other artists might have trouble relating to the songs or even understanding them. It's difficult to imagine Eddie Fisher or Tony Bennett singing "Masters of War." Many of these songs had no hooks; they were about feelings rather than specific events.

When you read books that are supposed to teach you how to write songs, keep all of the things described above in mind. Most of these instruction books ignore the Dylan revolution, as though its influence might disappear if it is not acknowledged. They tell you to use hooks, find catchy rhythms, experiment with chord progressions, come up with catchy titles, and use a notebook to write down titles or song ideas. There is nothing wrong with doing any or all of these things, nor is there anything bad about using a rhyming dictionary to come up with difficult rhymes. It's just that none of it seems very relevant anymore. The formulas have broken down, but the doctors are still selling the same prescriptions.

Songs can be written about anything. They can concern the writer's experiences, his fantasies, the experiences of friends, they can be about love, or hate, or society, an individual, or whatever he wants them to be about. He can write them with any melodies he wishes, but if he uses much more than an octave and a half, most singers and most listeners will have trouble performing them. Some people write the words first; others write the music first. Some writers do them both at the same time. Cole Porter supposedly wrote the rhythms of his songs first, then the words, and the music last. If you stop to think about a song like "Begin the Beguine," it makes more sense than you might initially think. Some people come up with an idea for a song first. This gets them started, and the words and music both flow from the concept. Many songs are written quickly, but a writer should not get discouraged if one part lags behind the rest of a song. Most writers have an easier time writing either the words or the music, so some work with a collaborator, who does what they find hardest.

Studying poetry is helpful, particularly if your songs rhyme. It will help to give you some feeling for the flow of lyrics and for the rhythms of syllables. A good deal of nonsense has been written about the poetry of popular music. In fact many of the lyrics don't stand up without the melodies. The music often needs a particular arrangement or performance to sound complete. Songs are at their best when words, music, arrangement, and performance work together. The whole is greater than the sum of its parts. Many contemporary songwriters write all of their melodies while playing guitar or piano, and their melodies seem more a function of chords than tunes that stand on their own. If this seems to be happening to your songs, try writing the melody in your head away from your instrument.

Songwriters who do not perform their own songs must be prepared for many rejections before their music is performed. Sometimes an artist or a producer simply cannot hear a song beyond the arrangement on a demo record. To sell a song you need to cast it, which means that you and your publisher need to determine what artist might be suitable for the song. Many songs get recorded because the artist and the songwriter are friendly, and in the course of their normal relationship the songwriter sings a few of his songs for the artist. Many songs that ended up being major hits were turned down a dozen or more times by famous artists and producers.

In making a demo the publisher usually wants the demo singer to convey the style of a song. If the singer imitates the style of a specific artist too closely, then it may be difficult to submit the song to other artists—especially if the original target doesn't like the song.

Many songwriters run up against the problem of dry periods, when they simply cannot write. One way to combat such periods is to try a new approach. If most of your songs are about personal experiences, experiment with subjects that are far from your own experience. Try writing a country tune or a novelty song, if these are things you haven't done before. BMI and ASCAP both have workshops for songwriters, and BMI has a weekly songwriters' showcase at The Improvisation in Los Angeles. Going to such a showcase or to the workshops gives you a chance to meet other writers and publishers and to get some feedback on your own work.

When you write a song you should try to record it as soon as possible on a cheap cassette recorder. This will save you the trouble of writing a

lead sheet immediately and enable you to have a copy of the song to refer to later. For a typical lead sheet see the Appendix of this book. Today
there are computer programs that will transcribe music in lead sheet
form. This is a great convenience for today's writers, especially those
who cannot read or write music down in notation.

Although it is advantageous for a songwriter to be able to perform his
own songs, there will probably always be artists who are primarily
singers, like Whitney Houston and Randy Travis. These people provide
the basic market for the prospective writer. Sometimes a songwriter will
collaborate with a recording artist. Songwriters Diane Warren and
Desmond Child have pursued this strategy.

It is increasingly difficult to separate a song from the actual record of
the song itself. Many rap hits have an incredible groove that may or may
not be part of the construction of the song. The groove may come from
the way the drummer or producer programmed the drum machine.
Producers like Jimmy Jam and Terry Lewis or L.A. and Babyface have
produced dozens of hit records. Chances are that when they write a
song they already have the artist and the musical groove in mind.
Narada Michael Walden prides himself on taking the sort of MOR
songs that Whitney Houston sings and building incredible rhythmic
grooves into them. In such cases it is difficult to separate the song from
the recorded performance. This is one of the reasons why cover records
are comparatively rare today. Can you imagine another artist covering a
song by Guns N' Roses or Def Jam?

There are several songwriters' contests that are open to both amateur
and professional songwriters. In chapter 7, "Record Company Contracts," I comment on similar contests for artists. In general, I feel that
such contests are a mixed blessing, for the reasons stated in that chapter.

Magazines and tip sheets listed in the Appendix can give you tips
about songwriting and addresses of publishers. *Songwriter's Market* is an
annual publication that is full of addresses and helpful hints about writing songs, jingles, etc. A number of organizations, especially the National Academy of Songwriters (NAS), the Songwriters Guild of
America, and the Nashville Songwriters Association International
(NSAI), provide seminars, showcases, and workshops for aspiring writers that feature top industry pros.

Another source of help is the performing rights societies. ASCAP and BMI sponsor frequent songwriters' workshops in Nashville, New York, and Los Angeles, and often in other cities as well.

There are a number of good books about songwriting listed in the Appendix. Most of all, it is a matter of perfecting your craft and making contacts with artists and producers who are making records. If you are able to write a hit song for someone else, there is a good chance that you will be able to get a recording contract for yourself, even if your career plans haven't focused on a career as a performer. If nothing else, such a record will be a great tool for exposing your own songs at someone else's expense.

Songwriting without performing is an increasingly tough profession. In California, the rule of thumb is that three-quarters of the songs recorded are written by the artist. Often when the artist isn't the writer, the producer, who may also be a songwriter, exercises a considerable amount of control over the selection of material. Nashville is still dominated by the songwriter, but country artists are writing an ever-increasing share of the material they record as we move into the twenty-first century.

23

COLLEGE: GETTING THE EDUCATION YOU NEED

A number of schools* offer degree programs with courses in the music industry. From one year to the next different schools enter the field and others drop certain courses. Be sure to write to the schools of your choice requesting current catalogs. Some colleges have high-level, professional-quality recording studios and electronic music facilities, some offer extensive courses in music merchandising, some offer courses in such subjects as copyright protection, musical instrument repair, and songwriting. Attending a college with a music industry program gives you a chance to experience the various facets of the industry. Many schools offer internships in actual jobs. In these programs the student works for a company that is in the music business, learns their procedures, and does the same kind of work that actual employees of the company are expected to do.

---

* See Appendix.

Such internships can be arranged with music publishers, record companies, music stores, radio stations, music instrument builders or restorers, recording studios, or whatever is available to the school. In her academic work the student is generally required to take a number of courses in various disciplines. Music history and theory are usually required, along with basic business and accounting courses.

The question of whether such a program will be useful for you is one that only you can decide. There are certain guidelines that I can offer to help you in deciding whether a particular music industry program will be advantageous to you in pursuing your career. Who is doing the teaching? Have the teachers in the program had much practical experience in the music business, or are they mostly teaching people to do something they themselves have never done? How recent is the teacher's experience? The music industry changes constantly, and you will want to feel that your instructors are in touch with current practices. How large are the classes? If you are studying engineering and you are promised the use of the school's 24-track studio, how many hours a week will you get to use the studio, and will you have to share that use with other students? In some schools the equipment itself may be fine, but there are so many people using it, including faculty members doing some of their own projects, that you might get only one or two hours a week of studio time. This is really not enough to be of much use. How personalized is the instruction? Is it oriented for the beginner, and is there someone around to answer your questions, or are all the classes too large and the teachers too busy or uninterested to devote any time to working out your individual problems? Be sure to talk to the teachers in the program so you can begin to develop a feeling for them as people. That feeling may in itself answer many of your questions.

It is also worth checking to see if the school offers classes in radio, television, or film. Today's record companies have close ties to or own companies that operate in these areas. A job in one division of the company may well lead to opportunities in another division.

If you get vague answers to your questions, then perhaps more questions are in order. How many students are there in the program, and how many teachers are there? Are the people teaching the business courses familiar with the music industry or do they simply have a general business background? Are studio and practice facilities open at night and on weekends so that you can work on some of your own projects? Is there a maintenance engineer for the recording studio to repair the equipment when something goes wrong? Are the teachers sympathetic to the type of music that you expect to play? Even today many of the people teaching music in the colleges are ignorant of or hostile to country and rock music. If you are taking music arranging and history classes, there should not be artificial limitations placed on the type of music studied. You should be working with as many different kinds of music as possible in order to get the experience that you will need in the real world of the music business.

What kinds of internships are available in the program? Ask to see a list of internships that students have done in the past several years. Does the music department at the school seem to have enough contacts to get you an internship in the area of your choice? Try talking to students already in the program to find out what the good and bad points of the program have been for them.

Try to find out where graduates of the program are now working. If possible, talk to them, and try to find out if they feel that the school provided them with a good foundation for their current jobs.

Most students do not realize how much power they possess in the colleges today. Private colleges are in almost desperate need of students, and most state universities are funded based on the number of students that are registered. Colleges are more eager to attract students today than they have been since the days of the Great Depression. If the college you are interested in attending doesn't offer everything you want, see if they can arrange independent study programs to fill in the blanks in their academic offerings. Is there someone on the staff who can teach you songwriting on a one-to-one basis? Sometimes individual studies programs can be more useful than a formal class situation. How far will the school go in helping you to work out a program? Will the college allow you to take summer courses for credit at another school, or will they give you credit for study-related work experiences, such as an apprenticeship at a recording studio?

If you find that a college emphasizes requirements for graduation more than it seems to want to deal with what the student wants to learn, my advice is to avoid that college. There are so many career possibilities in the music industry today that it would be foolish to lock yourself into a limited curriculum. You may not think of yourself as a future music critic, but a music criticism course might be highly beneficial for you. It might give you perspective on music performance and could also be useful in helping you to develop a writing style. If you are a communications major headed for a career in radio, you should choose a college that has a radio station. You should also plan to take some courses in music theory and in the history of jazz and popular music. If the school you are dealing with doesn't offer such courses, insist that they allow you to take the courses elsewhere. The more inflexible a school is, the less likely it is to train you for a diversified industry like the music business.

Business courses may sound grim to you, but in reading this book you should have realized by now just how important the business part of a career can be. If your records are not merchandised and promoted properly, your career will never get off the ground. An artist should develop a good general grounding in business to protect himself and to work more efficiently with the people whose prime responsibility is to merchandise his career.

If your orientation is toward the performing end of music, take a good look at what kinds of ensembles and instrumental instruction the school offers. A typical college today has the usual choral groups, a jazz-rock stage band that does occasional concerts, and in the larger schools a marching band for football and pep rallies. Have you heard these ensembles? Who writes the arrangements? Will membership in such a playing group help you to grasp a broad variety of musical styles or is the music limited to one idiom? If none of the school ensembles plays any music that interests you, there is a good chance that you shouldn't attend that school. If you are studying arranging and composition, listen to some of the work that your prospective teachers have done. The fact that they can write music well doesn't necessarily mean they will be great teachers, but if you hate their music there may be good reason to question whether you are going to be able to learn much of value from them.

If you are taking private lessons in a particular instrument, and you consider this to be an important part of your education, find out who teaches your instrument at the college. Is the teacher a versatile player? Will she understand what you are trying to do and help you to reach your playing goals, or will you be molded into some shape that is not relevant to your goals? If a teacher is good in one area but not another, can you take additional lessons for credit from another teacher? Is there someone your teacher can recommend if you can't find another teacher? Many jazz players do not have a good legitimate classical technique on their instruments, and many classical players can't play jazz. Virtually no college music teachers have a clear understanding of how to play country music, soul, or even contemporary popular music.

What I am trying to say is that your education should be tailored to your own needs and goals. If you are seventeen you may not have a complete picture of what you need to do to get into the music industry or how you stay there once you have gotten in the door. Following is a list of subjects that might be offered in an ideal music industry program. Consider how many of these courses are available at a college, and if they are not, ask whether the school will assist you in finding such course offerings elsewhere or in setting up independent study programs. Be sure you get college credit for anything that you are studying that relates to the music industry program.

There are many engineering-technical courses available in various parts of the country. These are usually nondegree programs that offer some sort of certificate of completion.

There are two large 18-to-24-month programs in the United States and Canada. The TREBAS Institute has schools in Montreal, Ottawa, and Vancouver. The Art Institutes of Atlanta, Dallas, Philadelphia, Phoenix, Fort Lauderdale, and Seattle have schools in those cities. TREBAS focuses on engineering and the music business; the art institutes teach video and audio production, with some business classes. Both of these companies are private schools, and tuition is quite expensive compared to that for public institutions. Another private school, called Full Sail, located in Altamonte Springs, Florida, has a well-known audio instruction program.

Vocational education tends to be more practical and hands-on. Whether you need a college degree or a vocational certificate depends on who you are, what you want, and what experience you have already had. Don't go to any school without some attempt to evaluate the validity of what they are teaching and the credentials of those who are teaching you.

MUSIC INDUSTRY COURSE AREAS

CREATIVE AREAS	GENERAL MUSIC COURSES *4-Year College Program*	BUSINESS COURSES	ENGINEERING AND VOCATIONAL COURSES *18-to-24-Month Program*
Composing and arranging	Music theory and history	Introduction to music business	Audio and video
Record production	Jazz and popular music	General business and accounting	Record production
Songwriting	Music criticism	Music merchandising, instrument manufacturing, repair, wholesaling	Music business
All styles on the instrument of your choice	Non-Western music	Retail music store operation	Film and TV editing
Electronic music	Music therapy	Music publishing	Sales
Film music	Music education and private teaching	Sales and promotion	History of popular music
Commercials	Music librarian careers	Advertising and copywriting	Legal aspects of the business
Music ensembles—vocal and instrumental		Copyright, legal aspects of the business	Record promotion
		Music in print	Concert promotion
		Arts management	Sound reinforcement
		Concert promotion	Lighting and concert production
		Radio and TV	Advertising
			Media careers
			Songwriting and music publishing
			Copyright law
			Music retailing and wholesaling

Liberal arts courses—mathematics, science, English, etc.

All that stands between you and getting the kind of music industry education you want is your willingness to aggressively pursue the things you need to make such a program work for you as an individual, rather than as one of 1,000 students. The more you study and learn, the more industry jobs you will be able to undertake. Ten years from now your present orientation may have evolved into new and unpredictable areas. The more you learn today, the more you can use tomorrow. Remember not to overlook your teachers as a source of jobs in the industry.

24

CAREERS IN MUSIC EDUCATION AND PRIVATE TEACHING

The training offered in music education in American music schools and colleges is somewhat standardized. There are required courses in music theory and history, ear training and sight singing, conducting and piano. There are some electives in music offered, a major instrument is required, and there are requirements to perform in vocal and instrumental ensembles. Other courses are required in education and psychology, and liberal arts electives must be selected from a large number of courses. During the last year practice teaching in the classroom is required.

There are many books available about music education, and it is not my intention to duplicate this information, but I do want to provide a brief survey of the careers in this area. Over the last ten years or so a number of music education systems have been introduced to this country that reflect fresh approaches to music education. Zoltán Kodály was a famous Hungarian composer who believed in teaching music in the schools by concentrating on the national heritage of the student, her nation's folk music. The Kodály system strongly emphasizes the development of music skills through sight singing. The Orff system was created by the German composer Carl Orff. It uses special instruments that are available for use with the Orff music. They are xylophones with limited scales and a large number of percussion instruments and simple wind instruments. The music taught to the younger children starts with very simple scales, leading to a considerable amount of music using the *pentatonic* (five-note) *scale*. The Dalcroze system is called *eurythmics*. It seeks to involve the student with music and dance simultaneously. The Suzuki system has created a great stir in music circles because it starts to teach children at a preschool age, on smaller-sized instruments. Suzuki even believes in introducing music to the baby's crib and claims success at getting the child to recognize and sing selections of classical works by the age of two or three.

In practice teaching the student goes into a classroom and teaches children under the supervision of a music teacher. It is here that a student can discover whether or not he has a feeling for teaching and what methods seem to work in the classroom. The teacher is responsible for evaluating the work of the student.

For the last few years the school-age population has been declining in proportion to the total population of this country, and it shows signs of continuing to do so. This means that music education jobs are going to be in short supply relative to the number of available teachers. Moreover, school music and art budgets have received moderate to severe cuts in many parts of the country as school budgets in general have been cut or prioritized to stress programs in mathematics, science, and English.

In junior high school and high school, music teachers usually specialize in either band or chorus. The band teacher is generally a specialist in string, brass, or woodwind instruments who has had some basic methods courses in other instruments. The band teacher is expected to put together a band and even to offer basic instruction on all of the instruments. Band teachers feel inadequate in any family of instruments with which they have had little experience. Both band and choral teachers are expected to be able to conduct their ensembles and give school performances. In a small school the same person may teach band and chorus. Large school districts employ music supervisors and administrators. They generally have master's degrees and sometimes doctorates in music. In a very large city the music supervisor may formulate music programs for the music departments of dozens of schools and supervise the hiring of music teachers for these schools. This also requires keeping up-to-date on the latest music education literature and instrumental method books.

College music teaching also suffers from an oversupply of teachers and an undersupply of jobs. College theory and music history teachers usually have doctorates. Teachers of specific musical instruments have at least a performance degree in their instruments, and often a master's degree as well. There are many specialized fields of music study, such as music industry or ethnomusicology. At the present moment there are only two advanced-degree programs available in the music industry in this country.* Ethnomusicologists may study at a half-dozen graduate schools that specialize in this subject, such as UCLA, the University of Michigan, and Indiana University. Professors in ethnomusicology generally have Ph.D.'s or at least master's degrees and have done research in the field. In college teaching it is sometimes possible, especially in private colleges, to substitute practical experience or published works for a degree. A composer who has a limited number of degrees but who has a number of performances by leading ensembles to her credit might be employed by a college. Cecil Effinger, who taught composition at the University of Colorado, has a B.A. in mathematics. Other credits that might substitute for advanced degrees are an outstanding career as a solo performer or the publication of books about music.

There is an increasing emphasis on jazz and rock in school bands. Some experience composing and arranging for such ensembles may be useful in getting a teaching job. Many schools are now offering class instruction in guitar in response to wide student interest. The ability to play and teach guitar is another saleable skill for the prospective teacher.

---

* Master's programs at the University of Miami and New York University are currently in place, and a new program is being planned at Belmont College in Nashville.

Each state has its own specific teaching requirements. There is some reciprocity, but often a teacher moving from state to state will find it necessary to take some additional courses to meet the requirements in the new state. Some colleges maintain personnel offices that help their graduates find employment. It is worthwhile to check with state employment services, and there are some private employment agencies that specialize in securing jobs for teachers.

PRIVATE TEACHING

Private teaching can be done in the teacher's home, the student's home, or at a music store or studio. Many stores have teaching facilities as a way of promoting the sale of instruments and sheet music. Many schoolteachers, symphony players, and free-lancers also teach part-time as a way of making some extra income. A good private teaching practice is usually built up by word of mouth. This is a process that may take some time. A teacher generally builds up a reputation in a town, and other teachers, students, or music store owners begin to recommend him to inquiring students or parents.

Private teaching can be enjoyable, but it can also be a frustrating profession if the teacher is counting on it as his major source of income. Cancellations, sickness, people forgetting lessons, late-paying clients, and people unwilling to practice are among the various frustrations that someone running his own private music studio must face. Some teachers prefer to work in a music studio run by a retail store because the store can then set cancellation policies. It is best for a private teacher to clearly limit the number of conditions under which lessons can be cancelled and to insist on makeup lessons. Even doctors and dentists have problems with cancellations, so it is no wonder that in a nonessential luxury profession like music the reliability of the students can be a problem. Private students pay anywhere from $10 to $35 an hour and even more, depending upon the city and the reputation of the teacher.

If you have special skills in songwriting or, say, the history of jazz, you may be able to teach courses at a local college or university, either through the music department of the department of continuing education, or at a local community college.

25

CAREERS RELATED TO MUSIC IN PRINT: THE WRITING, PUBLICATION, AND SALE OF WRITTEN MUSIC

*L*ess than a dozen music publishers produce the majority of sheet music and music folios that are published in the United States. Over the last thirty years print publishing has moved out of New York to various parts of the United States.* There are still two large publishers in the New York area, but others are in Miami, Milwaukee, Los Angeles, St. Louis, and Philadelphia.

---

* I am using the term *music publisher* in this section to mean a company that prints and sells written music, as opposed to its use as described in the section on music publishing.

Printed music is distributed in the same general way that records are sold. The print company actually prints the music and owns the music books. It then sells directly to stores, utilizing its own sales personnel and making many telephone calls, or it sells to a music jobber. A *jobber* is a wholesaler who carries music books of all leading publishers—in other words, the equivalent in music publishing of the one-stop in the record business. There are also rack jobbers who will completely stock a location for a store owner. These rack jobbers are important because they distribute music books to locations that do not have sufficient traffic to justify the necessary paperwork or telephone calls to order books from the individual publishers. Music publishers do not have branches in various cities in the way that record companies do because the dollar volume of the print business cannot support such overhead. Music is also sold through the mail by some companies that prepare catalogs and develop large mailing lists of consumers interested in music. Some music teachers also sell music to their students because it is convenient and profitable to do so.

Many of the major music publishers started out as one-person businesses, with a single author who was determined to distribute his own books. Such an operation is Mel Bay, which is headquartered in a suburb of St. Louis, Missouri. Over a thirty-five-year period the Mel Bay operation has expanded from Bay's own famous and pioneering guitar method to printing dozens of instructional publications for various instruments. Although he still specializes in guitar instruction books, Mel Bay has expanded his activities to include method books and studies.

Today we are seeing the beginning of desktop publishing in music. A few arranger-composers are starting to make their own band arrangements, print them through desktop publishing, and sell and promote them directly to schools. Since each state has an organization of school music teachers, and there are also regional and national conferences of teachers, promoting this product is not as difficult as you might imagine.

There are many styles and formats in the publications of the various music publishers. The major popular music hits are still published individually in sheet music form. The sheet music includes a basic piano arrangement with guitar chords diagrammed over the lyrics. There are also entire songbooks featuring the songs of specific artists. These collections capitalize on the popularity of a specific artist, including songs, pictures, and some biographical material about the artist. Sometimes these folios contain the songs on an artist's latest records; sometimes the songbook is a general collection that includes songs selected from a number of record albums. The artist, who is always featured on the cover of the songbook, may or may not be a songwriter. If the songs have been written by other writers, permission must be received from the appropriate music publishers to print the songs, and royalties must be paid to the various publishers represented in the book. They in turn pay the writers. A new wrinkle in music in print is greeting cards that use a hit song lyric and have illustrations of the situations described in the song.

The royalty paid for songbooks is generally 10 percent of the retail selling price of the book. If several writers and publishers are involved, the royalty is split proportionally. If the artist has not written any of the songs, some sort of agreement must be worked out where the artist, whose name and picture decorate the front cover of the book, also gets a royalty. This may lead to a total royalty of as much as 15 percent of the retail selling price. In some instances the music publisher leases the songs for a flat fee rather than paying royalties for them. Some artists even own their own music print companies in an effort to diversify their earnings and investment opportunities. In general publishers try to keep the total costs of music folios down to 20 percent of the retail selling price of the book.

Some other works that music publishers might print include method books for various instruments, educational arrangements for stage bands and choral groups, and general collections of music that are merchandised not on the basis of an artist's name but because of interest in a particular style of music. Such a book might be entitled *100 Great Jazz Tunes*, or *100 Best Hits for Easy Guitar*. There are also general collections called *fakebooks*, which are intended for bands and pickup groups that work one-night jobs. Fakebooks include the melody line, lyrics, and chords of a song. For many years these books were sold illegally under the counter and used by professional musicians all over the country. The reason that fakebooks were illegal was that their publishers did not obtain permission to use the songs or pay royalties to publishers or writers. Today a number of the larger music publishers have put together their own legal fakebooks by leasing material from many different publishers. Some of these books contain as many as a thousand songs and sell for as much as $30 to $40. The royalties on the songs are divided among the various publishers and writers. No one gets rich this way, but at least the creators share in the profits.

The author of a music instruction book should get a royalty of 10 percent of the retail selling price of the book, plus an advance. The advance may vary from zero to as much as $1,000. Some publishers pay half the advance on receiving a signed contract and the other half upon completion of the manuscript. Some pay the entire sum on completion or upon reaching contractual agreement. Some publishers try to pay the author a smaller royalty or to reduce the royalty when the publisher offers high discounts to jobbers or for special promotions. Under normal circumstances I do not feel that the author should accept a royalty of less than 10 percent. Whether a smaller royalty is acceptable for specially discounted books depends upon your relationship with the publisher and whether you have confidence that a higher discount structure will lead to sufficient sales so that your overall royalties will not suffer. Some publishers may seek the rights to your next manuscript or even your next two manuscripts. This is not unusual in the book publishing business, but is unnecessarily strict for a music publisher. Some publishers try to charge off the advances of one book to the royalties of another book. This is a poor deal for the author, unless the books are part of a series that logically falls into such an agreement. The publisher will probably pay only 50 percent of royalties for foreign sales, for the same reasons that this is done with records. If the publisher owns his own foreign affiliate, the artist should seek more than a 50 percent share of the foreign royalties. Some music publishers are taking a leaf from the record industry and attempting to charge some of the costs of a book against the author's royalties. The author should attempt to revise such provisions. The author is usually given a specified number of free books and is permitted to purchase additional copies at discounts equivalent to, or greater than, the discounts afforded retail stores. Some publishers pay royalties every three months, some pay every six months, and some once a year. There is even one music publisher, who shall remain nameless to protect me from potential libel suits, who is rumored not to bother paying royalties at all. In all fairness I should report that in my experience music publishers pay royalties more quickly and more consistently than do record companies.

If you do a collection of solos for an instrument that includes some songs owned by other publishers and written by other writers, those writers and publishers will share in your royalties, unless your publisher is able to lease the songs for a flat fee. This is why so many method books consist entirely of new compositions by the author or works in the public domain. These are works published more than seventy-five years ago whose copyright protection has expired, so the original writer and publisher no longer receive royalties.* Sometimes a publisher hires a music arranger to do arrangements of classical works or works in public domain. Often the publisher will try to hire the arranger by paying a flat fee instead of royalties. The arranger should resist this temptation because it is very difficult to predict how much in royalties a book will bring in over a number of years.

Let's go through the creation of a music book from conception to distribution. To sell such a book to a music publisher the author should have completed a table of contents, a rough outline of the book, and perhaps one sample chapter. It is unwise to submit a complete manuscript because the publisher may want you to make certain changes in your style or presentation, or even use some music that you hadn't included in your rough draft. The book should be submitted to the director of publications or editor in chief at one of the print music publishing companies listed in the Appendix. Once you have written some successful books you may be able to make a sale without a complete presentation of this nature, but as a beginning writer you need to submit some of your work to convince the editor that you are capable of delivering a legible finished manuscript that is intelligently constructed.

Once you have reached an agreement with the publisher, the editor will work with you on your manuscript. She will make suggestions and correct mistakes. Music books are bound in groups of eight pages, so it is wise to make your total number of pages divisible by that number. In many cases printing sixteen pages costs little more than printing eight, so a large number of books are forty-eight or sixty-four pages long. When you are preparing your book you must figure in space for any

---

* New works are protected for the life of the last surviving author and an additional fifty years.

necessary photos, drawings, or diagrams. The music publisher has a production manager who is responsible for working on the physical content of your book. A typeface must be chosen, and the book must be precisely laid out with spaces between the lines. This is skilled work and requires considerable experience. The production manager then sends the book out to a music engraver.* Engravers are experienced in working with written music; in fact the more experience they have, the more useful they will be to you. An engraver may find mistakes that you and your editor have overlooked. Some typical mistakes might include note stems written in the wrong direction, wrong number of beats in a bar, omission of rests, or wrong notes or chord symbols. Many music engravers are also musicians and can detect such mistakes. The engraver returns a copy of the engraved manuscript to the publisher, where the author and/or a proofreader check it over. Proofreading requires great patience, and it is very easy for an author to miss her own mistakes without realizing it. A good proofreader can even uncover conceptual errors, passages that are not technically incorrect but are not explained properly. The manuscript is then returned to the engraver for correction. The engraver makes the necessary corrections and then passes the manuscript on to a printer. The printer meanwhile receives the cover and any necessary artwork or photography. Some music publishers have their own art departments; others use free-lance artists. The printer shoots each page with a camera and prepares blueprints of the book. These are returned to the publisher for a final check by the author and/or editor. The printer then makes plates and prints the book. After printing, the book is collated and bound and shipped to the publisher's warehouse.

JOBS IN MUSIC PUBLISHING

Music publishing companies often have a copyright department manager, whose job is to lease songs from other publishers for print rights. Anyone negotiating copyrights needs a thorough knowledge of the copyright law. This may be obtained through college courses, consulta-

---

* All music today is prepared by music typing, but the term *music engraver* is still used to describe the work. This dates back to the time when the engraving process was actually used.

tion with lawyers, or on-the-job training procedures. Leasing foreign songs may be particularly complicated. Sometimes some negotiating skills are necessary, because the publisher of a current hit will seek outrageous guarantees or attempt to restrict the printing of a hit to one or two books. The copyright law does not force the publisher to lease the print rights for a specific period of time.

The sales department of the music publisher takes the new book and introduces it to music educators, retail stores, jobbers, and whatever markets may exist for a particular piece of music. The educational market can be reached through advertising in the national or regional music educators' journals, and the consumer can be reached through ads in popular publications such as *Guitar Player* or by in-store displays. Music stores can be contacted through press releases and brochures, catalogs, and personal visits by the sales staff. Some of the publishers have their own staffs to write copy for ads and brochures. The sales staff will visit their major accounts once or twice a year. Often the salespeople will cover a huge territory, such as the entire western United States from New Mexico to Washington and Oregon. Many salespeople are ex-musicians because it is easier to sell something that you understand, and many of the music store owners or managers are or were musicians.

More and more publishers are packaging cassettes or CDs with instructional folios. Some of the publishers operate their own audio or video facilities, thus providing another source of work for those seeking careers in the print business.

Many music publishers send their authors out as clinicians and lecturers. The authors give seminars, sometimes called clinics, for music teachers at conventions or do demonstrations at large music stores to attract customers and sales. Clinicians are paid fees and expenses, but the goal for the clinician as well as for the publisher is to increase sales. A successful clinic will affect book sales in the same way that a successful concert will stimulate record sales in a market.

26

MUSIC CRITICISM

$\mathcal{N}$ewspaper reviewing is the most readily available source of employment for the music critic. The trend in newspaper ownership today is consolidation. There are fewer newspapers almost every year as some go out of business and others join forces with other existing papers. Consequently there are fewer newspaper jobs available now than in previous years. On the other hand, there are some additional opportunities available for popular music critics because of the increase in the number of popular music concerts and records.

The music critics on a large newspaper usually has some sort of training in music history, performance, or composition. Critics who review classical music concerts seldom write about jazz and almost never cover popular music. The Newspaper Guild is a union for newspaper employees. It sets salary minimums for papers in which it bargains for the employees. Non-Guild papers also usually set some sort of minimum salaries for their writers. Part-time newspaper writers are called *stringers* and are paid per article. Often the stringers are hired by the regular music critic when that critic doesn't feel qualified to review a particular concert or when there are several competing concerts taking place on the same day at the same time.

The critic for a morning newspaper must be able to write quickly because a typical concert might end at 10:30 P.M. and the final deadline for the morning paper is around 11:00 or 11:15 P.M. The critic may call in at intermission to find out how much space the editor has left vacant for the night's review. When a concert takes place at a location far from the offices of the newspaper, the critic will have to leave the concert early or send it by E-mail using a laptop computer. Obviously in this sort of situation there is no time for careful rewriting and the copy editor may omit a key sentence or rephrase a sentence in such a way that the original thought is lost or distorted. Not everyone who is capable of writing well can turn out an acceptable review in thirty or forty minutes. A slower stylist might prefer to work for an afternoon paper, which generally has a deadline of 7 or 8 A.M. the next morning.

The critic is expected to know quite a bit about music and also is supposed to know how to write. The critic for a small-town paper may also review films, plays, art exhibits, and be a sportswriter when necessary. No human being is going to be able to perform all of these duties with equal facility. On such a paper there is not enough money or not enough work to support a full-time music critic.

On Sundays the regular critic usually writes a column in which she discusses some musical event or issue at length. This is a welcome change from the pressure of nightly deadlines for the thoughtful critic. Occasionally a music critic will interview an important figure who is passing through town or giving a special performance.

When the critic has a good musical background, reviewing concerts in the symphonic repertoire is not as difficult as it might seem. She has usually heard the work performed before because the symphonic repertoire as played by most orchestras is not very daring. New music presents more difficult problems. Sometimes she will try to get a copy of the musical score and read through it in advance or follow it as the orchestra plays. One of the problems in reviewing new music is that many pieces need to be heard more than once, but in the case of a new work the critic does not have that luxury. It is difficult for a critic to be totally objective—in fact, it is probably impossible. The critic must be aware of the specific performance problems as well as general aesthetic standards. A student symphony is not really comparable to a nationally known orchestra. When reviewing amateur or semiprofessional groups, the critic tries to strike a balance between being supportive and being objective. It is important for the critic to encourage the development of performing organizations in her city, and yet there is a responsibility to the reader not to praise a poor performance. The critic must also take into account the intelligence level and reading ability of the readership of her particular newspaper, which may be higher or lower than that of another publication.

Many critics have jobs besides their newspaper work. They may teach at a college or do a local radio show. Some critics write magazine articles or books about music. These books may be collections of their newspaper or magazine articles or they may be other works of music criticism or history.

Reviewing popular music is more difficult in some ways than writing about classical music. There are no universally supported standards for popular music performances, and many popular music critics have little or no musical training. The critic should be able to provide a historical context for the reader that will be helpful in understanding the roots and development of musical styles. To understand the early music of the Rolling Stones, it is really necessary for the reader to be familiar with Chicago blues and its development from the Mississippi delta blues styles of the rural black man. Unfortunately, many pop music critics lack a broad historical background in music, and the reviews may degenerate into a review of the audience rather than a review of the concert. A popular music critic should do homework before attending a concert in the same fashion that we have described this process in classical music. How does the present performance or record compare with previous ones? Are there any changes in musical style? Is the artist attempting to grow and to expand his musical horizons? One seldom sees a popular music review that comments on the harmonic or rhythmic structure of the music.

There are many regional and national popular music journals that can provide opportunities for writing reviews. Critics may even be offered payola in the form of free trips or extra records in return for reviewing concerts or records. Record companies may offer employment to critics to write album notes for records, and if a record company feels that a critic has a readable writing style, the critic may end up on staff as a record company publicist.

There is a great shortage and an expanding market for critics who are knowledgeable about folk music, blues, jazz, and soul music. Some of the better popular music critics, like the late Ralph J. Gleason, have even opened up new markets for musical styles by lending them credibility through informed reviews. The critic must continue to think, study, and listen throughout her career in order to be receptive to new musical experiences and to help introduce these experiences to new audiences.

There is no formal training available at this time for music critics, but the Music Critics Association does sponsor occasional seminars and meetings. This is a good way of meeting people active in the field. Such personal contacts may even lead to potential employment.

Below are some lists that describe some of the goals of music criticism, the factors that determine writing style, and how an editor deals with what the critic writes. Below is a list that categorizes different ways that critics look at musical events.

RATIONALE

1. Commentary: On an event, such as a specific concert.

2. Historical survey or think piece: An example is an article on the blues in Memphis today.

3. Explanation: An article that tries to define musical complexities in a way not apparent to the average reader. A piece concerning contemporary musical opinions about the performance practices of sixteenth-century music would provide such a context.

4. Evaluation: Should the consumer buy a particular record? This is often expressed by giving records varying numbers of stars, based on the author's opinion.

5. Muckraking: This is where a critic trashes a particular artist as being a copycat, unmusical, irrelevant, etc.

6. Cheerleader: Promotional pieces often written for fanzines/magazines that celebrate artists in an uncritical way.

WRITING STYLE

In determining the appropriate writing style, you must ask the question "Who is the audience that will read my article?" It can be based on such factors as:

1. Relative degree of education or sophistication.

2. An assumption of knowledge, as can be made in a specialty magazine like the *Journal of Ethnomusicology*.

3. The critic may have a primary goal of impressing the reader with her knowledge and erudition. This is often the case in articles in academic journals.

4. Is the article designed to raise questions rather than to entertain the reader, or vice versa.

5. Whether the article is designed to sell copies of magazine or newspaper—sensationalism.

6. Is the article designed to place the critic in the inner circle of musicians, record companies, etc. ("I am a tastemaker.")

7. Is the intent to inspire or assert standards of morality, politics, etc.

8. Whether the piece is a contextual—to place an artist's work in terms of the history of a specific musical style.

9. Egoistic. Some articles tell us more about how the writer feels than about an artistic event. Many "underground" papers, such as New York's *Village Voice*, feature such articles, which value subjective criteria over objective ones.

10. The reverse of the above category is the "oracle" role where the critic defines "objective" standards to judge an artistic event.

11. Gossip. This is a self-defining category.

ROLE OF THE EDITOR

1. Centralize the focus of an article.

2. Create title headings.

3. Rewrite to improve style or to fit an audience profile.

4. Suggest a new line of attack. For example: "What about X's new backup vocalist?"

5. Check spelling, grammar, style.

6. Verify facts to protect a publication from libel suits.

7. Provide possible references or contexts that a young writer may not know.

8. Set the policy of a publication. For example: "We don't do negative reviews."

9. Suggest new articles.

10. Get copyright permissions for lengthy quotes of lyrics.

11. Follow the production process. In a magazine, make sure pictures that accompany an article are appropriate.

12. Determine what page the article will be placed on.

13. In the case of books, an editor may help in getting a prestigious figure to write an introduction, and may call in old favors to get important reviewers to write about the book.

14. An editor may be involved in helping to create a promotional scheme. As with record companies, the fight for corporate promotional dollars can be an intense struggle.

FREE-LANCE WRITING

There are currently quite a few music publications. Some of them, like *Guitar Player*, are devoted to particular instruments. There are also many local and regional music papers, or weeklies, that include quite a few music reviews. There are also magazines that circulate within the music retail and manufacturing community, such as *Music Trades, Musical Merchandise Review*, and *Up Beat*. All of these publications offer opportunities for free-lance writing assignments. In recent years an amazing proliferation of magazines has occurred.

27

MUSIC LIBRARY CAREERS

$\mathcal{M}$usic librarians work for large university libraries or for libraries in large cities that maintain sizeable music collections. Degrees in library science and musicology are recommended for someone attempting entrance into this field. Many libraries also maintain circulating or special collections of records, so the contemporary music librarian must be knowledgeable about records as well as the written word or music score. A knowledge of foreign languages is also useful, depending upon the nature of a specific library and its collection and the ethnic composition of the particular city.

Another possible employment opportunity is working as a librarian for a symphony orchestra. The symphony librarian must order parts from publishers, check to make sure that all the correct parts are received and distributed to the orchestra, and collect the music for return to the symphony's library or, if the music is rented, for return to the publisher. An orchestra librarian will find the ability to read and write music crucial to the performance of such duties.

Some libraries have particularly strong collections in certain specialties, such as folk music, jazz, or popular music. A knowledge of these areas of music would prove helpful in working for such a library. When applying for a job the applicant should be aware of the areas of music that a library specializes in. Courses may be available at a local college that will provide specific information about the history and music of a specific ethnic group or musical style.

Radio and television stations have large record libraries, and some stations employ a record librarian. The type of music that a station plays will govern its concept of an expert music librarian. To be a music librarian at a radio station does not necessarily require academic expertise, but it does require the music librarian to be current on what records are available to the station and what is in the station library. At some stations a music librarian assists the programming director in music programming decisions.

Since many musicological publications are relatively obscure, it is important that the music librarian have an extensive biographical knowledge of music. This can be attained through academic study and by reading the many critical journals that deal with different musical styles and instruments.

In smaller libraries there may be no music specialist, but the same person might be in charge of an entire arts department, requiring a strong background in other art subjects such as painting, drama, and film. Some libraries offer concerts and film programs, and the music librarian may need to be a producer or consultant for such events.

One of the most difficult areas in music library work and in running a sheet music department at a music retail store is being cognizant of various editions of the same work and being able to recommend and describe the different qualities of the various editions. In some libraries it is the music librarian who will be ordering the specific editions of a work that the library purchases. Naturally knowledge of the performance of music is a prerequisite when the librarian is confronted with this kind of decision.

Some library training is useful to a person working in the sheet music department of a well-stocked music store such as Sherman Clay in San Francisco or Schirmer's in New York. Such an employee may even be able to recommend new or obscure repertoire to the concert artist.

Because training in music library work is not given in a single coordinated college program, a music librarian should have at least one degree in music and one in library science. To be a music librarian in a major library, both of these degrees should be at least on the master's level.

28

MUSICAL INSTRUMENT MANUFACTURING

*I*n 1994 music industry sales of instruments and music reached nearly $5 billion in the United States.* Acoustic piano sales hit 605.2 million, fretted instruments did $665.8 million, and various school music products grossed $489.9 million in the same year.

Concert bands and choral groups each number about 25,000 in American schools, and other music ensembles include marching and stage bands and various orchestral and vocal combos. The market for educational music and band instruments varies with the birthrate, but has been hurt in many parts of the country by cuts in school music programs.

Many of the manufacturers of band instruments headquarter in the Midwest, especially around Chicago, in Elkhart, Indiana. A number of

---

* "Marketing to Musicians," by Tibbett L. Speer, *American Demographics*, March 1996, pp. 28, 32.

the musical instrument manufacturers were bought by conglomerates in the 1970s, and since then have been subsequently bought and sold in the paper transactions that seem to be common in American business these days. Seventy years ago there were some 500 piano manufacturers in the United States—now there are fewer than a dozen. In 1986 we imported almost five times the value of musical instruments than we exported. As the value of the yen has increased relative to the American dollar, more instruments are being imported from Korea, Taiwan, and even India and China.

Many of the jobs in musical instrument manufacturing require a business background, and music skills are useful but not required. This is particularly true in the financial areas of a company—the people who deal with credit ratings, accounting procedures—and of personnel directors. In the actual making of musical instruments many handcraftsmen are still employed, but many of the production workers such as tool and die makers do not need any sort of musical skills.

Manufacturers of any kind are concerned with the development of new technical processes. This may involve the invention of new musical instruments or new designs or modifications of older ones. Engineers are employed to work out the technical problems, and product managers come up with new ideas. Engineering skills are particularly useful in the design of synthesizers or amplifiers. Musicians may be hired as consultants on new design ideas or to test the final product. Some of the engineers in the research labs have some musical training or background. Manufacturers also have a repair and service division. This department is maintained to service instruments that are damaged while covered by manufacturers' guarantees or as the result of accident or wear. Some playing ability is helpful for the repair people to assess customer complaints and to test the product after it has been repaired.

The sales department is organized much like that of record companies, with a national manager and regional people. There are periodic regional and even national sales meetings, where sales personnel exchange experiences of value, provide feedback to the company on consumer reaction to new products, and discuss competing products. Many musical instrument salespeople have had some formal musical training, or at least can play some of the instruments that they sell. This is particularly important in trying to interest a school district in the purchase of band instruments. The salesperson must be able to speak the language of the music educator in order to have any sort of dialogue.

To stimulate sales and promotion and to establish good public relations, many companies have an educational services manager. This person is usually an experienced music educator and is responsible for hiring educational clinicians. These player-teachers give free concerts and demonstrations at the music educators' national, regional, and even state meetings. Sometimes they give free performances at large music stores where there is sufficient interest in an instrument to attract a sizeable audience. Some of the instrument manufacturers also seek to get endorsements from top players in various styles. The endorsement by a top player can be of great value, if that player is known as a significant stylist on the instrument. Sometimes a musician may actually design musical instruments for the company, as Les Paul has done for the Gibson Guitar Company. In other instances the company might design an instrument after conferring with a musician about possible innovations in appearance or design. If a musician has actually designed a musical instrument, particularly if the model is named after the musician, the company may pay her a royalty on each instrument sold. Famous musicians may receive fees, free instruments, or large discounts and special services from the manufacturer in return for endorsements. The musicians also get additional free publicity from posters, magazine ads, and brochures featuring pictures of the musician playing the instrument. Occasionally musicians will make special records for the manufacturer demonstrating technique, with descriptive material on the jacket about the instrument.

Some of the instrument manufacturers act as distributors for foreign-made instruments in this country. An alternative is for an American manufacturer to buy a foreign company because they cannot manufacture a comparably cheap instrument in this country.

As the population shifts to an older age group and the school-age population declines, musical instrument manufacturers may have to adopt new measures in order to reach the adult population. Marching-band instruments will decrease in demand if this trend continues, but the piano, organ, and guitar would appear to be able to maintain their popularity without any great difficulties.

29

MUSIC RETAILING AND
WHOLESALING

 $\mathcal{T}$ here are more than
9,000 retail music stores in the United States at the present time.* Some
of them are full-service stores stocking band instruments, keyboards,
fretted instruments, percussion, sheet music, amplifiers, etc. Some are
specialty stores carrying only pianos or organs or guitars and other fretted instruments. In addition to these stores, there are dozens of discount
appliance and home entertainment stores that carry portable electronic
keyboards.

To operate a successful music store the owner must have a good location, a knowledge of music, good relationships with the music educators in the community, and some business ability. Sales personnel in
music stores may be paid a salary, a salary plus a commission, or they
may work on a straight commission basis. When the salesperson gets a

---

* *Musical Merchandise Review Directory of Musical Instrument Dealers*, 1995.

salary plus commission, the commission is usually based on sales over a certain amount of money. Because the retail price of pianos and organs is so high, a commission deal can be very lucrative.

Television advertising is effective, but too expensive for most retail outlets to attempt. They must rely on word of mouth, service, or discounting to attract customers. Some sponsor community music events in order to become known and respected in their town.

There are some colleges that offer degree programs that feature music merchandising. They include Bradley University in Peoria, Illinois, the University of Evansville (Indiana), the University of Miami, and the University of Wisconsin at Oshkosh. In these programs the student serves an internship while attending school. Such internships often lead to job offers when the student graduates.

A retail music store owner should have a variety of business skills mixed in with his music background. New editions of music and new instruments must be evaluated from an aesthetic and sales viewpoint, repair personnel and salespeople must be hired, and financing deals must be arranged. Many instruments are purchased on time payment plans. It is wise for the owner to have the bank finance these plans. If the store owner does the financing, he may find himself in a cash bind when a number of instruments have been sold, but no cash is available to replace them with new instruments. Without any retail stock the owner cannot possibly survive.

Some music stores supply instruments to public or private schools on a contract basis. This requires working closely with school administrators, and sometimes written bids must be submitted in competition with other stores. A school may buy or rent instruments, depending on the needs of the school district. Naturally the owner must be able to evaluate the school's needs and to select suitable instruments that are sturdy but playable.

Specialty music store operators often are ex-musicians who have a good working knowledge of how to play their instruments and possess considerable knowledge of who will buy such instruments. If the market in a particular area is sufficiently concentrated, such a shop can be quite successful. The most common specialty music stores sell pianos and/or organs and guitars.

Many music store owners operate teaching studios, hiring teachers from the colleges or high schools or music students from the colleges. The teaching is done after school and in the evenings and on Saturdays. Some store owners make tie-ins with instrument sales, giving several free lessons with the purchase of a new instrument. It is presumed that when a student comes to a studio inside the store or close to it, further sales will be made of instrumental accessories and music, and eventually a replacement instrument will be purchased as the student becomes more advanced. The teacher is paid most of the lesson fee, and the owner keeps a percentage—usually around 20 percent for providing the studio space and booking the student.

Whether or not the owner operates a music studio, he will try to make contact with local music teachers. Teachers are offered a professional discount, ranging from 10 to 20 percent. The store will seek to stock music books or even the instruments that the teacher recommends to her students. This represents a convenience for the teacher and a profit-making opportunity for the store owner.

The larger music stores maintain their own musical instrument repair services. There is a shortage of competent instrument repair personnel of almost every kind and also a need for amplifier repair people. Instrument repair can be a good business in itself, but it is also valuable because it brings traffic into the store, results in trade-ins and the subsequent sale of used instruments, and offers service to the consumer. Repair personnel may be paid a salary, or they may be paid in the same fashion as teachers in the owner's music studios, with the owner taking a small percentage of the bill. If a store does not have a repair service or if a new instrument has some defect in it, the store owner must sublet the work to another repair service or send the instrument back to the factory. This is time-consuming and will often irritate the customer.

In New York and Los Angeles and in some other large cities there are discount music stores. These stores sell to the public at steep discounts, relying on a large volume of business to produce some profit. In New York there is a concentration of some ten music stores on one block of West 48th Street. When so many stores are close to one another, discounting is inevitable. Discount stores often do not offer repair services, or they offer service on only the most minor repairs. The mid 1990s have witnessed the growth of a number of chain stores, such as Daddy's Junky Music and Sam Ash and Guitar Center.

WHOLESALING

The wholesaler buys large quantities of instruments and some sheet music and accessories from many manufacturers and offers a one-stop service to the smaller music store. The large wholesalers have salespeople who cover numerous states and specialize in servicing the small retail store. Wholesalers may also import instruments directly. In recent years acoustic guitars from Korea and Taiwan have been heavy import items. Wholesale salespeople have to have some knowledge of the instruments that they sell, and playing experience is helpful. To the small music store the wholesaler offers the convenience of ordering all of their merchandise from one or two sources instead of having to deal with dozens of manufacturers.

30

MUSIC THERAPY

*D*egree programs in music therapy are available at a number of colleges.* The majority of hours are taken in music, with some special music therapy courses, psychology, sociology, anthropology, and general electives. Study at an approved institution is required to complete a music therapy degree. Seven schools offer additional training for the master's degree. This training includes clinical experience.

After the student completes his college training, he becomes eligible for registration as a Registered Music Therapist. This certification is administered by the National Association for Music Therapy Inc. A certification exam is then administered by the Certification Board for Music Therapists Inc. Music therapy is used for physical and mental disorders. Playing wind instruments can be helpful in restoring proper breathing, and problems of speech and vocal articulation can be aided

---

* See Appendix.

by music therapy. Paralysis and heart patients are also treated with music as a form of physical therapy. Motor coordination and skills can be improved through the playing of musical instruments.

In a mental hospital situation music therapy can be used for soothing purposes, for purposes of drawing out the patient, or for general recreation and socialization procedures. Sometimes a particular song or style of music has associative value to the patient and may bring a flood of memories that can be helpful in treating her. Some amazing instances have been reported where patients who were regarded as hopeless incurables reacted so strongly to the work of a musical therapist that eventually the patient was discharged from the hospital.

Historically music has been used in a therapeutic way. Medicine men used singing as part of the healing process in many primitive societies. The Arabs have been reported to use flutes with mental patients, and the ancient Greeks and Chinese attached much philosophical value to music as a means of balancing the universe.

Music therapy can be done in a one-on-one situation with a patient, it can be practiced in small groups, or it may be used with large groups of patients. The intensity of the treatment may vary according to the patient's situation and the availability of the therapist. Music must be tailored to the needs of each patient. Some patients may respond to soothing music; others are attracted by dissonant music. Some exceedingly restless psychotic children have been observed concentrating in music lessons for periods of over an hour. Certain chords or musical intervals can produce measurable changes of respiration in patients.

The music therapist should be able to play the piano and also a more portable stringed instrument, such as the guitar. The ability to play other musical instruments may also prove helpful in performance or instruction. The broader the therapist's knowledge of music is, the better. A patient may have some secret locked in him that a particular piece of music will reach. A music therapist must be able to read music fluently and should also be able to improvise freely. In playing a particular piece of music the therapist may find that the patient has a reaction to it. In such cases the therapist should be able to elaborate on the theme while observing the patient as closely as possible. It is valuable for the treatment facility to have an extensive collection of records and tapes of all styles of music because a patient's response to different styles of music can be so unpredictable. In working with geriatric patients music can bring life and purpose to the generally depressed world of the patient.

At the present time opportunities in music therapy are somewhat ambiguous. The field is growing conceptually, but as the budgets of state facilities continue to be cut, experimental programs are not looked upon with favor. A student who is in doubt about her career might consider volunteering in a treatment facility to get a taste of what a music therapy career offers. A part-time job might be another way of testing the waters before making a more serious commitment.

Another academic possibility is a psychology major with a music therapy minor. The student could then do some music therapy work as an adjunct to her normal clinical work. Such a degree program might provide a good background for a job at a typical state mental hospital. Check with your local treatment facilities to see if they employ any full-time music therapists or if they have any plans to institute a music therapy program.

Job opportunities for music therapists exist in mental hospitals, in geriatric treatment facilities, mental health centers, day-care centers, schools for the retarded, special-education facilities, hospitals for the physically disabled, nursing homes, and in private practice. Teaching opportunities are available on the college level.

31

PIANO TUNING, INSTRUMENT REPAIR, MUSIC IN THE ARMED FORCES, CHURCH MUSIC, AND CAREERS IN LAW

PIANO TUNING

A considerable number of jobs are available for piano tuners. The piano tuner serves an apprenticeship, usually about two years. During this period she learns technical skills. Some piano tuners are in business for themselves; some are on staff with schools or music stores. Self-employed tuners may have part-time contracts to tune pianos for particular schools, concert halls, or recording studios. Although there is no legal regulation of piano tuners at this time, there is a Piano Technicians Guild, which gives an examination as a prerequisite for membership. Guild members charge fees for a tuning, while nonmembers may charge lower fees. To maintain a normal piano it should be tuned twice a year, but pianos used in recording studios or at the concert hall must be tuned more frequently. Many performers specify in their contracts with a nightclub or a concert hall that the piano must be tuned before they perform.

Some piano tuners work part-time, and there is an increasing opportunity for women in the field. Clients are usually gained through word of mouth and by advertising in the Yellow Pages. Some piano tuners also do repair and restoration work, but in larger cities such craftsmen have sufficient work, so they need not spend their time tuning pianos. In smaller cities tuners may have to make or adapt parts if replacement parts are unavailable.

INSTRUMENT REPAIR AND BUILDING

There is a great shortage of instrument repair personnel in almost every family of instruments. Some schools offer courses in string and fretted instrument repair. Some of the music merchandising programs offer repair courses in various families of instruments. The repair of high-quality instruments is a highly paid and skilled job available wherever these instruments are owned. Repair people may own their own businesses or work for a music store on a salary or commission basis. Some instrument manufacturers endorse specific shops to do their guarantee work. Such an endorsement provides prestige and some assured income for the repair person.

There are a number of people who build instruments and sell them directly to the consumer or through consignments at local music stores. A successful instrument maker often has customers in excess of his ability to make instruments. Advertisements for courses or apprenticeships in instrument making may be found in the journals of the various instruments.

MUSIC IN THE ARMED FORCES

All of the branches of the armed services have some full-time music organizations. This includes some playing opportunities for women. To enter an armed service band an audition is required. The service requires a three- or four-year term of enlistment. Several thousand jobs are available in the armed services. Some of the bands are stationed in the United States, some at American installations abroad. There is some rotation of personnel, but this can sometimes be avoided by the better players. Positions are available on almost every instrument, and there are symphonic and marching bands, string ensembles, and even vocal groups and small combos. Some jobs are available for arrangers and music librarians. There is an armed services music school at Little Creek, Virginia. It provides an opportunity to receive formal music instruction at government expense. All of the services except the Marine Corps require basic training as a condition for membership in the bands. Some of the bands do tours in addition to their regular service. Medical benefits and thirty days of paid vacation annually are part of the contract with the armed services.

Careful consideration should be given to a military career before signing the contract because the full term of enlistment must be served. Information about military music careers is available from your local military recruiting service.

CHURCH MUSIC

Full- and part-time careers are available in church music. The salary and duties of the job will vary with the size of the church. Large urban churches may have a full-time music director, who conducts the choir, writes some music for services, and is responsible for planning a concert series. Smaller churches may employ a part-time choir director or organist. Composers of church music submit new music to a committee of the church for approval, and sometimes the committee commissions new works. Additional part-time work is available at weddings and funerals for vocalists and keyboard musicians.

A job in a large church may be sought by numerous applicants. The music director may need to have a Ph.D. degree with extensive study in music literature and history. Sometimes the church music director is also responsible for working with dramatics and dancing, so acquiring such skills may also be useful. Church music organizations hold music workshops and offer courses in church music at regional meetings or denominational colleges.

MUSIC LAW

Los Angeles, New York, and Nashville are the cities most likely to employ music business attorneys. In smaller cities part-time opportunities may be available to a lawyer in general practice. At the present time there are no music industry specialty programs offered, although U.S.C. and a handful of other schools do have courses in show business law. The usual way to break into this field would be to work as a young lawyer in a firm that specializes in the entertainment business or to get a job as a staff attorney for a major record company. Music business lawyers charge high fees. In the major music markets they can exceed $300 an hour. Some lawyers work for clients on a percentage basis, taking a portion of the client's gross, or on retainer for a monthly fee. Some music business attorneys act as business advisers for their clients, doing investment and tax work for additional fees. Many music business lawyers have numerous personal contacts in the industry and may undertake functions usually performed by personal managers, such as selling an act to a record or music publishing company. A few music lawyers have gone on to become personal managers or record company executives.

32

ARTS MANAGEMENT

*A*rts management specialists must have a background in business procedures together with a deep love and knowledge of the arts. The large number of symphony orchestras and the size of these orchestras makes a job with a symphony one of the more obvious career possibilities for an arts management specialist. Other opportunities exist with federal and state arts commissions, opera companies, and in jobs related to the other arts, such as working with theater groups or ballet companies, or working at an art museum. A number of colleges offer degree and advanced-degree programs in arts management.*

The large symphony orchestras employ a number of people in their offices. There is a general manager, who has the title of president or vice president of the orchestra; there is an orchestra manager and a director of development. The orchestra manager deals with contracts for the orchestra members and must negotiate with the musician's union and with

---

* See Appendix.

the first-chair players, the conductor, guest conductors, and soloists. The personnel manager is responsible for sending out notices of vacancies in the orchestra, screening applicants for these positions, and setting up auditions. The director of development coordinates fund-raising activities and attempts to expand the audience for the orchestra. As the larger orchestras have gone to fifty-two-week seasons, new concert series are developed in adjoining communities, residencies are undertaken in colleges, and tours are set up. Tours in neighboring towns and communities, playing for hospitals, and outdoor concerts are some other activities that symphonies are beginning to pursue. Many of these performances are financed by grants from state arts councils, city governments, or private foundations. Some of these grants call for matching funds by the group applying, and the development director must also do a considerable amount of paperwork in preparing the grant applications. Fund-raising is an important activity for arts organizations because most of them run at a deficit even if their performances have 100 percent attendance.

Arts management personnel must have a thorough knowledge of their community. The audience for performances should be thoroughly researched and the art manager should seek to reach an increasing number of community members. With the board of trustees, the head of the arts management team must select new conductors, and with the help of the conductor of the orchestra, guest conductors and soloists must be selected. These guests are generally contracted at least two years in advance, so considerable scheduling is involved. Many orchestras have symphony guilds. Guild members are often wives of prominent community leaders. Through their enthusiasm, attendance at events can be improved and the financial support of corporate leaders and community business people can be obtained. The trustees themselves can constitute an important source of funds, and an active trustee group is of inestimable aid in fund-raising activities. Familiarity with the symphonic repertoire is useful because it gives the manager a clear idea of what budgetary problems may arise in the scheduling of a particular piece. Public speaking skills and the ability to write press releases or brochures are helpful in the fulfillment of arts management jobs. Many of the arts management programs include internships, and these are also sometimes available to high school students with some interest in arts management careers.

The highest salaries in the field run in excess of $50,000, but the beginner is apt to find employment in a small orchestra where the salary may start at about $10,000. In a small orchestra the arts management team may consist of one or two people who handle all of the responsibilities outlined in the preceding paragraphs. The American Symphony Orchestra League lists job openings in orchestra management in its newsletter, and the Associated Council for the Arts also lists vacancies in its publication. Some regional arts organizations, such as the Western States Arts Foundation, may have additional listings for their particular regions in their publications.

Since 1965 the National Endowment for the Arts (NEA) has funded state arts councils and artists through grants procedures. Many jobs are available working for the state councils or the national endowment. The National Endowment for the Humanities (NEH) operates similarly, although its programs focus on critical aspects of art and on the social sciences. There are also humanities councils in each state.

State arts councils vary in size. The New York State Council for the Arts is a large organization with a major budget that a small state could not duplicate.

Many areas have local arts councils, and some cities provide grant support administered by arts managers. There are also numerous private foundations, from small family funds to the giant Ford Foundation, that administer all sorts of grant programs in the arts and humanities. Some foundations are extremely specialized in purpose and some are quite broad.

In recent years, the budgets for both the National Arts and Humanities Councils have been severely cut by the United States Congress. Congress appears to want to phase out both of the endowments. At the present time it is not clear where federal funding will continue in the twenty-first century.

33

GRANTS

$\mathcal{S}$ome form of grant is available today for doing almost anything. There are even people making a living teaching others how to write grant proposals. Grants are available from state, regional, and occasionally local arts councils all over the United States, from the National Endowment for the Arts, the National Endowment for the Humanities, and through numerous other federal programs. Most grants require some sort of matching funds, sometimes contributed in cash, sometimes provided by contributions of services or equipment. The latter sort of match is called "in kind." There are some grant programs and some foundation support from private foundations available for the individual artist, but the bulk of grant support demands a good deal of paperwork and administrative supervision and is therefore channeled through nonprofit organizations. The concept of matching funds is that the government is not in the giveaway business, and it is considered to be the responsibility of the applicant or applying organization to come up with some community support by utilizing the resources of the applying person or group. The crux of the problem for many artists is that many of those who need grant support do not have the public relations or business skills to find such a sponsor or even the writing ability to complete the grant proposal. The majority of grant applications are rejected because there simply isn't enough money to fund them. Many other grants are funded only in part, and the applicant should realize that this is a strong possibility before she applies.

National funding in the arts dates from 1965, except for the temporary WPA programs in the thirties. The amount of funding rose from $2.7 given to the NEA in 1967 to approximately $160 million given to the NEA in 1987; almost as much has been given to the NEH. In 1996 this funding was cut back to less than $100 million for each program. The difference between the NEA and the NEH is that the arts council funds creative projects, such as an original piece of music, while the humanities group funds projects like a critical study of the music of Charlie "Bird" Parker. In Canada the Canada Council has a number of excellent and interesting grant programs. Together with Canadian radio stations the FACTOR program currently provides $5 million a year for artists to make records. When you consider that Canada has about one-tenth the population of the United States, this means that there is available the equivalent of $50 million just for artists to make records. Since the NEA covers music, dance, drama, film, creative writing, and video, there is more money proportionally in the Canadian fund for the making of records than there is in the NEA's entire music program!

State arts councils were mostly founded in order to take advantage of matching funds granted to the states by the NEA. There are two levels of members of the state commissions—the professional full-time staff and the unpaid appointees. The full-time staff comprises people with some arts management background, general knowledge of the arts, or with administrative experience; the appointees are selected by the state's governor. New York started its arts council in 1961. It is the best-funded state council, although there is some sentiment in the state government for cutting these funds. During the Reagan era, President Reagan made several attempts to cut NEA and NEH funding. Congress strenuously resisted these cuts, because many senators and representatives favor the widespread dissemination of the arts, but by 1995, the Republican-led Congress succeeded in instituting severe cuts in these programs.

In New York and California the organization of the state arts councils is quite large and the staff is divided up into panels that deal with the various art forms. State and national councils can only act on applications—they are not authorized to plan specific programs. This procedure is followed to minimize any sort of favoritism. Similarly, grant panels may include judges from out of state who have no personal knowledge of applicants or familiarity with their styles. This is done to safeguard fairness.

Grant forms include descriptions of the grant proposal and complete budgetary data as to where and how the money will be spent. After the grant form is filled out, it is read by one of the full-time staff. The reader makes sure that the application fulfills the terms of the grant and makes notes on the proposal. The grant is then judged by a panel of people with expertise in the particular art form. The panel usually assigns some sort of point score to each grant based on such factors as the merit of the program, the panel's best guess as to whether the proposal can be carried out as described, and the question of who the grant will benefit. The panel tries to apportion grants so that they cover different areas of the state, different art forms, urban and rural groups, and various ethnic groups. Some grant requests are funded in toto, some are partially funded, and some might receive a token contribution as a form of moral support. The governor's appointees must approve the grants, but they generally treat this as a formality, relying on the panelists' expertise. The appointees are a combination of artists, business patrons of the arts, and political supporters of the governor who wish to receive the honor of a council appointment. The council appointees will generally represent different regions of the state and will include at least some minority representation.

At this point we come to some knotty matters of policy. What is the function of grants? Should they support established excellence in the arts through working with a proven group, such as the Metropolitan Opera, or should they be new programs designed to bring the arts to ghetto areas or rural areas where people have relatively little contact with the arts? Should grants concentrate on funding teaching experiences, such as artists-in-residence in the public schools, or should they support general cultural programs designed to bring high-level professionals into the community? Should dollars be spent on new and untried programs and artists or should the bulk of the money support existing programs? Are amateur groups worthy of funding? Should grants focus on young and promising professionals or should they be given to encourage proven practitioners to continue careers that are already in motion? Should the focus be on large institutional groups such as a symphony orchestra or on the work of individual artists? Should jazz or folk arts be supported or should the traditional classical art forms such as the opera and ballet predominate?

I feel that it is necessary to bring up the issues not in order to express my own point of view but because when you write a grant proposal the context in which it will be read will have a strong influence upon whether or not your program will be funded. No two state councils or, for that matter, two readers will have exactly the same views. Before writing a grant proposal it is a good idea to check with the funding agency to see what proposals they have funded in the last five years.* The particular proposal that you have in mind may already have been funded or rejected. Or you may discover that your particular state arts council is not interested in funding a jazz performance in a rural area, to give an example. The people at your state arts council will probably be very cooperative in helping you to better formulate your proposal.

NEA, NEH, and some state arts councils do give individual grants to composers and artists. They are usually for the completion of a specific work and do not require matching funds. This type of grant is for relatively little money, and a comparatively small number of individual grants are given.

Other funding is available through corporate or foundation support. Under the current tax law corporate deductions for gifts to the arts are somewhat curtailed, but private foundations offer many grants programs that are roughly similar to what NEA has. There are books and organizations, mentioned in the Appendix, that provide information on accessing this support. Many states have small foundations set up to provide grant support for specific programs or specific parts of a state. Many of these foundations have an educational focus, so if you are able to combine your music grant with an educational purpose, you may be eligible to receive some support. Consult the best library in your hometown for information on grant programs available in your locale.

San Francisco, Denver, and a handful of other cities have grant pro-

---

* Usually headquartered in the capital city of the state.

grams for the arts. The Music Performance Trust Fund (MPTF) of the American Federation of Musicians also provides grants in the form of matching funds that sponsor free concerts throughout North America.

Several other sources of funding are available through the federal government, particularly projects that relate to arts education. These are funded through various educational titles passed by the U.S. Congress. The emphasis in these programs is on measurable criteria for the improvement of education in specific subject areas. This type of grant may be difficult for artists to conceive and execute because art and music by their very nature may not provide readily testable, specific data.

Several private organizations, such as Young Audiences and Affiliate Artists, provide performances or residencies in the schools or communities for performers. Young Audiences is active in more than thirty states, and its programs generally pay union scale. They can provide a supplementary source of income for the musician or singer. Groups perform in every medium, from chamber music to folk music. To become accredited, an audition and some paperwork, including a comprehensive program outline, are required. Affiliate Artists provides young concert artists with paid eight-week residencies in various communities. Both Young Audiences and Affiliate Artists receive funding from a variety of sources, including the government, corporations, and the musicians' union.

Your chances of receiving a grant depend upon careful planning and thought in the preparation of the grant proposal. If you do your homework on the history of the issuing agency, and if you prepare your proposal with care and receive proper references and recommendations, with some luck you may receive the grant. I recommend patience and a sense of humor as a corrective in dealing with what is necessarily something of a bureaucratic structure. Try to get some help from people who have already gotten grants from the organization you are applying to or from people who have had experience with similar organizations.

The beauty of grant programs is that they make it possible for an artist to be supported while doing projects that have no commercial potential, but have real artistic merit. As a person who has received several grants and failed in getting others, I can say that I am truly grateful for the grant support that I have been fortunate enough to get.

34

MINORITIES IN THE MUSIC BUSINESS

THE POSITION OF WOMEN

At the present time men occupy almost all of the major positions of responsibility and power in the music business. Recently, women have begun to make inroads into middle-range executive positions. Many aspects of the business have a "macho" air surrounding them. Aggressiveness is valued as a prime trait, for example, in the case of record promotion. Since aggression has been customarily identified as a masculine trait, a woman is caught in the "Catch 22" routine. If a woman is not aggressive, then she must not be an industry heavyweight, which means she doesn't have to be taken seriously. If she is aggressive, there must be something wrong with her. Either she is hostile, a lesbian, or a misfit. Generally speaking, a job in the music business requires that you project a positive self-image and also that you be aware of when being positive creates such a strong image of self-confidence that you may be threatening to others. To the extent that it is feasible, a prospective employer should be interviewed in the same way that he or she is examining you. Anyone who is a continual hassle to work for or with may be better left alone, unless you have absolutely no options.

This is a good time for women to seek jobs in the music industry. Most companies are aware that they have discriminated against women in the past and are quite ready to make amends, if only at a fairly basic level. In the case of the broadcast media, the FCC has compelled radio and television stations to become equal opportunity employers, and women and other minority group members are finding jobs as air personalities and in sales, promotion, and technical areas that were partially or totally closed to them in the past.

It needs to be said that part of the enthusiasm for hiring women or other minority group members is that they generally offer a cheap labor supply. Women must demand wage increases, job promotions, and added responsibilities in order to advance beyond the role of secretary. It is not an inevitable condition for women to be treated as sex objects. Some record company and music publishing executives have hired exotic-looking women as promotion people, but what is going to happen to these people when they no longer look young or attractive? Women should not have to behave according to the preconceptions or prejudices of men. Many men are unaware of their prejudices but may be willing to listen if you choose the proper time and place to express your feelings.

There are numerous male prejudices against women involving flightiness, irresponsibility, inability to function under pressure, inefficiency, etc. These charges can be equated with portrayals of men as being overly aggressive, insensitive, boorish, or always delegating their work to others. Clearly there are men and women whose limitations are described by the above clichés and those who in no way relate to the stereotypes. When people can relate to one another with their minds released from stereotypes, real cooperation, friendship, and a successful business relationship can evolve. At the present time men and women on the job are not treated as equals, but this state of affairs is improving.

Perhaps it is time for corporations to make use of some of the special qualities of women. Women seem to have a talent for teamwork and an ability to consider the feelings of their coworkers in pressure situations. Efficiency is often dependent on the ability to work with others rather than the use of manipulative power. In more and more cities there are conferences and workshops on the special problems of women in business. Consult your local college, newspaper, or chapter of NOW (National Organization for Women) for more information. If you feel you are being denied job opportunities because of sex discrimination, NOW or the ACLU (American Civil Liberties Union) can offer advice or even legal aid.

When I first began working in the music business in the late 1950s the most prestigious jobs available to women were as executive secretaries to top-ranking male officials. Gradually women have eased into middle-management roles. In looking at job announcements and promotions in the music industry trade papers, I have noted that more women are regularly appearing in such jobs as product manager for a major record company. A&R coordinator, local promotion rep, marketing and media coordinator, national press and publicity director, professional manager for music publishers, disc jockey, or trade paper staff writer. More women have moved into jobs in engineering, record production, and radio station management. Women are obtaining more obvious notoriety as television air personalities, particularly with the prominence of Oprah Winfrey and a variety of newscasters.

In general this influx of women into the music business has been happening at a slower rate than acceptance in the advertising and book-publishing industries. There are no women in the record business with the clout of Mary Wells in advertising or Sherry Lansing in motion pictures. The presidents of all the major record companies continue to be white males, with the single exception of Sylvia Rhone, who is the president at Elektra Records. However, Elektra is only one company in the WEA hierarchy, with many other people positioned in a higher spot on the executive ladder. Monica Lynch at Tommy Boy and Missy Worth at Revolution Records are also important record company executives.

Careers in music performance have been open to women for some time. In the thirties and through the fifties such performers as the Andrews Sisters, Doris Day, Peggy Lee, and Jo Stafford were quite popular, as were such classical musicians as Wanda Landowska and the famous teacher and composer Nadia Boulanger. Today we have a greater representation of female musicians, many of whom are also songwriters. In pop music such people as Tracy Chapman, Aretha

Franklin, Madonna, Whitney Houston, Janet Jackson, Joni Mitchell, K. T. Oslin, Dolly Parton, and Linda Ronstadt immediately come to mind. It is true that male stars still predominate, especially in heavy metal or rap groups, but more and more women artists are achieving success. The image of the present-day female performers is also on a higher level. Many of these performers are clearly intelligent and creative people.

An ever-increasing number of women are establishing careers as symphony orchestra players, although the five most prestigious orchestras still lag behind the less famous ones in hiring women. Women in the symphonies are most often found in the string, harp, and woodwind sections. This concentration on particular instruments has much to do with tradition. As these walls break down we can anticipate seeing more women employed as bass or percussion players, for example. In jazz, women have traditionally been accepted as piano players. Barbara Carroll, Marion McPartland, and the late Mary Lou Williams are examples. Only a few women, such as Carla Bley and Melba Liston, have received recognition as composers and arrangers. Ira Jane Bloom is a saxophone player who is recognized by her male peers, but she is the exception to the rule. Elizabeth Swados is renowned for her Off-Broadway and Broadway music, and some other prominent female composers of show music are Gretchen Cryer and Nancy Ford.

A few women have made significant strides in the field of conducting. Sarah Caldwell is the artistic director, conductor, and producer for the Opera Company of Boston; Eve Queler is well known on the New York classical scene; and Marin Allsop, Margaret Harris, Sylvia Carduff, and Jo Ann Falletta are other conductors making an impression. Judy Collins and Jill Godmilow directed and produced an award-winning movie about the struggles of Antonia Brico to be accepted as a conductor.

There are some 850 women composers in the United States. These include such people as Barbara Kolb, Pauline Oliveros, and Pulitzer Prize winner Ellen Taffe Zwilich. Sophie Drinker's book *Music and Women* details the prejudice against women in music, especially in the church and synagogue. Although this book was written in 1948 we are just now beginning to respond to the conditions it describes.

The same sort of discrimination mentioned in the discussion of symphony orchestras applies to the hiring of female music teachers in the academic world. Several studies have shown that the following conditions prevail:

1. Women are not hired to teach at the college level at a level commensurate with the number of women qualified to teach music.

2. When women are hired they are most apt to be stuck at the lowest academic teaching level, as instructors.

3. As you go up the academic ladder to the rank of full professor, which carries the most prestige and the highest pay, the percentage of women holding positions at this level is considerably less than at the instructor level.

Women artists have never been as popular as their male counterparts in American popular music. This may stem partly from the large sale of records to teenage girls. The emphasis in the United States in the fifties and sixties was on the male culture, and the role of the woman was seen as taking care of the children, doing housework, and making the husband comfortable. The flower power ideology of the sixties led to a more searching examination of the role of women in the culture, as presented in such songs as Carly Simon's "That's the Way I've Always Heard It Should Be," or Joni Mitchell's "Little Green," or even Helen Reddy's "I Am Woman." These songs asserted women's independence, or at least questioned the traditional roles attributed to women in our culture.

Women played little part in the disco music movement, except as objects, and they are seldom present in today's heavy metal, thrash, or rap music scenes. It seems as though there is a part of rock 'n' roll that remains a sort of perverse male bastion. Sexpot artists like Madonna and Sheena Easton play kind of traditional "starlet" female roles even when they appear to be making fun of the very idiom that glorifies them. Several other late eighties artists, especially Tiffany, were more child stars than female sex objects or rebels.

There are several feminist record labels, notably Olivia Records and Holly Near's label, Redwood. Olivia was established in 1973 and is committed to working with music at all levels of the industry, including production, engineering, distribution, graphics, and sales. It distributes its product through feminist bookstores and at concerts, as well as through record outlets. Olivia also publishes songbooks and has a tape library of women's music available to other women. Redwood started out as Holly Near's outlet for her own music, but has expanded through her success to include the music of other performers as well.*

An organization called Women in Music functions in the major music towns in an attempt to bring women together to network job skills and to provide a support group for one another.

Should there be women's record companies, pressing plants, and the like? I would hope that in the future such alternatives will cease to be necessary, but the hard facts are that the major record and music publishing companies are owned and operated by men. This didn't prevent a major record company, Capitol, from promoting and manufacturing Helen Reddy's "I Am Woman" any more than it prevented the giant CBS corporate structure from selling Bob Dylan's records, even though they expressed social views it didn't support. If a product is deemed salable, the record company will put it out and promote it. Principles in the corporation are defined by profit and loss statements. If women's liberation goes out of fashion, record companies will quickly lose enthusiasm for songs about it. The primary issue is money, not politics. Of course, there are some exceptions to this, but even they may be influenced by marketing factors. It is doubtful that a direct and fervent plea for racial integration would be promoted on Top 40 radio by a major record company in the southern United States. At times the airplay of records has been restricted because of protests by offended groups or because the artist has been caught engaging in some immoral activity. By and large, the question remains, Will the record sell?

The point that I am trying to make is that large companies support activities that produce income. Small companies like Olivia are based on ideology rather than money. Nevertheless, some money must be made or the smallest company cannot survive. In the next chapter we will return in depth to the subject of alternative media.

There is no question in my mind that eventually there will be more

---

* Redwood recently went out of business.

women presidents of major record companies. At the present time women can take pride in their expanding role in middle management and as performers, conductors, arrangers, personal managers, record producers, etc. Those who wish to go further must "keep on pushing."

BLACK PARTICIPATION IN THE MUSIC BUSINESS

Discrimination against black musicians in the music business dates from their very entry into the business. In the 1920s and '30s black music was separately classified under the category of "race records," and these records were not even distributed to most record stores. In the forties the term became an embarrassment and was replaced by the title "rhythm and blues." When rock 'n' roll became popular in the mid-fifties many of the early hits were rerecordings by white artists of rhythm and blues hits. Radio and record people felt that the originals were too hard for white teenagers to understand. Some of these rhythm and blues records did sell in white markets, but without much regularity. Black musicians were consigned to lower-priced bookings for largely black audiences. There were some exceptions, such as Nat "King" Cole, who was quite popular with white audiences, but the majority of black musicians did not earn money comparable to their white compatriots.

In the 1930s many black musicians waived their writer's royalties when recording. Sometimes token payments were given for these rights, sometimes no payment at all was given. They were also paid flat fees for recording, without subsequent royalty payments. The rights to the songs written by these artists were owned by the record companies or by the A&R men, who often copyrighted them in their own names. Sometimes these A&R men also served as managers of the artists. Chapple and Garafalo, writing in *Rock 'n' Roll Is Here to Pay*, describe how Arthur "Big Boy" Crudup had his royalties for two of Elvis Presley's biggest hits ripped off by Lester Melrose, a famous record producer, and Crudup's manager. Many other black writers complained of receiving irregular royalty payments or no royalties at all.

Most of the musicians who succeeded in making big money in jazz, like Paul Whiteman, Benny Goodman, and Artie Shaw, were white, even though the origins of the music and most of the really innovative players have always been black. Until the late 1930s there was no integration in jazz groups, except for a handful of recordings on which the musicians sometimes used pseudonyms.

When the folk music boom emerged in the late 1950s and early '60s, a number of the older black blues singers were rediscovered by young white blues enthusiasts and were brought up north and employed at colleges and coffee houses, playing for young white audiences. When the English rock groups became popular many American disc jockeys and fans were astonished to find that the favorite entertainers of many of these English groups were the old black blues singers. Some of these rock groups recorded songs by these bluesmen and even toured with them.

Motown was the first black-owned record company, and many of its artists achieved popularity in the broad pop market. Now Motown is owned by Polygram, and there are no comparable large black record companies. Although there are still records that are popular only on black "soul" or rap music stations, an increasing number of black popular and jazz artists, like Herbie Hancock, Lionel Ritchie, Prince, Michael Jackson, and Whitney Houston, have been able to achieve universal popularity. A number of outstanding black record producers achieved success in the late eighties and nineties, especially Jimmy Jam and Terry Lewis and "Babyface." Some of the successful black producers now have their own labels, set up by the major record companies. This is particularly true in the field of rap, where most white executives acknowledge that they don't have the expertise to compete in this area.

The employment of black executives lags behind in the large record companies. Most of the major companies have Black Music divisions, and it is here that black executives are employed in production, sales, and promotion. Many black format radio stations are owned by whites and pay notoriously low wages. Blacks are also underrepresented in the large booking agencies, as personal managers, and in many other important industry roles.

In 1987 the NAACP published a report that made two specific indictments of the lack of equal opportunity in the music industry. The report maintained that blacks were not being hired as executives at record companies and that when they were hired their opportunities for promotion were severely limited. The report next charged that black entertainers were contributing to the problem by invariably hiring white managers to supervise their careers rather than giving any black personal managers the opportunity to play in the big leagues of the entertainment industry. Since the music industry has always thought of itself as a sort of liberal egalitarian operation, the report was quite an annoyance to the industry. Shortly after the report was issued, A&M Records announced a plan to hire fifty inner-city adolescents to work in a summer program at various jobs in the company. A&M denied any relationship between the report and their program. This program has now expanded to include other record companies, but no information is available that would verify any long-lasting results.

Whether or not the relationship between the NAACP report and the start of A&M's program was direct or not is almost irrelevant. The NAACP report hit a nerve in the industry and among black entertainers, but at this writing it is not possible to say that there have been any specific results because of it.

The classical music establishment has not readily accepted black musicians either. There have been so many charges of discrimination against black symphonic musicians that some orchestras have taken to auditioning the musicians behind screens, as I mentioned in writing about symphonies. Several years ago the Detroit symphony hired a black bass player as a result of political pressure in a city that has a large black population. The trouble with this action is that it leaves the musician, the orchestra, and the audience wondering whether the player could have gotten the job at a normal audition. At present it is one solution to a seemingly inevitable dilemma. Many of the urban orchestras ask for governmental support in cities that have a large black community, even a majority of black citizens.

Some of the finest black musicians in ragtime and jazz—Scott Joplin and James P. Johnson come immediately to mind—wrote classical music that they were unable to get performed. Long after Joplin's death, the opera *Treemonisha* has finally received several major performances, and conductor Marin Allsop has recently recorded a CD of Johnson's orchestral works.

Although black musicians were somewhat shut out of lucrative studio work for many years, this is less true today. This is partly because a number of black composers and arrangers, such as Quincy Jones and Herbie Hancock, have become active as composers. There are also several major black executives who work on music in advertising.

OTHER MINORITY GROUPS

In the same fashion that black executives are hired to deal with black music, the few Hispanic employees of the major companies are generally relegated to the field of Latin music. While such practices may appear to make sense at first glance, they really do not. Enforcement of this concept would limit Jewish and Italian executives to promoting or selling Jewish or Italian music, positions not too many music business executives would favor.

35

POWER IN THE ARTS AND ALTERNATIVE MEDIA

*M*ost of us are accustomed to thinking of art as an individual expression of an artist's deepest feelings. When you examine the ownership of the six multinational record companies, a wholly different picture emerges. BMG, the German owner of RCA, also owns Arista Records, a sizeable record company in itself. The parent company is also one of the largest book publishers in the world. Capitol is a subsidiary of EMI, which is itself a division of British electronics giant Thorn. To give you an idea of their corporate clout, Thorn a few years ago purchased SBK Music Publishing, who themselves had acquired CBS Songs, formerly the music publishing division of CBS Records. The purchase price for SBK was an astronomical $350 million! MCA, 80 percent Canadian- and 20 percent Japanese-owned, is very actively involved in booking entertainment at a handful of giant facilities around the country. Fiddler's Green in Denver, for example, has a capacity of about 20,000 people and does a large number of shows in the summer (it is an outdoor facility). Polygram is a jointly owned Dutch-German giant, a combine of German Polydor and Dutch Philips. The latter is a giant electronics and appliance firm that advertises heavily all over Western Europe. CBS Records is now a division of Japanese giant Sony, a massive company involved in numerous phases of the electronics industry.

Finally there is Warner Communications, now amalgamated with Time-Life. Both companies are active in book and magazine publishing; Warner Communications owns MTV and Time-Life owns HBO. Warner Brothers Music is a giant music publisher. It now owns Chappell Music, no small company in its own right.

Even some of the medium-size companies, like Island, Virgin, and Geffen Records, which are themselves subsidiaries of the six giants, are involved in the film business and a number of other enterprises.

On the retail front there are half a dozen chain stores like Musicland, which owns hundreds of stores in the United States. They generally do all of their buying out of a central office and do not encourage special orders.

The concentration of power in books, records, and the media provides enough material for several books, and in fact several large books, mentioned in the Appendix, have been written on the subject. Media connections extend further through newspaper chains and newspaper companies owning radio and television stations, as well as through book and magazine publishers. Music and media are big business, and they seem to get bigger all the time. In 1995 the record companies did over $12.3 billion worth of business, according to the Recording Industry Association of America. The sales of CD players, records, blank cassettes, VCRs, car stereos, and other electronics seem to climb year after year, and soon high-resolution TV sets will appear. Their supposedly excellent improvements in the picture quality of TV will probably cause TV sets to sell in great quantities as consumers scurry for the latest toys. But they are not available yet, except in Japan. Cable television is finally becoming a profitable business, and we can expect to see more consolidation of existing cable networks and investment by other entertainment business enterprises in cable. MTV, which has become a major player in contemporary television, is now operating in most parts of the world.

The significance of this information for you as an artist is that the more you understand about the music industry and the media, the more you begin to realize that unless you are working on a project that has the potential of earning large amounts of money, major companies are simply not interested in you.

A similar picture emerges from a close look at the major private foundations, such as the Ford, Rockefeller, and Mellon foundations. Foundations in the arts in effect set policy and help determine the future of the arts through their financial support. The Ford Foundation, for example, virtually established the standards for contemporary American symphony through its gifts of over $80 million to symphonies during the period 1957–73. The policies of foundations reflect the business backgrounds of their board members, who tend to be around sixty years old. Foundation dollars will generally tend to go to the old and proven forms of art rather than to new or experimental ones. Yet if art is going to grow and thrive, it must be treated as an exciting and experimental area of human endeavor, not as a living museum of forms that basically represent the creative efforts of the past. This is not to deny the validity of traditional art but simply to suggest that newer forms must be nurtured for the arts to truly grow and flourish.

ALTERNATIVE MEDIA

Warner Communications and CBS-Sony currently account for about 50 percent of tape and record sales in the United States. There are also hundreds of small record labels operating in North America, many of which sell only a few thousand or fewer records. The young artist is confronted with some complicated decisions. Virtually all of the books about the music business are written with the view of how to succeed in rock 'n' roll, big-time. "Is that all there is?" to quote the Leiber-Stoller song recorded by Peggy Lee. No, it is not. All over the United States and Canada artists are developing innovative ways of financing their recordings. Some of these tapes are beautiful, eclectic records well recorded in professional studios, and others are modest productions put together in semiprofessional home or basement studios. What they have in common is that the artists retained total control over the product from beginning to end and simply ignored the mass distribution network that makes and merchandises recorded product.

There are small specialty record companies that record classical music of all periods, avant-garde and traditional jazz, blues, bluegrass, and heavy metal music, or, for that matter, any kind of music you can name or imagine. These companies are spread out all over the United States and Canada, often in medium-size cities that you wouldn't associate with the music industry. It is these small record companies that have helped to keep jazz and folk music alive when they were not profitable items. Nanci Griffith recorded for Rounder for years before MCA signed her.

The artist should consider what constitutes intelligent goals in the performance and sale of his music. No one is forcing you to be processed through the media apparatus that so much of this book has described. It really is a question of goals. Do you have music that you wish to communicate in a specific way that is unique to you, or are you after a large dollar return and mass distribution? Some artists are fortunate enough to have it both ways, probably because the record companies don't understand them. I doubt that the Dutch-German owners of Polygram are musically or ideologically on a line with Michelle Shocked, but they appreciate the fact that she has an audience and that this represents income for them. Recently Shocked announced her intention to leave Polygram and to start her own record company. The point is that this is her choice, not the decision of the record company.

I am not posing questions with any presupposition of what your answers may be. I am simply suggesting that there is more than one way to approach the process of building a career. The artist who is primarily concerned with pursuing his own goals as opposed to receiving the maximum dollar return should consider dealing with alternative media.

To sustain a successful career in music it may be necessary to be able to do more than one thing. This is the point that I have tried to stress in discussing a college education. At this point in your life you may want to make records. In five years you may be more interested in producing records or writing songs without performing them. The more you can experience and learn, the better chance you have of making a living in the music business without turning into the grotesque stereotype that so many music and media people seem to become.

In dealing with alternative media it is important to understand what you are giving up, as well as what you can accomplish. If you publish by yourself a book of your songs, you cannot expect to walk into a music store in North Platte, Nebraska, and see a dozen copies of your book alongside *The John Denver Songbook*. If you record for a record company that presses 1,000 copies of your record, it will not get on every radio station in North America. Most of the frustrated musicians whom I know have a basic misapprehension of the business processes. If you record for RCA or Warner Brothers, they want to sell thousands or hundreds of thousands of records. If the initial response to your record does not produce significant sales, they will probably not continue to record you. Yes, there are occasional exceptions. There are companies that have stayed with a group that did not sell, or that have retained an artist because the artist has great prestige in the community of musicians and may lead to interest from other, more commercial artists. But the bottom line is the bottom line. No major company will continue to plow money after lost money indefinitely. This is also true in classical music or jazz. Some artists sell better than others. Some classical composers have dozens of their works recorded, and some have a single record that goes out of print almost instantly.

I have a friend who has tried to produce pop records for alternative record companies. He is terribly frustrated because he records with minute budgets, and he feels that he doesn't get enough distribution or promotion. But in reality he is in the wrong place. An alternative record company cannot compete with a major label any more than someone who makes handcrafted guitars can compete with the Gibson or Fender guitar companies. The skills, goals, ambitions, and products are simply not comparable.

There is even an alternative to alternative media: Operate your own business. I have a friend named Happy Traum who lives in Woodstock, New York. Happy started out with a small mail-order tape business, offering his own instruction tapes on folk guitar. He has built this company into a large business, selling audio and video tapes that instruct banjo, fiddle, guitar, and mandolin players, as well as blues pianists, singers, and other musicians. He now utilizes the services of several dozen top professionals on these tapes and does national advertising of his excellent products. The Canadian group String Band once sold subscriptions to raise money for a recording. Mark Hanson has written and self-published some excellent guitar books, one of which is now distributed nationally by Music Sales Corporation.

Many artists write so-called vanity books or do vanity records. These are books or records financed by the artist. There are companies that specialize in putting out such books or records; they will even provide some promotional and production assistance if the artist desires help. Before entering into an agreement to have such a company produce a book or record, be sure that you have a specific idea of what it is going to cost you.

Below is a chart of two albums, one produced by a major record company, the other self-financed by the artist. A close examination of the costs and profits may show you why so many artists are now self-producing their own product.

	MAJOR-LABEL ARTIST	SELF-PRODUCED PRODUCT SOLD DIRECTLY BY ARTIST
Cost	$125,000	$8,000
Royalty	10% minus packaging deductions—real royalty about 7%	100% less costs ($18,000 including pressing)
Sales	100,000	5,000
Net Profit	0	$53,000

My final bit of advice is that you try to control your artistic destiny as much as possible. Be honest about your goals. How important is money to you? How important is it that you retain control over your music? How do you balance these two factors? As you answer these questions, keep in mind that you may change your mind at a later date. Perhaps what you want right now is success. If you do achieve it, or if you don't, try to keep your options open. Consider changing the thrust of your attack on the business if you decide you do not like the people determining your destiny. It may well work in the opposite way, as you move from a desire to present your music on its own terms to the need to make a reasonable income. Neither goal is the right one. The right goal is to do what you want to do.

My goal has been to explain the way the music business operates. The way you deal with that process is your own decision. To illustrate the idiosyncratic nature of the music business I would like to share one last story with you. A friend of mine has an audition tape that Laura

Nyro did for Mercury Records in 1966. During this audition she sang "And When I Die," which several years later became a tremendous hit record performed by Blood, Sweat and Tears. She then sang several other songs that became quite successful on her own recordings some years later. After Laura had gone through several of these songs, the A&R men said over the studio intercom, "Laura, do you sing songs by other people? Do you know 'Stardust'?" There is a moment of silence on the tape, followed by obvious despair. Laura says yes, she can sing some songs that she hasn't written, but she doesn't really play them and hasn't worked them out. She goes through a couple of false starts, including a brief version of "Kansas City." It is clear that she is close to tears. The producers, the people who are supposed to know what's happening in the business, come back on the intercom and say, "Okay, do another of your songs." She sings one more song.

Imagine the scene. Laura must have been about eighteen at the time—young, enthusiastic, eager to perform her music. Two unsympathetic and unimaginative hacks hear her unique songs and quickly decide the songs will never sell.

People in the music business love to apply pat formulas. Don't let them oversell you on that approach.

36

ENTREPRENEURSHIP:
TAKING CARE OF BUSINESS

Note: This chapter is based on extensive research assembled by my friend and colleague Associate Professor Frank Jermance. Both of us teach in the Music Management Program at the University of Colorado at Denver.

Many musicians and songwriters harbor some secret dream of creating a company to provide a service or to merchandise a new product that they have created but have not yet produced. This brief discussion is intended to provide such budding entrepreneurs with a few guidelines for starting a business.

THE PRODUCT AND THE MARKETPLACE

In planning a business, the first thing to ask yourself is whether you have a product or service that can carve some sort of niche in the marketplace. Is this market share limited? For example, a device to be used only by oboe players obviously can only be marketed to a comparatively small group of musicians. Below is a list of things to consider:

1. Is the product unique?

2. If the product is *not* unique, why would the consumer want it? Is it more efficient than anything else currently available? Is it cheaper? Are there significantly innovative design features that will capture the consumer's attention?

3. If the product is competitive to something already on the market, how well established is the version that is already available? Is the competing product attractive, is it inexpensive, and does it have good distribution?

4. Will your product appeal to a specific section of the population that isn't buy the competing product? How can you focus on that demographic?

5. How are you going to finance the production of your product or the location of your business?

6. Do you have a plan to advertise your product to reach the maximum number of people who will be interested at a minimal cost to you?

SETTING UP THE BUSINESS

The very first step in setting up the business is to establish a name for your business, product, or service. If you are creating a new product, you will need to do a trademark search to make sure that the name is not currently in use. This search, which will cost you several hundred dollars, should be done by a lawyer or law firm that has experience in trademark law. One such firm is Thompson and Thompson, based in

Washington, D.C. They specialize not only in trademark searches, but in copyright work as well.

Now you need to determine whether your business will be operated as a proprietorship, partnership, or corporation. A proprietorship is a business that is operated by one person, the sole proprietor. The advantage of this setup is that the person operating the business has total control. The disadvantages are that the ability of the business to expand is limited by the proprietor's lack of financial support, and furthermore, the proprietor assumes all legal liabilities arising from lawsuits or financial claims against the business.

There are two kinds of partnerships, general and limited. In a general partnership the business is operated by two or more partners, and they have joint liability should any legal problems arise. The inclusion of other individuals in an ownership role adds to the financial resources of the business; also, risk and possible continuity of the business are shared rather than limited to one person. Assets of individuals can be sheltered from the liabilities of the company. On the other hand, if the partners disagree on policy, there will be conflicts and potential bitterness, and the liability of the partnership is unlimited. Policy disagreements can occur as easily in family-owned businesses as in general partnerships formed by two people who are unrelated by blood. Divorces and family feuds can also play a role in demolishing a general partnership.

A limited partnership occurs when partners contribute capital but do not manage a business. The liability of limited partners is restricted to the amount of their financial contributions to the partnership. The advantages of a limited partnership are that the investment has limited liability, and ownership can be readily transferred. On the other hand, partners have no control over policy, yet still have considerable risk. Other options include limited-liability companies and joint ventures.

Corporations include regular corporations, also known as C types, and subchapters, or S types. Corporations are owned by shareholders, and every corporation has officers. The principle disadvantage of corporations is that they require extensive paperwork, state reports, and bylaws. Corporations pay their own taxes, and shareholders do not have specific liability, but must pay individual taxes on income received from the corporation. Smaller corporations that consist of a small group of shareholders sometimes form the S type of corporation because it has the advantage of avoiding corporate taxes. It also enables a person to actually work for his own corporation. The biggest drawback of the S corporation is that the IRS and the United States Congress constantly look at anything that enables an individual who is primarily selling his own services to do it in a corporate context. Be sure to get advice from a competent attorney who keeps abreast of current tax regulations.

If you are planning to operate a short-term business, the responsibilities that go with incorporation may make that an unwise choice. In any case, you should consult a competent tax attorney to assist you in deciding on the format of your business.

TAXES AND COSTS

If you plan to start your own business, you need to familiarize yourself with local and state licensing requirements and tax procedures. You may need a sales tax license, and you will certainly need to purchase insurance. Federal Social Security taxes, as well as withholding taxes, may also need to be paid. Bookkeeping procedures must be followed and accurate records must be kept to satisfy governmental requirements. If your business involves a retail location, you will also be confronted by fire and zoning regulations, and certain accessibility requirements in order to accommodate the handicapped. You need to be aware of whether employees can be hired as independent contractors or you'll need to withhold taxes from their paychecks. These regulations are complex and change from year to year.

BUSINESS PLANS

When a business is in the start-up phase, the proprietor often puts together a business plan in order to raise additional capital, and to actually create a strategy for the expansion of the business. Business plans can range from slick 100-page brochures to two- or three-page outlines. They include such matters as the background of the company, the background of the founder, the business direction of the company (proprietorship, partnership, or corporation), the track record of the product or the founder, a time line that indicates when the business was started and what plans there are for expansion, and a clear statement of what this particular business has to offer. Statements involving product image, concept, merchandising plans, and a guide to the competition will also be important to prospective investors.

CAN IT BE DONE?

At this point you are probably feeling a bit discouraged. You didn't really want to think about the amount of planning and paperwork that a new business involves. Generally the thought of taking on additional tax burdens to your local, state, and federal government is also something less than exciting. To restore your faith in the pot of gold at the end of the rainbow, here are stories of three businesses that I have encountered in some of my free-lance writing endeavors.

Bill Rich graduated from the University of Texas with a business degree, and assumed that he would be happy going into his father's real-estate business in Tulsa, Oklahoma, but although the business went well, he had no particular interest in it. In thinking back on his college days, he realized the one thing he had always loved was to play guitar. But Bill is a realist, and understood that he was no Eric Clapton or Jimi Hendrix, so he did the next best thing: he went into business creating products that related to the guitar.

His first product was guitar pins. This concept evolved from a trip to the state fair where he saw people wearing pins publicizing farm products. Bill designed several guitar pins, featuring sought-after and popular guitars. He got them manufactured, and was lucky enough to contact Billy Gibbons of ZZ Top. Billy was his first customer, buying a large quantity of pins for personal use and as gifts. Subsequently Bill has designed and sold vintage guitar calendars, inflatable "air" guitars, a limited edition of "Batman" guitars, and the Guittool, a sort of Swiss knife that contains screwdrivers, wire cutters, and other tools that guitar players use on a daily basis. Today he has hundreds of dealers and exhibits at the annual NAMM (National Association of Music Merchants) show in Anaheim.

Herb Blayman was a clarinet player with the orchestra of the Metropolitan Opera. Like most woodwind players, he was often required to play additional instruments, in his case bass clarinet. Because many orchestral musicians perform in small performing "pits," they have little space for additional musical instruments. Naturally they utilize musical instrument stands that are intended to hold the instruments. Blayman found that the existing stands were often poorly made and would often fall over. This resulted in expensive repairs to priceless musical instruments, which musicians could ill afford. Out of this observation process Blayman came up with a very substantial metal stand that is virtually impregnable to accidental elbow shoves. Eventually he retired from the orchestra and now has a very successful business, Blayman's Last Stand, in suburban Albuquerque. Like Bill Rich, he also has developed many dealers all over the country and exhibits at the Anaheim show.

A final and fascinating example of an individual entrepreneur is Tom Bee, who owns SOAR Records in Albuquerque. Tom was a performing musician in XIT, a successful American Indian rock group of the seventies. By the late eighties, he'd decided to start his own record company. He sold an expensive Rolex watch, maxed out his American Express card, and today has a nationally distributed company that operates in every genre of American Indian music. He has some thirty CDs in his catalog, and also distributes some product for other companies.

Tom started out selling cassettes from the back of his station wagon, and last year he sold more copies of Robbie Robertson's *The Red Road* than did Robbie's own record company, Capitol. Capitol distributes its own records through the company-owned CEMA Record Distribution, yet through niche marketing Tom merchandised Capitol's product better than the giant company itself did. Now Tom has compiled a sampler of his recordings for European release by Virgin Records, and has other similar deals in the works.

The point that I am trying to make in telling these stories is that if you have a truly unusual product or idea, you may quite possibly succeed in establishing your own business. Down the line you may or may not give up some control of the company in order to obtain additional financing or distribution of your product.

MUSIC PARAPHERNALIA MERCHANDISING

Paraphernalia refers to T-shirts, sweatshirts, tour jackets, bumper stickers, neckties, mugs, caps, or any other merchandise connected to a particular artist or musical group. Just as popcorn constitutes the most lucrative profit center for the movie theater operator, the selling of tour merchandise can represent the highest percentage of profit for the artist of anything that she does. Remember, recording contracts all contain extensive deductions from royalties, and artist royalties pay for the cost of making records. Tour engagements involve commissions to agents and managers, and the large tours incur incredible costs for travel, meals, road crews, trucks, lights, sound, etc. Tour merchandise can be shipped in boxes and sold at the venue where the artist plays.

Today most of the larger record companies have merchandising subsidiaries. The bottom line is that an $18 T-shirt costs just over $3 to manufacture. Superstar acts virtually name their own percentages on deals, but even new-artist merchandise royalties are in the 30 percent range. On an $18 item this amounts to $5.40. Smaller percentages are made on the sale of merchandise in retail stores, but these represent no overhead at all for the artist. In a live venue the venue usually collects a percentage of the take. Of course, some superstars are involved in their own promotion, and are able to enjoy superior terms with the promoters, booking agent, and venue owners or renters. A few acts receive multimillion-dollar advances for merchandising rights.

One of the items that is negotiated in a record contract is who owns the graphics and artwork on an album cover. More often than not the record company owns these rights and will share the merchandising rights of the artist's tour merchandise.

The artist's personal manager usually seeks bids for handling tour merchandise. Superstar artists get sizable advances against the sale of this merchandise. According to Lawrence J. Blake's article on merchandising agreements in *The Musician's Business and Legal Guide*, superstars like Pearl Jam can make over $4 per person in merchandise sales at a major concert appearance. Sales of New Kids on the Block tour merchandise supposedly averaged $12 per concert patron.

Music merchandising rights can be a lucrative source of revenue for the successful touring artist. These rights should be guarded as closely as more obvious revenue streams, such as publishing rights or record royalty percentages.

37

ASSISTING THE MUSICIAN'S BUSINESS: COMPUTER AND INFORMATION RETRIEVAL SYSTEMS

By Frank Jermance, Associate Professor of Music Management, University of Colorado at Denver

"Multimedia," "cyberspace," the "Web," "enhanced CDs," "virtual reality," and "the information superhighway" will be dominant catchphrases for the remainder of this century, and into the next. Yet they may be nothing more than mere technological curiosities for the uninitiated. In the pages that follow, I will discuss how some of these new resources made available by technology might be used by the musician or songwriter.

The basic technological marvel at the center of the "information revolution" is the personal computer, or PC (or Mac if you are so inclined!). The personal computer will be the home stereo and entertainment center, recording studio, information resource, business manager, and (for some) companion of the future. For those in the music business, the impact of emerging technologies will provide unparalleled new opportunities. The technology exists whereby the "musical entrepreneur" of the future will create his music on the PC, market it via the information superhighway, and possibly even distribute recordings direct to the homes of an audience in "cyberspace." As an example, a songwriter can accomplish the following using today's technology:

1. Demo your songs at home and have access to hundreds of musical instruments.

2. Print professional lead sheets even if you can't read music.

3. Track song pitches. This includes a record of where each song is and how long it has been there (see the information on the Song-Tracker, page 255, and Right Track, page 257, later in this chapter).

4. Organize expense records for tax and business management purposes.

5. Send songs anywhere in the world, at virtually no cost.

6. Prepare professional cover letters and correspondence.

The more sophisticated user can employ certain more complex programs and industry-based resources to accomplish the following:

1. Direct letters of inquiry and correspondence to industry personnel by accessing lists or databases of industry contacts (see information on the Sourcebase, page 252).

2. Keep track of other publishing-related issues—for example, copyright status and automatic printing of copyright registration forms, catalog tracking, royalty payments, song licensing and songwriter contract forms, etc.

3. Track production costs, plan recording projects, and negotiate the financial aspects of record deals (see information on the Record Mogul, page 260).

4. Keep track of "gigs"—for example, scheduling, contact persons, song lists, tax data, etc. (see information on the GigMaster, page 256).

The capabilities expand daily, limited only by the imaginations of the users!

SOFTWARE "SPECIES"

For managing the musician's business, there are generally two types of software she may use: "off-the-shelf" types, which can be immediately used to better manage and organize any type of business, and "proprietary" programs, which have been designed for certain industry-specific applications. "Off-the-shelf" programs, which can be very useful in basic business management applications, include spreadsheets, databases, word processors, and programs such as Quicken and Microsoft Money, which combine several aspects of financial management, reporting, and small-business accounting processes. "Proprietary" programs specific to the music business comprise software packages custom-designed to manage operations of certain music industry entities, including recording studio management software, publishing company management software, record company financial software, etc. Some of these proprietary programs are essentially templates, designed to run "off-the-shelf" word processor, spreadsheet, and/or database programs. Template-based software typically incorporate the unique format, formulas, layout, etc., corresponding to specific music industry applications and are designed to "nest" within another program, which in turn provides the base operating software for the particular application.

"OFF-THE-SHELF" PROGRAMS

Spreadsheets

The spreadsheet is a marvelous tool for handling any type of numerical data. It automates the types of tasks that were once done manually with pencil and calculator. The spreadsheet allows the user to enter financial, statistical, and even scientific information into its various boxes or "cells" and manipulate the information in a vast number of ways. It is possible to experiment with different numbers and let the spreadsheet recalculate automatically, lending itself to be used in "what if" types of scenarios. Finally, when the user is satisfied with the results, the spreadsheet can be printed. It is also possible to instruct most modern spreadsheet programs to print charts and graphs based upon certain select information. This is particularly useful in giving a distinct visual representation of typically sterile data.

A variety of financial statements can be prepared from the spreadsheet, including balance sheets, income statements, various sorts of business ratios with associated analysis, etc.

Databases

A database is essentially an electronic filing cabinet, Rolodex, phone book, and information directory all in one. It can be set up to contain a great number of records containing a great deal of information. Lists of clients and contacts can be entered and cross-referenced in such a way as to isolate certain information or to access only files meeting certain criteria. Calculations can be done on individual records, and reports can be created that summarize mathematical and statistical data on the given files. One may also set up the database to merge with word processor software to create customized form letters, mailing lists/labels, etc.

Various templates and data-sets can be acquired that can be made to run on most modern database programs. Databases of contacts, contracts, vendors, and other resources are currently available which focus upon the music and entertainment business. Examples include the Recording Industry Sourcebase* and more sophisticated template-based programs like the SongTracker for Filemaker Pro and the Gig-Master for Filemaker Pro.

PROPRIETARY TEMPLATES

Database Template: The Recording Industry Sourcebase

The Recording Industry Sourcebase is a comprehensive set of databases containing listings of more than 12,000 records in fifty-five categories of information related to the national and international music and entertainment industries. It is designed to run on most common off-the-shelf database software. Specifically, the Sourcebase includes names, addresses, telephone numbers, fax numbers, and contact names of music business vendors and services from studios to record labels to agents, managers and publishers.†

---

* The Recording Industry SourceBase, Ascona Communications, 1995.
† See Appendix.

The Sourcebase is typical of comprehensive databased information systems the contemporary businessperson may access. In addition to names and addresses, each record listing contains information on the contact person. One may isolate specific information through the use of most common databases' "query" (or "find") function. "Query" allows one to instruct the database to search for certain conditions or perimeters, such as by city, state, range of zip code, or a variety of combinations. We merely type in the information we wish the query function to search and assemble and instruct the computer to "apply query." The database will then call up a list of those records fulfilling the query criteria. We can get even more sophisticated by the use of "wildcard" function, which instructs the database to search for any records that even partially satisfy the stated condition. For example, say we were told that a certain publisher in Nashville was particularly interested in our catalog, but all we can remember is that the company name starts with the letter F. We then type in the "name" cell the information F*, instructing the computer to search for any Nashville publisher whose name begins with the letter F. We then instruct the query function to search and assemble the needed information (by an "apply query" command). The database will then call up a list of those records fulfilling the query criteria, which in this case will give us a list of Nashville publishers whose name begins with F:

Famous Music Corp. (ASCAP) (615) 329-0500
65 Music Square East, Nashville, TN 37203

We can also use numerical ranges to search for certain numerical data. Say we want all of the publishers within a certain zip code range—for example, Orange County, 90035 through 90135. Using the query function of most modern database programs, we can isolate in the ZIP box the logical criterion for the needed data, =zip>=90035&<=90135. Literally we have just instructed the computer to find all zip codes that are greater than or equal to 90035 and are less than or equal to 90135. By instructing the computer to "apply query," the database will then call up a list of records fulfilling the query criteria, which, in this case, will give us a list of Orange County publishers.

The database is capable of many other types of searches and data collation as well. The real beauty of this capability is in the various uses that can be made of the information—assembling contact lists, mailing lists, key information, etc. One can write a form letter in the word processor, instruct the computer to merge the form letter with the records chosen by query in the database, and automatically print personalized letters, press releases, invoices, etc. One may also then print mailing labels on label stock or print addresses directly to envelopes.

One of the most common uses of this integration capability is creating form letters. A form letter is a standardized text or letter that can be made to contain individual information unique to a given person/record. If the database being accessed is comprehensive enough, form letters can be sent to each selected record that contains information exclusive to that record, all automatically. These letters can take the form of invoices, letters of inquiry, promotional and sales cover letters, etc.

A sample letter would look like this:

> May 20, 1996
> «Contact»
> «Name»
> «Address»
> «City», «State» «Zip»
>   Dear «Contact»,
>   The Speedy Orchestra, fresh from a successful tour of the hottest West Coast Venues, is currently planning their next tour. We would very much like to include «City» or other stops in «State». Please read the attached press release and promotional materials. We can be reached at 1 (800) 222-2222, or if you could please fill out the enclosed reply card, we will personally contact you to discuss possible bookings.
>
> Sincerely,
>
> Helmut Horatio
> Manager, The Speedy Orchestra
> HH/FJ/Encl.

The « » brackets are the database fields that will be inserted in the actual letter. These fields will contain the individual names, addresses, etc., of the mailing list database chosen. Once the above letter is created, the query function in the database can be used to assemble a list of contacts that meet whatever given criteria this particular mailing dictates.

Word Processor Template: The Entertainment Source Library

The Entertainment Source Library, or ESL, is essentially an extensive compilation of contract samples covering such topics as booking and agents, music publishing, artist management, artist recording, raising capital, etc. With the use of most common word processor software, the contract forms can be accessed and modified to fit your particular needs. Note: The reader is advised to always have an attorney review the finished draft.

Database Template: SongTracker for FileMaker Pro

The SongTracker* is a set of integrated templates that combine to create a full-featured publishing/song shopping system. By accessing the powerful and sophisticated database capabilities of FileMaker Pro, the SongTracker Software has the capability of automating the myriad tasks involved in managing a song-publishing company and administering a song catalog. The program is comprised of five modules, including:

1. *Catalog.* Tracks and monitors an entire song catalog, to include cowriter, writer, and copublisher percentages, demo costs, licensing information, song styles, and general song data.

2. *SongShopper.* Where and to whom songs have been pitched, feedback from contacts, etc.

3. *Author/Copublishers.* Information on authors affiliated with your publishing company—for example, writer status, performing rights affiliations, etc.

4. *Royalties.* Computation of various royalty statements and generation of reports of song activity and royalties due, etc.

---

* SongTracker, Working Solutionz Software, 2191 Rosecrans St., Simi Valley, CA 93065, (805) 522-2170, fax (805) 527-7787.

5. *Company.* Information on your individual company, as well as other vendors and publishers your company may deal with, etc.

The above modules interact to effectively:

1. Allow for application to multiple companies, as well as writers and copublishers per song.

2. Generate performing arts and sound recording copyright forms from blank forms or blank paper.

3. Print a variety of reports, including quarterly financial reports, tracking reports, licensee and royalty reports, and many others.

4. Print a variety of agreements and licenses, including mechanical and synchronization licenses, songwriter contracts, publishing administration rights and collaborator agreements, etc.

The SongTracker is designed to effectively handle the business side of the songwriter profession. It also is capable of creating and printing everything from cassette inserts (J-cards) to pitch cover letters to lyric sheets, all in a very professional and attractive format. The Song-Tracker makes it possible to automate and simplify the difficult task of song-shopping and maintaining a publishing catalog—at a (relatively) economical price! It is a competent example of the way computer technology can be used to benefit the musical entrepreneur.

Database Template: GigMaster for FileMaker Pro

GigMaster is a database designed specifically to assist musicians in keeping track of music jobs. The GigMaster comprises a comprehensive system for automating the business and organizational aspects of the working musician's career. It consists of five distinct sections: the Calendar, the GigBook, the People file, the Reports file, and the Mailing list. Like the SongTracker, the GigMaster is a template-based system designed to run on FileMaker Pro. The GigMaster allows the musician to:

1. Enter all details of each gig in the electronic GigBook.

2. View booking schedules on the electronic calendar.

3. Print monthly calendars, contracts, travel details, reports, set lists, etc.

4. Print reports on income, expenses, mileage, and wages for any time period.

5. Keep files of musicians, agents, contacts, etc.

6. Maintain up-to-date mailing lists.

GigMaster is unique in that the program has been developed with a specific application to all aspects of managing and coordinating the working musician's career. Although GigMaster was designed for the working musician, it can also be useful to anyone who is responsible for booking his or her act, budgeting those bookings, hiring independent contractors, reporting on bookings, earnings, wages, etc. It can be extremely helpful for keeping track of everything from bookings to personnel to contracts to tax records.

PROPRIETARY PROGRAMS

Right Track
Right Track* is a free-standing proprietary program that is gaining widespread acceptance in the professional community. It is not a template-based program, but rather incorporates its own operating system and format based upon a state-of-the-art "relational database" program. One of the main advantages of Right Track is that, unlike many industry-specific computer programs, it is designed to run on any PC-based platform or hardware system,† including LAN's (Local Area Network—a means of linking several PCs to share data and systems in real time). Therefore, it provides a level of power and sophistication previously available only in custom-designed "mainframe" systems. Because of its sophisticated "relational database" technology, Right Track enables its users to instantly "zoom" in and out of the various modules and screens without having to move through the menu system.

---

* Right Track, Right Track Solutions Inc., 6901 Hayvenhurst Ave., 2nd Floor, Van Nuys, CA 91406-4632. 1995 E-mail: Compuserve 102136,2422.
† Minimum hardware requirements: 486/33 processor with 8 MB RAM; 30 MB available hard disk space; 3.5 high-density floppy drive; 9600 Baud modem (for remote support)

Right Track is an example of the "high-end" type programs at use in the industry. At the time of this writing, Right Track is being used by numerous publishing and recording companies, including such prominent players as Cherry Lane Music, MGM/UA Music, and Tommy Boy Music, as well as by many national and international licensing agencies, publishing companies, record labels, and attorneys.

The program is comprised of a series of "modules" that interact to form a comprehensive system for administering all the ways a property (song, video/film, master recording property, etc.) may be managed. The base modules of Right Track include RT Copyright, RT Licensing, RT Publisher Royalties, RT Professional Manager, RT Advanced Reporting and RT Product Royalties. The modules can be configured to specifically meet the needs of various users, from large international record/publishing companies to small, independent publisher/administrators.

The publishing system configuration would consist of the RT Copyright, RT Licensing, and RT Publisher Royalties modules, with the (recommended) option of adding the RT Professional Manager module. This particular system configuration incorporates all of the financial, administrative, and managerial functions involved in running a modern music publishing company. The basis of the publishing system is the RT Copyright module, which is where all writer, publisher, and song information (e.g., copyright registration information, ASCAP/BMI clearances, ownership status, etc.) as well as client (payee) information is stored. The RT Licensing and RT Publisher modules provide the information and capacity to track licenses and income, process royalties, generate writer and publisher royalty statements, and track advance recoupment. The RT Professional Manager module is designed to effectively manage a company's song-pitching efforts.

A system configured for record/publishing companies and producers would also begin with the RT Copyright, RT Licensing, and RT Publisher Royalties modules. Together, these base modules integrate to keep track of compositions, publishers, writers, licenses, and all other necessary information for processing writer and publisher royalties. These three modules provide the base of information for the RT Product Royalties module, which defines a product (or that which is being sold) as a collection of licenses (any combination of mechanical, synchronization, print, and master licenses). For example, a CD product would include mechanical licenses for each song on the CD and master licenses for each master recording on the CD. This product flexibility allows the system to process the types of products that may be popular in today's marketplace. Using the Right Track system, the record company or producer can track and manage:

Rate Structures. For a variety of licenses and licensees, including payout rates by unit, percent of wholesale, or retail selling price. Rates can be made to vary by product type, territory, date, or number of units sold.

Reporting of Units Sold. After entering sales figures for various products, the system will automatically compute reserves and "free goods" proportions based on sales, update inventory, generate product royalty transactions based on license fees for each product, and render royalty statements for each client.

The record company/producer configuration allows the executive or producer to:

Define a Product. Budgets, expenses, configurations released.

Track Artist/Producer Contracts. Advances, royalty caps, release of reserves.

Facilitate Master Licensing. Either to or from another company.

Generate Mechanical Royalties. After entering sales figures for various products, the system automatically computes publishing royalties, factoring in reserves, free goods, packaging deductions by configuration, territory, and type of sale, and processes royalties on any composition they own or control.

The program even has the ability to automatically recoup outstanding advances as sales accumulate and statements are created.

The user can access data from the system via more than seventy-five standard reports, as well as through use of the query function. The RT Advanced Reporting module provides the ability to create sophisticated custom reports.

Using the record company and producer system configuration, it is possible to not only manage the above, but to effectively administer publishing interests.

Right Track has developed similar application-based configurations for publishing administration, contact management for song pitching, and copyright management. The beauty of the Right Track concept lies in the modular approach—that is, using the same basic modules to configure various application-specific systems. This strategy allows for extensive and logical evolution for a company's system as needs change.

The Record Mogul

The Record Mogul is a sophisticated but easy-to-use simulation of the finances of the record business. The program is designed for record companies, entertainment lawyers, producers, artists' managers, and other individuals who plan and manage recording projects or negotiate record deals.

The Record Mogul is a computer model of the finances of the record business. It is also a free-standing program, containing the calculations needed to determine which people make how much money from a recording project. The purpose is to help plan recording projects and negotiate the financial aspects of record deals. The program can also be used to track a project that is under way and calculate royalties.

The Record Mogul allows for the examination of assumptions about a project, the estimation of how much money it might make (or should have made) under different conditions, and the illustration of how income would be divided among the record company, artist, and producer. Specifically, it allows the user to:

1. Estimate the costs involved in producing, manufacturing, and marketing records, cassettes, and compact disks.

2. Determine the income that the artist, producer, publishers, and record company will each receive under different levels of sales, given your assumptions about royalty rates and the expenses involved in recording, manufacturing, promoting, and distributing the product.

The Record Mogul can help answer important questions, such as the following:

• What is a reasonable budget, given expected sales, royalty rates, and product mix?

- What is the likely effect on income when negotiating changes in royalty rates, packaging discounts, percentage of records upon which royalties are paid, the percentage of a video budget recoupable from royalties, and so forth?

- What happens if several of the above items are changed at once?

- What is the break-even point on total expenses? What is considered break-even in regard to alternative promotion budgets, given a particular mix of production costs and royalties?

- If we change list or wholesale prices, what's the effect on the bottom line, given sales levels are likely to change and royalty payments increase?

- As an artist or producer, can I produce a good product within a given advance? What effect will a higher advance have on when I start to receive royalties?

- As a singer/songwriter, what happens to my income if the company imposes a mechanical royalty cap?

With this program you can answer nearly any "what if" question that relates to the finances of the record industry. You control:

Product Configuration. The Record Mogul handles three simultaneous release configurations (such as album, cassette, and CD). It can also account for expenses in more than 100 categories organized into the following logical units:

- Overhead/general expenses (legal, A&R, etc.)

- Advances (to artist and/or producer)

- Preproduction

- Production

- Graphics

- Mastering

- Manufacturing and shipping (both initial and reorders)

- Promotion

- Distribution, collection, and accounting

Expenses Advanced Against Royalties. For twenty-seven major categories, the user determines the percentage of that expense deemed an advance against royalties. The program calculates and displays the amount of the advance associated with each category, as well as the total advance.

Sales Channels Used and Prices Charged. Includes wholesale, direct to retail, mail-order, direct to artist, and discount sales (e.g., foreign, record club, etc.).

Mechanical Royalties. You distinguish among cuts controlled by the artist, producer, record company, and independent publishers, and the rates and deductions for each cut.

The user has complete control over the royalty basis, including:

- whether recording royalties are calculated on list or wholesale price

- the percent of units sold that the rate is based on

- whether or not CD royalties are capped, and, if they are, two ways to cap them

- percentage deducted for packaging

- for discount sales, the percentage of the full rate that will be paid

The program calculates and displays the per-unit basis on which royalties will be paid, and the per-unit dollar amount of the royalty. It also includes:

Manufacturing. User control of the size of initial runs, the size and number of reorders. The program calculates and displays the total manufacturing run for each configuration.

Distribution and Sale. The number of promo copies, the number sold to retail, the number sold wholesale, the number of bonus goods, the number sold through mail order, the number sold to the artist, and the number sold at discount. The program calculates the total units manufactured, the total units distributed and sold, and, for each product configuration, the number of copies remaining in inventory.

Based on the figures you input, the Record Mogul calculates and displays the following:

For the record company:

- gross income (from all sales sources, plus publishing on cuts it controls)

- amount paid out in mechanical royalties (after adjusting for any mechanical royalty caps)

- amount paid out in recording royalties (after allowing for advances and cross-collateralization, if used)

- overhead, general, and production costs

- manufacturing costs

- promotion and distribution costs

- net income

- total investment and return on investment

For artist and producer:

- gross royalties

- amount deducted for royalty advance

- net royalties

- mechanical royalties on controlled cuts and/or writers' share on noncontrolled cuts

- net income from artist sales

- artist's total income from recording royalties, mechanical royalties, and artist sales

- producer's total income from recording and mechanical royalties

I have used the Record Mogul for a number of years in our Music Business program at the University of Colorado at Denver. It provides an invaluable illustration of record company dynamics, budgeting, contractual issues, and serves as a "simulation" program for applying case study situations.

THE INFORMATION SUPERHIGHWAY, "CYBER-MARKETING," AND THE "WEB"

Probably the most exciting aspect of computer technology as related to the music business is the development of the "Web." The Web (or more correctly, the World Wide Web—WWW) is a component of the Internet, a worldwide computer network that is accessed by more than 30 million users (from 1 to 10 percent of U.S. citizens are estimated to be on-line via the Internet and/or similar services). The "Net" can be used to exchange mail and conduct research into literally thousands of online data archives, containing everything from text to video and sound clips. The Web is an extensive collection of Web sites, or addresses, each of which can contain the above sorts of data archives and forums.

The music industry has established an increasing presence on the Web, with offerings including:

- Fan clubs
- MIDI (Musical Instrument Digital Interface) files
- Direct marketing of CDs and other recordings
- Business issues, including industry contacts, contract databases, legal advice, etc.
- Record sales charts, concert receipts, and other industry information

All major record companies, as well as numerous indie labels and distributors, have established Web sites. Labels are using the Web primarily for marketing and R&D (Research and Development). Record label Web sites typically consist of a home page with artist information, new products, contests, tour schedules, and video and sound clips. The R&D

aspect is possible in that the labels are able to acquire much information on the potential market, including mailing and E-mail addresses, favorite local clubs, number of CD purchases a month, etc. Labels can also determine the effectiveness of certain promotion strategies, with near-instantaneous feedback from a motivated audience.

Music industry trade associations and professional organizations, including ASCAP, BMI, NARAS, AFM, NMPA, AES, NAMM, and many others, can be accessed to provide information and resources for the intrepid musician and songwriter. A casual examination of one such Web site, the BMI (or Broadcast Music Incorporated*) home page, would illustrate the services it provides, including the ability to:

- Determine the writer(s) and owner of a given tune through "title search," as well as extensive information on a particular writer's catalog of tunes

- Address correspondence and questions to staff

- Access "The Art and Business of Songwriting," where the visitor can download copyright registration forms and many other informational brochures.

- And much more

One of the more interesting of the music-related Web sites is the Internet Underground Music Archive, or IUMA. The IUMA claims to be "the first and largest high-fidelity Internet music outlet." The IUMA is immensely popular, with more than 300,000 accesses per day. As of July 1995, the IUMA offers the works of more than 800 independent musicians to an estimated 30 million-plus Internet users. According to the IUMA, this on-line community "represents a global audience of fans, radio station programmers, club promoters and music industry representatives."†

---

* Note: BMI is a performing rights society whose main function is to license and collect public performance royalties for its writer and publisher members.

† Internet Underground Music Archive (IUMA), 303 Potrero #7A, Santa Cruz, CA 95060.

The songwriter or musician can use the IUMA to showcase their tunes and talents to a vast audience with text, graphics, sound, and video capability. In addition to providing on-line merchandising of their recordings, the unsigned act can reach an enormous, previously inaccessible audience through the IUMA and other similar Internet or proprietary-based services. This form of "cyber-marketing" can give an unprecedented edge to the musician or songwriter of the future!

Accessing the "Net"

If you're interested in checking out the on-line world, you'll need the following minimum equipment:

1. Personal computer (PC or Mac) of relatively recent design, running at least 33 Mhz.

2. Phone line with modem (modem speed of at least 14.4 meg. BPS [Baud per second] speed is recommended).

3. Subscription to an Internet access provider, such as Compuserve, America OnLine, Prodigy, Delphi, etc., or a "dedicated" local Internet access provider. The above access providers often offer many music-related forums and E-mail capability in addition to Internet access. Most of the access providers will also supply communication software to allow for easy navigation of the Net.

Once connected, one can easily follow the simple navigation instructions, screens, and menus for "surfin' the Net"!

There are now literally hundreds of sources of information on computer technology and information retrieval, from MIDI uses and files to specific software programs to information on creating your own Web page, and more are being developed daily! These technologies can truly open a wealth of benefits and opportunities for the musician.

FRANK JERMANCE is an associate professor of music management and jazz guitar at the Department of Music, University of Colorado at Denver. He holds graduate degrees in both music merchandising and business, and has worked in telecommunications marketing and as a talent agent and contractor. He is in demand as a freelance guitarist, and has performed with a variety of Broadway shows, name artists, and projects. His articles have appeared in *Recording* magazine, *Mix* magazine, and *Guitar Player* magazine.

CYNTHIA BARRINGER, research assistant, is the publicity director at the School of the Arts, University of Colorado at Denver. She received her B.S. in music management from the University of Colorado at Denver.

Afterword: The Music Business in the Twenty-first Century

*W*hat will happen to the music industry in the twenty-first century? I expect to see the six multinationals consolidate even more, down to three or four companies. My guess is that only one of the super-companies will remain under American ownership. Video and some sort of interactive storage medium combining quality video and audio will emerge as the central format of the twenty-first century. I expect to see rock groups on stage who are actors, with one musician hidden from the audience actually generating most of the music through computers and emulators and prerecorded tapes while the performers do their thing. I also expect to see a group of musicians who come from different continents, speak a variety of languages, and come up with a unique blend of musical styles.

The success of Windham Hill Records proves that there is an audience out there for acoustic music. World music will assume an increasingly important role, through performances by authentic groups and an increased amount of sampling. There will be new forms of rock 'n' roll; I wouldn't even venture to say what forms it will take. Heavy metal music has become an accepted, almost conservative style. At this writing rap appears headed in the same direction. The beauty of rock 'n' roll is that it represents a continual injection of youth and energy into the musical mainstream controlled by older executives who have little understanding of what they are actually merchandising. That is why there is room for a Tracy Chapman in our polyglot music scene. I try never to confuse musical artistry with commerciality. They have little if any direct correlation. There are always going to be wonderful musicians and writers out there, and there will be others copying them. There also will be artists whose main impetus is to manipulate the media, who in turn are manipulating them. It is hard to say whether the tail is wagging the dog or vice versa. There will be wonderful musicians who can't sell records because they have no visual appeal, no management, or don't get lucky. And there will be wretched musicians who contribute only gloss and slickness to the scene and are in this business only for the money, power, and attention that they generate to feed their egos.

What I really like about the music business is that no one really knows what is going to happen. That's why it's more fun to be involved in the "starmaker machinery" than to sell Scotch tape. Unless, of course, that's what you want to do.

Dick Weissman is available for music business seminars. For information contact Skye Griffith, Skyline Talent, 1424 Larimer St., Ste. 300, Denver, CO 80202, (303) 595-8747.

APPENDIX

Relevant College Programs

MUSIC BUSINESS PROGRAMS

Previous editions of this book listed colleges offering music business programs. Rather than reprinting that list, this edition includes more comprehensive sources of this information. The list below should offer more current and updated material. Currently a detailed guide to such programs is available for $14 from Dr. Scott Frederickson, President, MEIEA (Music and Entertainment Industry Educators Association), College of Fine Arts, University of Massachusetts at Lowell, Lowell, MA 01854. It is a 130-page guide entitled *Complete List of Music Business Programs in the United States and Canada* and includes two- and four-year programs. Many colleges offer special programs or courses in the music business.

MUSIC MERCHANDISING PROGRAMS

Music merchandising programs are college programs that deal with careers in the manufacturing, wholesaling, and sale of musical instruments, accessories, and sheet music. A free brochure listing these schools is available from the National Association of Music Merchants, 5140 Avendida Encinas, Carlsbad, CA 92008-4391.

AUDIO ENGINEERING PROGRAMS

The June issue of *Mix* magazine features schools offering audio courses. Another source for such information is the book *New Ears: A Guide to Education in Audio and the Recording Sciences*. It is compiled and edited by Mark Drews and is available from New Ear Productions, 1033 Euclid Ave., Syracuse, NY 13210.

MUSIC THERAPY PROGRAMS

A free brochure listing college programs in music therapy is available from the National Association for Music Therapy, 8455 Colesville Rd., Suite 930, Silver Spring, MD 20910.

COLLEGES OFFERING CHURCH MUSIC PROGRAMS

Liturgical Music:	Alverno College, Milwaukee, WI. B.A. in Liturgical Music
Music and Religion:	Athens State College, Athens, AL. B.A.
	Boston University, Boston, MA. M.A.
	Dallas Christian College, Dallas, TX. B.A.
	Greensboro College, Greensboro, NC. B.A.
Sacred Music:	Kansas City Community College, Kansas City, KA. A.A.

COLLEGES OFFERING ARTS MANAGEMENT PROGRAMS

The American Council on the Arts in New York City publishes a book discussing various undergraduate and graduate programs in arts management. These programs deal with nonprofit arts management.

SCHOOLS OFFERING PROGRAMS IN INSTRUMENT BUILDING AND REPAIR

Chicago School of Violin Making, Chicago, IL

Dutchess Community College, Poughkeepsie, NY

Eastern School of Musical Instrument Repair, Irvington, NJ

Five Towns College, Seaford, NY

Lord Fairfax Community College, Middletown, VA

Mount Vernon Nazarene College, Mount Vernon, OH

Pitt Community College, Greenville, NC

Red Wing Technical Institute, Red Wing, MN

Trinidad State Junior College, Trinidad, CO

Western Iowa Tech Community College, Sioux City, IA

Some other schools that are not affiliated with colleges as such offer this training, such as Peter Paul Prior's School of Violin Making in Salt Lake City.

For information about academic programs, consult the annual *College Bluebook*, published by Macmillan, or *Lovejoy's College Guide*, among others. Some colleges offer self-directed and interdisciplinary majors which enable you to create your own program emphasis.

Music Business Organizations

UNIONS (NATIONAL HEADQUARTERS)

Local chapters of these unions exist in many cities. This is especially true of the AFM, which has some 300 locals in the United States and Canada.

AFM (American Federation of Musicians)
1501 Broadway, Ste. 600, New York, NY 20036

AFTRA (American Federation of Television and Radio Artists)
260 Madison Ave., New York, NY 10016

SAG (Screen Actors Guild)
5757 Wilshire Blvd., Los Angeles, CA 90036
    Consult the above for local or regional offices

PERFORMING RIGHTS ORGANIZATIONS

ASCAP (American Society of Composers, Authors, and Publishers)
2nd Floor, 3500 W. Hubbard, Chicago, IL 60610
Suite 300, 7929 Sunset Blvd., Los Angeles, CA 90046
2 Music Sq. W., Nashville, TN 37203
1 Lincoln Plaza, New York, NY 10023

BMI (Broadcast Music Inc.)
8730 Sunset Blvd., Los Angeles, CA 90069
10 Music Sq. E., Nashville, TN 37203
320 W. 57th St., New York, NY 10019

SESAC Inc. (Society of European Stage Authors and Composers)
55 Music Sq. E., Nashville, TN 37203
421 W. 54th St., New York, NY 10019

Canada now has one performing rights organization that represents Canadian writers and publishers. It is called SOCAN, the Society of Composers, Authors and Publishers of Canada. The main office is at 41 Valleybrook Dr., Don Mills, Ontario M3B 2S6, Canada.

SONGWRITERS' ORGANIZATIONS

There are local and regional songwriters' organizations all over the United States and Canada. A list of them appears in my book about local and regional music markets, *How to Make a Living in Your Local Music Market*. There are several key organizations in the music business centers that can help you, especially if you live in or near these centers. They are:

Los Angeles

National Academy of Songwriters, 6381 Hollywood Blvd., Ste. 780, Hollywood, CA 90028

The Songwriters Guild of America, 6430 Sunset Blvd., Hollywood, CA 90028

Nashville
Nashville Songwriters Association International, 803 18th Ave., S., Nashville, TN 37203

Songwriters Guild of America, 1222 16th Ave. S., Nashville, TN 37203

New York
The Songwriters Guild of America, 1500 Harbor Blvd., Weehawken, NJ 07087

OTHER ORGANIZATIONS

Audio Engineering Society, 60 E. 42nd St., Rm. 2520, New York, NY 10065

American Composers Alliance, 170 W. 74th St., New York, NY 10023. Maintains a music library and assists composers with legal matters.

American Council for the Arts, 1 E. 53rd St., New York, NY 10022

American Music Center, Inc., 250 W. 154th St., Ste. 300, New York, NY 10019. Maintains a library of serious music and assists composers.

American Music Conference, 5140 Avenida Escinas, Carlsbad, CA 92008

American Symphony Orchestra League, 777 14th St. NW, Washington, DC 20015

Canada Council, PO Box 1047, 350 Albert St., Ottawa, Ontario K1P5U8 Canada. Gives arts grants.

Canadian Academy of Recording Arts and Sciences (CARAS), 124 Merton St., 3rd Floor, Toronto, Ontario M4S 2Z2 Canada

Center for Black Music Research, c/o Columbia College, 600 S. Michigan Ave., Chicago, IL 60605

Country Music Association, 1 Music Circle S., Nashville, TN 37203

Country Music Foundation, 4 Music Sq. E., Nashville, TN 37203. An exhibition hall, with a great research facility in the basement.

Ford Foundation, 320 E. 43rd St., New York, NY 10017

Foundation Center, 79 5th Ave., 8th floor, New York, NY 10003-3076. An excellent source for grant information.

Gospel Music Association, 7 Music Circle N., Nashville, TN 37203

Harry Fox Agency, Inc., 205 E. 42nd St., New York, NY 10017

International Conference of Symphony and Opera Musicians (ICSOM), c/o American Music Center, listed above

Music Critics Association, 7 Pine Ct., Westfield, NJ 07090. Holds workshops and publishes newsletter.

Music Educators National Conference, 1806 Robert Fulton Dr., Reston, VA 22091. The national organization of school music teachers.

Nashville Songwriters Association International, 14 Music Sq. W., Nashville, TN 37203

National Academy of Recording Arts and Sciences, 3402 Pico Blvd., Santa Monica, CA 90405. Chapters in Atlanta, Austin, Chicago, Memphis, Nashville, New York, Philadelphia, and San Francisco.

National Academy of Songwriters, 6381 Hollywood Blvd., Suite 780, Hollywood, CA 90028. Recently combined with the Los Angeles Songwriters Showcase.

National Association of Broadcasters, 1771 N. St. NW, Washington, DC 20036. Members subscribe to a code of ethics.

National Association for Campus Activities, 13 Harbison Way, Columbia, SC 29260

National Association of Independent Record Distributors and Manufacturers, PO Box 988, Whitesburg, KY 41858

National Association of Music Merchants. See American Music Council.

National Association for Music Therapy, Inc., 8455 Colesville Rd., Ste. 930, Silver Spring, MD 10910

National Association of Record Merchandisers, 9 Eaves Dr., Suite 120, Marlton, NJ 08053

National Music Publishers Association, 711 Third Ave., 8th Floor, New York, NY 10017

National Endowment for the Arts, Nancy Hanks Center, 1100 Pennsylvania Ave. NW, Washington, DC 20506. Offers grants in the arts to organizations and individuals. Each state also has an arts council, usually located in the city that is the state capital.

National Endowment for the Humanities, Washington, DC 20506. Gives grants that involve critical scholarship on the arts.

Piano Technicians Guild, 3930 Washington, Kansas City, MO 64101

Recording Industry Association of America, 1020 19th St. NW, Washington, DC 10036. An industry organization that compiles statistics on records and gives gold and platinum awards.

Society for Ethnomusicology. Moves with election of each new president. Publishes a magazine, books, and recordings in the field.

Society of Professional Audio Recording Studios, 4300 Tenth Ave. N., Lake Worth, FL 33461. An association of studio owners and engineers.

Volunteer Lawyers for the Arts, 1 E. 53rd St., 6th Floor, New York, NY 10022. Many states have low-cost legal services for artists available through their branches of this organization.

Publishers of Printed Music

Below is a list of the most active publishers of printed music. Hal Leonard and Warner Bros. are most active in the publication of hits. The others concentrate on educational uses, including school band and choral folios, and instructional methods for specific instruments.

Alfred Publishing Co., 16380 Roscoe Blvd., PO Box 1003, Van Nuys, CA 91410

Mel Bay Publications, #4 Industrial Dr., Pacific, MO 63069

Cherry Lane Music, PO Box 850, Valley Forge, PA 19482

Hal Leonard, 777 W. Bluemound Rd., Milwaukee, WI 53213

Music Sales Corp., 222 Park Ave. S., New York, NY 10003

Warner Bros. Publications, 15800 NW 48th Ave., Miami, FL 33014

Union Scales

Since union scales change annually, it is suggested that you contact the appropriate union—AFM for instrumentalists, AFTRA or SAG for singers, etc. Addresses appear on page 273 of this Appendix.

Schirmer Brochure for Piano
Howard Kasschau Piano Course

NEWLY REVISED
HOWARD KASSCHAU
PIANO COURSE

The *Howard Kasschau Piano Course* covers the entire range of piano study from the young beginner to the college preparatory level. The beginner is introduced to the new musical experiences of notation, technic, and repertoire in interesting, entertaining and gradually progressive steps. Each new musical experience is approached in four ways to insure complete understanding: by Reading; by Writing; by Reading Music; by Playing Music. As the course progresses, there is a gradual expansion of technical ability, performance and recital repertoire, knowledge of musical forms, musical history and harmonic understanding.

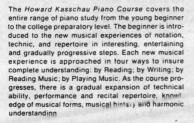

Teach Me to Play (2336)	1.50
First Book (2347)	2.25
Second Book (2348)	2.25
Third Book (2395)	2.25
Fourth Book (2404)	2.25
Fifth Book (2405)	2.25

SUPPLEMENTARY MATERIAL

Ensemble Book *(to be used with "Teach Me To Play")* 1 Piano, 4 hands or 2 pianos, 4 hands (2349) .75
First Grade Pedal Book (2350) .85
Note Speller (2381) 1.50

The next three collections are the latest compositions by Mr. Kasschau. Each collection is designed as a group for the beginning, early and intermediate grades. They may be used singly as teaching pieces or in conjunction with the Howard Kasschau Piano Course.

Five Beginner's Pieces (2973) 1.50
Six Easy Pieces—Recital Music for the Early Grades (2966) 1.75
Seven Recital Pieces for the Intermediate Grades (2965) 2.00

73 Favorite Pieces For Piano (with Guitar chords)—Arranged by Howard Kasschau. A marvelous new collection of familiar tunes ranging from Aura Lee, Ciribiribin, Glow Worm and Joy to the World to Country Gardens, Greensleeves, Londonderry Air and Pomp and Circumstance. A real value (2917) 2.50

Keyboard Interpretation (2592) 1.50
Reading Through Intervals (2735) 3.00

SCHIRMER'S SELECT PIANO MUSIC SERIES
Compiled from Best Sellers by Howard Kasschau
For Early Grades (2343) 2.00
For Intermediate Grades (2344) 2.00
For Advanced Grades (2345) 3.00

106 GREATEST PIANO STUDIES
Compiled and Edited by Howard Kasschau
Vol. I (No.'s 1-62) (2429) 2.50
Vol. II (No.'s 63-106) (2430) 2.50

25 VENTURES IN ROCK, WESTERN & BLUES (3054) 2.50

Please send copies as indicated beside each title.
Name
Address
City
State   Zip

Schirmer Brochure for Rock Guitar

The Great New Rock Book Has Arrived!

HOW TO MAKE MONEY PLAYING ROCK GUITAR
by Bruce Bergman

Bruce Bergman is generally recognized as the most sought after club date rock guitarist in the busiest music market in the United States, the New York Metropolitan area. He is leader-guitarist-bass player with the Peter Duchin Orchestras and Musical Personalities, Inc. and has done extensive work with all the top club date orchestras in New York including Ray Bloch, Meyer Davis, Lester Lanin, Skitch Hendersen, Ben Cutler, and many others. This book is based upon all the author's years of on the job experience in the exciting world of professional guitar playing.

CONTENTS

Introduction
Who This Book is For
Where the Money Is
Why Play Where the Money Is?
The Rise of the Guitar Player
The Role of the Guitar Player
What to Expect on the Job
The Unique Style of Club Date Rock Playing

Basic Rock Progressions
One-Chord Songs
The 1-4 Progression
The 1-6-4-5 Progression
Common Variations of the 1-6-4-5
The 1-3-2-5 Progression
The 1 Minor-Flat-7-Flat 6-5 Progression
The Blues
The Venerable 1-4-5 Progressions
The Cycle of Fifths

Twenty Rock Rhythms

Guitar Solo Playing
The Chord Solo
Solo Figures

Tricks Of The Trade—The Mechanics Of What To Do On Stage

Repertoire
The Three Types of Music the Club Date
Guitarist is Expected to Play
Tempos and Rhythms
What Rock Songs to Play
How to Handle Requests
"Singles"
What Key to Play in
How to Really Know What Key is Best for You
How to Call Your Keys

Equipment—Your Guitar And Amp
The Guitar
The Amplifier
Accessories
How to Set the Controls on Your Amp

Doubling On Bass Guitar

What To Wear
Demeanor on the Job

Taxes For Guitar Players

How To Get Into The Business

The Rock Glossary

G. SCHIRMER, INC., 866 THIRD AVENUE, NEW YORK, N.Y. 10022
Please send _____ copies of "How To Make Money Playing Rock Guitar" @ $6.95
NAME _____
ADDRESS _____
CITY_____ STATE _____ _____ ZIP _____

Printed by permission of G. Schirmer, Inc.

Note the contrast between these two sales brochures, both printed by the same publisher. The emphasis in the Kasschau piano books is strictly academic, while the Bergman book is intended to sell to the working musician. The graphics are straight and serious for the piano book, eye-catching and a bit playful for the rock guitar book. These are judgments that the publisher has made about the audience for the two books. The Bergman book, by the way, is an excellent guide to the performance of rock music, useful to other musicians as well as guitarists.

Sample Lead Sheet

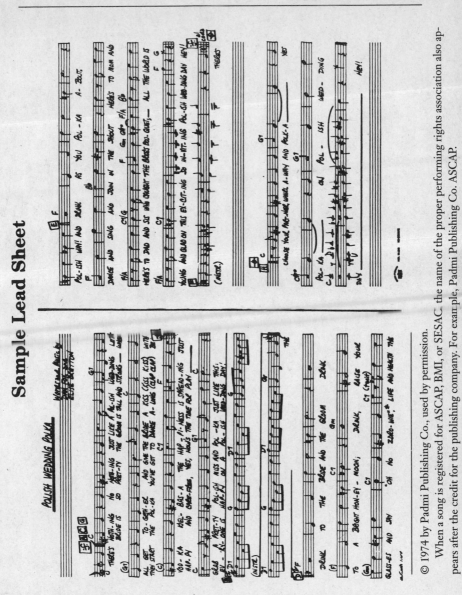

When a song is registered for ASCAP, BMI, or SESAC, the name of the proper performing rights association also appears after the credit for the publishing company. For example, Padmi Publishing Co. ASCAP.

_____

_____

_____

_____

_____

GLOSSARY OF
MUSIC BUSINESS TERMS

Agent Someone who gets work for singers or musicians. Also called a booking agent.

Aircheck Tape of a disc jockey's show used for audition purposes

Analog recording Older technology, expressing data by measurable quantities rather than numerically. See **digital recording**.

A&R Artist and Repertoire.

ASCAP See **Performing rights**.

Bed Instrumental background for a vocal commercial.

BMI See **Performing rights**.

CD Compact disc.

C&W Country and Western.

Chart A musical arrangement; Top 40 chart (a list of hits).

Click track A click fed through headphones to musicians in a recording studio in order to provide a perfect tempo.

Contractor The person who hires musicians. Usually a musician, but may not play on the session he is booking.

Control room The area where an engineer and a producer monitor the sound from a recording session.

Controlled composition clause A clause in a recording contract whereby the record company attempts to control the rate paid for publishing rights, usually at three-quarters the normal fees.

Copublishing When the publishing rights to a copyright are shared by more than one publisher.

Cross-collateralization Two types: (1) Where the record company charges the royalties of an artist against the unrecouped costs of a previous album; and (2) when the record company pools artist and songwriter royalties into one pot and charges recording costs against both sets of royalties. Only possible if the record company owns the artist's publishing.

Crossover record A record that achieves popularity in more than one style of music, e.g., a rap record that also goes pop.

Cutout A record that is discontinued from the catalog and remaindered at a heavy discount.

DAT Digital audio tape.

DBX A system for noise reduction used in recording.

Demo A demonstration record. It is a sample of the finished product, used to sell an artist or a song.

Demographics Population breakdown by age, sex, and other factors.

Digital recording A recording that uses digital computer technology expressing data numerically.

Direct to disc Recording directly to a master record without the use of tape.

Dolby A system for noise reduction in recording.

Donut A music bed used as background for narration in a commercial.

Fakebook A collection of tunes by many authors and different publishers.

Head arrangement An arrangement done with little or no written music. It is usually worked out in the recording studio.

Hook A repetitive phrase designed to hook the listener's attention. Can be a lyric or an instrumental phrase.

Jingle A commercial for radio or television.

Jobber A wholesaler that sells music books of many publishers.

Key man clause A clause in a recording company or management contract that lets the artist out if the "key man" leaves the company.

Lead sheet The words, music, and chords of a song. Lead sheets are required for copyright purposes.

Lip sync When a singer mouths to words of a song to match a record without actually singing the song.

Logging Literally means writing down in a radio log. Also used to indicate a way of keeping track of air play by performing rights societies.

Master A finished product that can be turned into a record.

Mechanical license The license that a record company applies for from a publisher to legally issue a song on a record.

MIDI Musical instrument digital interface.

Mix To take a multitrack master and reduce it to a finished product.

Modulation Changing the key of a song in the middle of the song.

MOR Middle-of-the-road—noncontroversial music. Sometimes called easy-listening or beautiful music.

Noise reduction Systems to reduce tape hiss. **DBX** and **Dolby**.

One-stop A wholesaler that carries records of many companies.

Overdub To add parts on a multichannel recording—technically this process is called sel synchronization.

Payola Illegal payments to radio station personnel so they give extra play to records. In a general sense any kind of illegal payments for favors.

Performing rights Composer rights for play on radio and television. These rights are governed by ASCAP, BMI, and SESAC.

Personal manager A career guide for the artist.

Push record A record that a record company is particularly eager for its promotion staff to push.

R&B Rhythm and blues.

Record producer The person who puts together a record; corresponds to the director of a movie. A producer may hire the musicians, rent a studio, hire an arranger, rehearse the artist, and mix the product.

Remix To mix a multichannel product again.

Scale Union minimum pay.

Secondary market A market of some size, but not a giant population center—for example, Milwaukee as opposed to Chicago.

Sound track library Service that sells music from preexisting tapes to radio stations, television stations, or low-budget movie productions.

Source licensing A plan promoted by television broadcasters where instead of licensing music for local and syndicated television from ASCAP, BMI, and SESAC, the producer of the show would license the music directly from the composer.

Standard A popular song that remains popular over an extended period of time, such as "Stardust."

Studio musician A free-lance musician who makes a living by playing in the recording studios.

Subsidiary rights Rights for media other than the one specifically being contracted.

Synchronization rights The rights for synchronizing of music to a picture, paid to the composer.

Taking care of business Payola.

Tour support Record company subsidies to an artist to support promotional tours.

Track record A person's history in the business.

Voice-over The voice of an unseen announcer for a commercial, or a narrator in a documentary film.

ANNOTATED BIBLIOGRAPHY

RECORDING AND RECORD PRODUCTION

Carlin, Robert. *The Small Specialty Record Company in the United States*. John Edwards Memorial Foundation Quarterly. Summer 1976.

Chapple, Steve, and Garafalo, Reebee. *Rock 'n' Roll Is Here to Pay*. Chicago: Nelson Hall, 1977. A radical critique and analysis of the record business—stimulating and argumentative.

Davis, Clive. *Clive Inside the Record Business*. New York: William Morrow & Co., 1975. Alive and intelligent, if egomaniacal.

Denisoff, R. Serge. *Solid Gold: The Popular Record Industry*. New Brunswick, N.J.: Transaction Books, 1975.

Eisenberg, Evan. *The Recording Angel: Explorations in Phonography*. New York: McGraw-Hill, 1987. A series of interesting and odd essays on the record business and fanatical record collectors.

Gillett, Charlie. *Making Tracks: The Growth of a Multi-Billion-Dollar Industry*. New York: E. P. Dutton, 1974. The fascinating story of Atlantic Records.

Hammond, John, and Townsend, Irving. *John Hammond on Record*. New York: Ridge Press/Summit Books, 1977.

Hammond, Ray. *How to Get a Hit Record*. Poole, U.K.: Javelin Books, 1985. The British record business.

Hurst, Walter E., and Hale, William Storm. *Record Industry Book: Stories, Texts, Forms, Contracts*. Entertainment Industry Series, vol. 1. Hollywood: Seven Arts Press, 1974. The same publisher has numerous books available on managers, recording company contracts, etc. The books are readable, although poorly printed and designed.

Jahn, Mike. *How to Make a Hit Record*. Scarsdale, N.Y.: Bradbury Press, 1976.

Karshner, Roger. *The Music Machine*. Los Angeles: Nash Publishing, 1971. More about payola than you'd ever want to know.

Kashif. *Everything You'd Better Know About the Record Industry.* Venice, Calif.: Brooklyn Boy Books, 1995. Most useful in its discussions of Top 40 music.

Morse, David. *Motown.* New York: Collier Books, 1971.

Shemel, Sidney, and Krasilovsky, M. William. *This Business of Music.* New York: Billboard Publications, 1995. Be sure to get the 7th revised and enlarged edition. Invaluable.

——. *More About This Business of Music.* 5th edition. New York: Billboard Publications, 1994.

Smith, Joe. *Off the Record: An Oral History of Popular Music.* New York: Warner Books, 1988. Interviews with more than 200 music industry figures in the creative and business areas. Entertaining and informative.

Spitz, Robert Stephen. *The Making of a Superstar: Artists and Executives of the Rock Music World.* New York: Anchor Press, 1978.

Stokes, Geoffrey. *Star-Making Machinery: The Odyssey of an Album.* Indianapolis: Bobbs-Merrill, 1976. A useful book. Contains an excellent description of recording and mixing.

Stone, Terri, ed. *Music Producers: Conversations with Today's Top Record Makers.* Emroyville, Calif.: Mix Books, 1992.

Sweeney, Tim, and Geller, Mark. *Tim Sweeney's Guide to Releasing Independent Records.* Torrance, Calif.: Tab Books, 1996.

Wade, Dorothy, and Picardie, Justine. *Music Man: Ahmet Ertegun, Atlantic Records, and the Triumph of Rock 'n' Roll.* New York: W. W. Norton, 1990.

Wexler, Jerry, and Ritz, David. *Rhythm and The Blues: A Life in American Music.* New York: Alfred Knopf, 1993.

HISTORY OF RECORDING

Altman, Rick. *Sound Theory, Sound Practice.* New York: Routledge, 1990.

Gelatt, Roland. *The Fabulous Phonograph.* New York: Collier Books, 1977. An absorbing history.

Harvith, John, and Harvith, Susan Gowards. *Edison, Musicians and the Phonograph: A Century in Retrospect.* New York: Greenwood Press, 1987. Interviews with critics, composers, and classical music performers.

Read, Oliver, and Welch, Walter L. *From Tin Foil to Stereo.* 2nd edition. Indianapolis: Howard W. Sams, 1976.

Williams, David Brian, and Webster, Peter Richard. *Experiencing Music Technology.* New York: Schirmer Books, 1996.

Two publications are available that provide listings of records. *Phonolog Reporter,* Trade Service Publications, 1710 Beverly Blvd., Los Angeles, Calif. 90057, is a loose-leaf index of records, with supplements regularly added to reflect new record releases. It can be found in most large record stores. The

Schwann Record & Tape Guide, 137 Newbury St., Boston, Mass. 02116, is a monthly catalog of records and tapes, available by subscription.

AGENTS AND MANAGERS

Csida, Joseph. *The Music Record Career Handbook.* Studio City, Calif.: First Place Music Publications, 1973.

Dumler, Egon, and Cushman, Robert F. *Entertainers and Their Professional Advisers.* Homewood, Ill.: Dow Jones–Irwin, 1987. A fairly complex, far-ranging book, with an excellent chapter on personal management by the well-known manager Dee Anthony.

Farragher, Scott. *Music City Babylon: Inside the World of Country Music.* The only book that I know of written from the agent's viewpoint.

Frascogna, Xavier M., Jr., and Hetherington, H. Lee. *Successful Artist Management.* New York: Billboard Books, 1978.

Glatt, John. *Rage & Roll: Bill Graham and the Selling of Rock.* New York: Birch Lane Press, 1993.

Graham, Bill, and Greenfield, Robert. *Bill Graham Presents.* New York: Doubleday, 1992.

Rose, Frank. *The Agency: William Morris and the Hidden History of Show Business.* New York: Harper Business, 1995.

Shagan, Rena. *Booking and Tour Management for the Performing Arts.* New York: Allworth Press, 1996.

Williams, Mike. *The Hop of the Small-Time Toad: Booking Yourself in the College Entertainment Market.* Denver: Bread and Butter Press, 1981. An amusing guide to a performer's adventures in booking himself.

PUBLISHING, PERFORMING RIGHTS, COPYRIGHT

Chickering, Robert B., and Hartman, Susan. *How to Register a Copyright and Protect Your Creative Work.* New York: Charles Scribner's Sons, 1987.

Erickson, J. Gunnar; Hearn, Edward R.; and Halloran, Mark E. *Musician's Guide to Copyright.* New York: Charles Scribner's Sons, 1983. A clear guide, unfortunately out of print.

Kohn, Al, and Kohn, Bob. *The Art of Music Licensing.* 2nd edition. New York: Prentice Hall Law and Business, 1996. Expensive and invaluable.

New York Law School Review. *The Complete Guide to the New Copyright Law.* New York: Lorenz Press, 1977.

NSAI. *The Essential Songwriter's Contract Handbook.* Nashville: NSAI, 1994.

Poe, Randy. *Music Publishing: A Songwriter's Guide.* Cincinnati: Writer's Digest Books, 1990. A useful explanation.

Racklin, Harvey. *The Songwriter's Handbook.* New York: Funk & Wagnalls, 1977. An excellent guide.

Roth, Ernest. *The Business of Music: Reflections of a Music Publisher.* New York: Oxford University Press, 1969.

Strong, William S. *The Copyright Book: A Practical Guide,* 2nd edition. Cambridge, Mass.: MIT Press, 1976. A good book, includes material on taxes and international copyright protection.

Taubman, Joseph. *Performing Arts Management.* Book VI. *Forms—Music Publishing.* New York: Law Arts Press, 1977.

Weinstein, David A. *How to Protect Your Creative Work: All You Need to Know About Copyright.* New York: John Wiley & Sons, Inc., 1987. Easy to follow, includes information about patents and trademarks.

COMMERCIALS

Cone, Fairfax. *With All Its Faults.* Boston: Little Brown, 1963.

Diamant, Lincoln. *Television's Classic Commercials: The Golden Years, 1948–1958.* New York: Hastings House, 1970.

———, ed. *The Anatomy of a Television Commercial: The Story of Eastman Kodak's "Yesterday."* New York: Hastings House, 1970.

Galanoy, Terry. *Down the Tube.* New York: Pinnacle Books, 1972. Simultaneously amusing and frightening.

Karmen, Steve. *Through the Jingle Jungle: The Art and Business of Making Music for Commercials.* New York: Billboard Books, 1989. An absorbing although occasionally repetitious book by one of the top jingle composers in New York.

Key, Wilson Bryan. *Subliminal Seduction.* New York: Signet Books, 1974. Key finds sex is being used to sell us everything from alcohol to dark glasses.

Miller, Fred. *Music in Advertising.* New York: Music Sales Corp. A useful guide.

Norbach, Peter and Craig. *Great Songs of Madison Avenue.* New York: Quadrangle Books, 1976. Words and music for many famous commercials.

Robinson, Sol. *Radio Advertising: How to Sell It and Write It.* Blue Ridge Summit, Pa.: TAB Books, 1974.

Savan, Leslie. *The Sponsored Life.* Philadelphia: Temple University Press, 1994.

Schwartz, Tony. *The Responsive Chord.* New York: Anchor Books, 1973. Techniques of persuasion and communication.

Teixeira, Antonio, Jr. *Music to Sell By.* Boston: Berklee Press, 1974.

Wainwright, Charles A. *Television Commercials.* New York: Hastings House, 1970.

Welling, Si. *How to Sell Radio Advertising.* Blue Ridge Summit, Pa.: TAB Books, 1970.

Woodward, Walt. *An Insider's Guide to Advertising Music: Everything You Must Know for TV & Radio.* New York: Art Direction Book Co., 1982.

RADIO

Barnouw, Erik. *A History of Broadcasting in the United States.* 3 vols. New York: Oxford University Press, 1966–70.
Dolan, Robert Emmett. *Music in Modern Media.* New York: G. Schirmer, 1967.
Exploring Theatre and Media Careers: A Student Guidebook. Washington, D.C.: U.S. Government Printing Office, 1976.
Hall, Claude and Barbara. *This Business of Radio Programming.* New York: Billboard Publications, 1977. An extended analysis of programming followed by interviews with significant figures. Recommended.
Hoffer, Jay. *Radio Production Techniques.* Blue Ridge Summit, Pa.: TAB Books, 1974.
Ladd, Jim. *Radio Waves: Life and Revolution on the FM Dial.* New York: St. Martin's Press, 1991. An impressionistic history.
Lujack, Harry. *Super Jock.* Chicago: Henry Regnery, 1975.
Passman, Arnold. *The Deejays.* New York: Macmillan; 1971.
Quaal, Ward L., and Brown, James A. *Broadcast Management.* New York: Hastings House, 1976.
St. John, Robert. *Encyclopedia of Radio and Television Broadcasting.* Milwaukee: Cathedral Square, 1970.

The public relations department of the National Association of Broadcasters (NAB), 1771 N. St. NW, Washington, D.C. 20036, offers the following free publications: *Careers in Radio, Careers in Television, If You Want Air Time, Radio and Television Bibliography,* and *Radio U.S.A.*

The Chronicle-Guidance Publications, Inc., and the U.S. Government Printing Office publish a number of career guides to media and music careers. Their addresses are: Chronicle Guidance Publications, Inc., Moravia, N.Y. 13118, and U.S. Government Printing Office, Washington, D.C. 20402.

STUDIO WORK

Blaine, Hal, with David Goggin. *Hal Blaine and the Wrecking Crew: The Story of the World's Most Recorded Musician.* Emoryville, Calif.: Mix Books, 1990.
Faulkner, Robert R. *Hollywood Studio Musicians: Their Work and Careers in the Recording Industry.* Chicago: Aldine Atherton, 1971. A superb sociological study of studio musicians.

TELEVISION, CABLE TV, MUSIC VIDEO

Bishop, John. *Making It in Video: An Insider's Guide to Careers in the Fastest Growing Industry of the Decade*. New York: McGraw-Hill, 1989. Well written, easy to follow.

Costello, Marjorie, and Katz, Cynthia. *Breaking into Video: A Guide to Career and Business Opportunities*. New York: Fireside Books, Simon & Schuster, 1985. A practical guide.

Denny, Jon S. *Careers in Cable TV*. New York: Barnes & Noble, 1983. Job descriptions.

Frith, Simon; Goodwin, Andrew; and Grossberg, Lawrence, eds. *Sound & Vision: The Music Video Reader*. London: Routledge, 1993.

Kaplan, Ann E. *Rocking Around the Clock: Music Television, Post-Modernism and Consumer Culture*. New York: Methuen Books, 1987. A searching critique, sometimes difficult to follow.

Reed, Maxine K., and Reed, Robert M. *Career Opportunities in Television, Cable and Video*. 2nd edition. New York: Facts on File, 1986. Various careers outlined, with job prospects, salaries, job descriptions, etc.

Shore, Michael. *The Rolling Stone Book of Rock Video*. New York: Quill, 1984.

Wiese, Michael. *Film & Video Budgets*. Westport, Conn.: Michael Wiese Film Productions, 1984. An intelligent guide to budgets, easy to understand.

———. *Home Video: Producing for the Home Market*. Westport, Conn.: Michael Wiese Film/Video, 1995. Wiese's books are excellent.

———. *The Independent Film & Videomakers Guide*. Westport, Conn.: Michael Wiese Film Productions, 1995. Investors, distribution, budgets, etc.

Winston, Brian, and Keydel, Julia. *Working with Video: A Comprehensive Guide to the World of Video Production*. A how-to book, easy to follow, with many pictures.

Zimmerman, Caroline A. *How to Break into the Media Professions*. Garden City, N.Y.: Doubleday, 1981. How to get a first job in broadcasting, advertising, public relations, etc.

An earlier book that is still worth reading is Bob Shank's *The Cool Fire: How to Make It in Television*. New York: Random House, 1976.

AUDIO ENGINEERING, SOUND SYSTEMS

Backus, John. *The Acoustical Foundations of Music*. 2nd edition. New York: W. W. Norton, 1977. A guide to acoustics. Excellent.

Borwick, John, ed. *Sound Recording Practice: A Handbook Compiled by the Society of Professional Recording Studios*. 3rd edition. New York: Oxford University Press, 1987.

Burroughs, Lou. *Microphones: Design and Application*. Plainview, N.Y.: Sagamore, 1974.

Clifford, Martin. *Microphones: How They Work and How to Use Them.* Blue Ridge Summit, Pa.: TAB Books, 1975.

Eargle, John M. *Handbook of Recording Engineering.* 3rd edition. New York: Van Nostrand Reinhold, 1986.

Everett, F. Alton. *How to Build a Small Budget Recording Studio from Scratch.* 2nd edition. Blue Ridge Summit, Pa.: TAB Books, 1988.

———. *Sound System Operation.* Blue Ridge Summit, Pa.: TAB Books, 1985.

Huber, David Miles, and Runstein, Robert E., eds. *Modern Recording Techniques.* 4th edition. Indianapolis: Sams Publishing, 1995.

Pohlmann, Ken. *Advanced Digital Audio.* New York: McGraw-Hill, 1991.

———. *Principles of Digital Audio.* 3rd edition. New York: McGraw-Hill, 1995.

Vasey, John. *Concert Sound and Lighting Systems.* Stoneham, Mass.: Butterworth Publishers, 1989.

Woram, John. *The Recording Studio Handbook.* Plainview, N.Y.: Sagamore, 1983.

Be sure to get current material in this field, because the technology advances so rapidly.

FILM BUSINESS

Faulkner, Robert A. *Music on Demand: Composers and Careers in the Hollywood Film Industry.* New Brunswick, N.J.: Transaction Books, 1982. Describes how film composers get work and the life cycle of their careers. A superb book.

Gregory, Mollie. *Making Films Your Business.* New York: Schocken Books, 1979. A practical guide.

Kindem, Gorham, ed. *The American Movie Industry: The Business of Motion Pictures.* Carbondale, Southern Illinois University Press, 1982. A complex, well-informed book.

Litwak, Mark. *Dealmaking in the Film & Television Industry.* Los Angeles: Silman-James Press, 1994.

Resnik, Gail, and Trost, Scott. *All You Need to Know About the Movie and TV Business.* New York: Simon & Schuster, 1996.

Squire, Jason E., ed. *The Movie Business Book.* New York: Fireside Books, Simon & Schuster, 1983. Every step of the financing and production of movies, with chapters by such authorities as Mel Brooks and Robert Evans.

FILM MUSIC

Baker, Fred, and Firestone, Ross. *Movie People: At Work in the Business of Film.* New York: Douglas, 1972.

Bazelon, Irwin. *Knowing the Score: Notes on Film.* New York: Van Nostrand Reinhold, 1975.

Eisler, Hans. *Composing for the Films.* New York: Oxford University Press, 1947. Controversial and stimulating thoughts on the aesthetics of film music.

Evans, Marc. *The Music of the Movies.* New York: Hopkinson & Blake, 1975.

Flinn, Caryl. *Strains of Utopia: Gender, Nostalgia and Hollywood Film Music.* Princeton, N.J.: Princeton University Press, 1992.

Fredericks, Marc. *A Summary of Film Mathematics.* New York: Comprehensive Publications, 1974.

Gorbman, Claudia. *Unheard Melodies: Narrative Film Music.* Bloomington: Indiana University Press, 1987. A detailed analysis of various film scores, with extensive musical examples.

Hagen, Earle. *Scoring for Films.* New York: Criterion Music, 1971.

Kalinak, Kathryn. *Settling the Score: Music and the Classical Hollywood Film.* Madison: University of Wisconsin Press, 1992.

Limbacher, James L., ed. *Film Music from Violin to Video.* Metuchen, N.J.: Scarecrow Press, 1974. A series of articles describing the history and craft of film score composition and a long list of film scores with their composers.

Prendergast, Roy M. *Film Music: A Neglected Art.* New York: W. W. Norton, 1977.

Skiles, Marlin. *Music Scoring for TV and Motion Pictures.* Blue Ridge Summit, Pa.: TAB Books, 1976.

Thomas, Tony. *Music for the Movies.* New York: A. S. Barnes, 1973.

PROMOTION AND PUBLICITY

Gibson, James. *Getting Noticed: A Musician's Guide to Publicity and Self-Promotion.* Cincinnati: Writer's Digest Books, 1987. A useful guide with many practical suggestions.

Greene, Bob. *The Billion Dollar Baby.* New York: Signet, 1974. An enjoyable book describing the merchandising of Alice Cooper.

O'Brien, Richard. *Publicity: How to Get It.* New York: Barnes & Noble, 1977. A basic guide.

Pinskey, Raleigh. *The Zen of Hype: An Insider's Guide to the Publicity Game.* New York: Carol Publishing Group, 1991.

Plummer, Gail. *The Business of Show Business.* New York: Harper, 1961. How to promote concerts.

Rosenman, Joel; Roberts, John; and Pilpel, Robert. *Young Men with Unlimited Capital.* New York: Harcourt Brace Jovanovich, 1974. The peculiar story of the Woodstock festival, told by its backers.

Spitz, Robert Stephen. See Recording.

Stein, Howard, and Zalkind, Ron. *Promoting Rock Concerts.* New York: Schirmer Books, 1980. A useful guide.

MUSIC PERFORMANCE

This is a list of books on various facets of music. Not all of these books deal specifically with the performance of music, but all should be of some use to performers in the various styles listed.

Classical Music

Arian, Edward. *Bach, Beethoven and Bureaucracy: The Case of the Philadelphia Orchestra*. University, Ala.: University of Alabama Press, 1971. A hard look at symphony playing and the organization of this orchestra by a player who quit to pursue a career in political science.

Becker, John. *Discord: The Story of the Vancouver Symphony Orchestra*. Vancouver: Brighouse Press, 1989.

Bing, Rudolf. *Five Thousand Nights with the Opera*. Garden City, N.Y.: Doubleday, 1972.

Chase, Gilbert. *The American Composer Speaks*. Baton Rouge, La.: Louisiana State University Press, 1966.

Epstein, Helen. *Music Talks: Conversations with Working Musicians*. New York: McGraw-Hill, 1987. Interesting interviews with famous and lesser-known classical musicians.

Furlong, William Barry. *Season with Solti*. New York: Macmillan, 1974. A realistic picture of life in the Chicago Symphony.

Gammond, Peter. *The Harmony Illustrated Encyclopedia of Classical Music*. New York: Harmony Books, 1988.

Hart, Philip. *Orpheus in the New World*. New York: Norton, 1973. A study of American symphony orchestras, their organization, history, and finances. An important book.

Hurok, Sol. *Impresario*. New York: Random House, 1966.

Jacobson, Robert. *Reverberations: Interviews with the World's Leading Musicians*. New York: William Morrow & Co., 1974.

Kingsbury, Henry. *Music, Talent & Performance: A Conservatory Cultural System*. Philadelphia: Temple University Press, 1988. An analysis of the training of classical musicians.

Papolos, Janice. *The Performing Artist's Handbook*. Cincinnati: Writer's Digest Books, 1984. The only book that explains the business of classical music. Written with verve and intelligence.

Vigeland, Carl A. *In Concert: Onstage and Offstage with the Boston Symphony Orchestra*. New York: William Morrow & Co., 1989.

Woodhull, Marta. *Singing for a Living*. Cincinnati: Writer's Digest Books, 1991.

Blues and Soul Music

Albertson, Chris. *Bessie Smith*. New York: Stein & Day, 1972.

Blesh, Rudi, and Janis, Harriet. *They All Played Ragtime*. New York: Oak, 1971.

Broven, John. *Rhythm & Blues in New Orleans.* Gretna, La.: Pelican Publishing Co., 1978. An absorbing regional portrait.

Charters, Samuel. *The Bluesmen.* New York: Oak, 1967.

Dixon, R. M., and Godrich, John. *Recording the Blues.* New York: Stein & Day, 1970.

Garland, Phyl. *The Sound of Soul.* Chicago: Henry Regnery, 1969.

George, Nelson. *The Death of Rhythm & Blues.* New York: Pantheon Books, 1988. The author's notion that soul music is being diluted by the financial incentives to make records that cross over into white radio stations.

———. *Where Did Our Love Go?: The Rise and Fall of the Motown Sound.* New York: St. Martin's Press, 1985.

Guralnick, Peter. *Feel Like Going Home: Portraits in Blues & Rock 'n' Roll.* New York: Random House, 1981.

———. *Lost Highway: Journeys & Arrivals of American Musicians.* Boston: David Godine, 1979.

———. *Sweet Soul Music: Rhythm & Blues and the Southern Dream of Freedom.* New York: Harper & Row, 1986.

Note: Three excellent books. The first and second are about blues, and occasionally country music, and the third book is about soul.

Hannusch, Jeff. *I Hear You Knockin': The Sound of New Orleans Rhythm and Blues.* Ville Platte, La.: Swallow Publications, 1985.

Heilbut, Tony. *The Gospel Sound.* New York: Simon & Schuster, 1986. The only thorough history of gospel music to date.

Jones, LeRoi. *Black Music.* New York: William Morrow & Co., 1967.

Leadbitter, Mike. *Nothing But the Blues.* New York: Oak, 1971.

Lomax, Alan. *The Land Where the Blues Began.* New York: Pantheon Books, 1993. An invaluable book on delta blues.

Oliver, Paul. *Aspects of the Blues Tradition.* New York: Oak, 1970.

———. *Conversations with the Blues.* New York: Horizon Press, 1965.

Palmer, Robert. *Deep Blues.* New York: The Viking Press, 1981.

Shaw, Arnold. *Honkers and Shouters: The Golden Years of Rhythm and Blues.* New York: Collier Books, 1978.

———. *The World of Soul.* New York: Warner Paperback Library, 1971.

Southern, Eileen. *Music of Black Americans.* New York: W. W. Norton, 1971. A marvelous book, intelligent and readable.

Tilton, Jeff Todd. *Early Downhome Blues: A Musical and Cultural Analysis.* Urbana, Ill.: University of Illinois Press, 1977.

Vincent, Rickey. *Funk: The Music, the People, and the Rhythm of the One.* New York: St. Martin's Griffin, 1996.

For more books on blues, and about country music and American music in general, check out the University of Illinois Music in American Life books, an excellent series of several dozen books about various aspects of American music.

Also see the recent reissue edition of the book I coauthored with Larry Sandberg, *The Folk Music Sourcebook*, Da Capo, 1989.

Country & Western Music

Artis, Bob. *Bluegrass*. New York: Hawthorn Books, 1975. An intelligent and well-balanced book.

Bart, Teddy. *Inside Music City*. Nashville: Aurora, 1970.

Cornfeld, Robert, with Farwell, Marshall, Jr. *Just Country*. New York: McGraw-Hill, 1976.

Country Music Foundation. *Country Music*. New York: Abbeville Press, 1988. A massive book with many pictures and articles.

Dellar, Fred, et al. *Illustrated Encyclopedia of Country Music*. New York: Harmony Books, 1977.

Ellison, Curtis W. *Country Music Culture*. Jackson, Miss.: University of Mississippi Press, 1995.

Grissom, John. *Country Music: White Man's Blues*. New York: Paperback Library, 1970.

Hemphill, Paul. *The Nashville Sound: Bright Lights and Country Music*. New York: Pocket Books, 1971. An excellent guide to the music business in Nashville.

Malone, Bill C. *Country Music, U.S.A.: A Fifty-Year History*. Austin, Tex.: University of Texas Press, 1968.

Rosenberg, Neil. *Bluegrass: A History*. Urbana: University of Illinois Press, 1985. Essential reading.

Shelton, Robert, and Goldblatt, Burt. *The Country Music Story*. Portland, Me.: Castle Books, 1966.

Stambler, Irwin, and Landon, Grelun. *Encyclopedia of Folk, Country and Western Music*. New York: St. Martin's Press, 1969.

Tichi, Cecilia, ed. *Readin' Country Music*. Durham, N.C.: Duke University Press, 1995.

Wacholtz, Larry E. *Inside Country Music: The Guide to Success in Country Music*. Marshall, Wash.: Thumbs Up Publishing, 1984. The business of country music.

For further references see *The Folk Music Sourcebook*, discussed above, and the University of Illinois Press series, especially Neil Rosenberg's book on bluegrass.

ELECTRONIC MUSIC: COMPUTERS AND MUSIC

Note: I have deliberately not included much material about synthesizers, which would be outdated by the time it is in print. For material on synthesizers consult the various music publishers, especially Hal Leonard Publishing in Milwaukee.

Bigelow, Steven. *Making Music with Personal Computers.* La Jolla, Calif.: Park Row Press, 1987.

Deutsch, Herbert. *Synthesizer: An Introduction to the History, Theory, and Performance of Electronic Music.* Port Washington, N.Y.: Alfred, 1976.

Douglas, Alan. *The Electronic Musical Instrument Manual.* Summit, Pa.: TAB Books, 1977.

Friend, David; Pearlman, Alan R.; and Piggott, Thomas D. *Learning Music with Synthesizer.* Winona, Minn.: Hal Leonard, 1974.

Gurle, Ted M., and Pfefferle, W. I. *Plug In: The Guide to Music on the Net.* Upper Saddle River, N.J.: Prentice Hall, 1996.

Howe, Hubert S. *Electronic Music Synthesis.* New York: W. W. Norton, 1975.

Krepack, Benjamin, and Firestone, Rod. *Start Me Up! The Music Biz Meets the Personal Computer.* Van Nuys, Calif.: Mediac Press, 1986. Programs for music composition, budgets, etc.

Schwartz, Elliott. *Electronic Music: A Listener's Guide.* New York: Praeger, 1973.

Strange, Alan. *Electronic Music.* Dubuque, Iowa: William C. Brown, 1972.

Wells, Thomas, and Vogel, Eric. *The Technique of Electronic Music.* Manchaca, Tex.: Sterling Swift, 1974.

FOLK MUSIC

Ames, Russell. *The Story of American Folk Song.* New York: Grosset & Dunlap, 1960. A good brief history.

Brand, Oscar. *The Ballad Mongers.* New York: Funk & Wagnalls, 1961.

Cantwell, Robert. *When We Were Good: The Folk Revival.* Cambridge, Mass.: Harvard University Press, 1996.

Cohen, Ronald. *Wasn't That a Time.* Metuchen, N.J.: Scarecrow Press, 1994. A reader on the folk music revival of the 1960s.

Lieberman, Robbie. *"My Song Is My Weapon": People's Songs, American Communism, and the Politics of Culture, 1930–1950.* Urbana: University of Illinois Press, 1989.

Nettl, Bruno. *An Introduction to Folk Music in the United States.* Detroit, Mich.: Wayne State University Press, 1972.

Sandberg, Larry, and Weissman, Dick. *The Folk Music Sourcebook.* New York: Da Capo, 1989.

Seeger, Pete. *The Incompleat Folksinger.* New York: Simon & Schuster, 1972. A fascinating memoir by America's leading folksinger.

Traum, Happy. *Folk Guitar as a Profession.* Saratoga, Calif.: Guitar Player Books, 1977. Includes sample performer's contracts, which will be useful to anyone booking himself.

Numerous biographies of folksingers have appeared in the last ten years, along with more collections of songs and regional studies. For more information see *The Folk Music Sourcebook*.

JAZZ

Berliner, Paul. *Thinking in Jazz: The Infinite Art of Improvisation*. Chicago: University of Chicago Press, 1994. A detailed musical study.

Case, Brian, and Britt, Stan. *The Illustrated Encyclopedia of Jazz*. 3rd edition. New York: Harmony Books, 1987.

Collier, James Lincoln. *The Making of Jazz*. New York: Macmillan, 1978.

Feather, Leonard. *Inside Jazz*. New York: Da Capo, 1977.

Finklestein, Sidney. *Jazz, A People's Music*. New York: International Publishers, 1949. Concentrates on the social history of the music.

Gabbard, Krin, ed. *Jazz Among the Discourses*. Durham, N.C.: Duke University Press, 1995.

Giddins, Gary. *Rhythm-A-Ning: Jazz Tradition and Innovation in the 80's*. New York: Oxford University Press, 1906. Giddins is a fine writer who has won numerous awards for his critical writings. See his earlier book, *Riding on a Blue Note*, for more of his work.

Gray, Herman. *Producing Jazz: The Experience of an Independent Record Company*. Philadelphia: Temple University Press, 1988.

Hodeir, Andre. *The Worlds of Jazz*. New York: Grove Press, 1972. Translated by Noel Burch.

Leonard, Neil. *Jazz and the White Americans*. Chicago: University of Chicago Press, 1962.

———. *Jazz, Myth and Religion*. New York: Oxford University Press, 1987.

Ramsey, Fredric, Jr., and Smith, Charles E., eds. *Jazzmen*. New York: Harcourt Brace Jovanovich, 1977.

Schuller, Gunther. *Early Jazz: Its Roots and Musical Development*. New York: Oxford University Press, 1968. Essential.

———. *The Swing Era: The Development of Jazz, 1933–1945*. New York: Oxford University Press, 1988.

Shapiro, Nat, and Hentoff, Nat, eds. *Hear Me Talkin' to Ya: The Story of Jazz by the Men Who Made It*. New York: Dover, 1966.

Spellman, A. B. *Black Music: Four Lives*. New York: Schocken Books, 1970. A beautiful if terrifying book about the lives of four jazz innovators.

Stearns, Marshall. *The Story of Jazz*. New York: Oxford University Press, 1956.

Taylor, Arthur. *Notes and Tones: Musician to Musician Interviews*. New York: Perigree Books, 1982.

Ulanov, Barry. *A History of Jazz in America.* 1955. Reprint. New York: Da Capo, 1972.

Williams, Martin. *The Jazz Tradition.* New York: Oxford University Press, 1970.

RAP

Costello, Mark. *Signifying Rappers.* Boston: Ecco Press, 1989.

Nelson, Havelock, and Gonzales, Michael A. *Bring the Noise: A Guide to Rap Music and Hip-Hop Culture.* New York: Harmony Books, 1991.

Rose, Tricia. *Black Noise: Rap Music and Black Culture in Contemporary America.* Hanover, N.H.: Wesleyan University Press, 1994. An excellent book.

Sexton, Adam, ed. *Rap On Rap.* New York: Dell Publishing, 1995.

Toop, David. *Rap Attack 2.* Boston: Consortium Press, 1992.

ROCK

Bacon, Tony, ed. *Rock Hardware: The Instruments, Equipment and Technology of Rock.* New York: Harmony Books, 1989. Many illustrations.

Belz, Carl. *The Story of Rock.* 2nd edition. New York: Oxford University Press, 1972.

Christgau, Robert. *Any Old Way You Choose It.* Baltimore, Md.: Penguin Books, 1973.

Clifford, Mike, consultant. *The Harmony Illustrated Encyclopedia of Rock.* New York: Harmony Books, 1989.

Friedlander, Paul. *Rock and Roll: A Social History.* Boulder, Colo.: Westview Press, 1996. An intelligent guide, especially to 1950s and '60s rock.

Frith, Simon. *Sound Effects: Youth, Leisure, and the Politics of Rock 'n' Roll.* New York: Pantheon Books, 1981. Frith is a sociologically inclined rock critic and historian.

Gillett, Charlie. *The Sound of the City: The Rise of Rock and Roll.* New York: E. P. Dutton, 1970. The best history of rock I have seen.

Gleason, Ralph J. *The Jefferson Airplane and the San Francisco Sound.* New York: Ballantine Books, 1969.

Guralnick, Peter. *Last Train to Memphis: The Rise of Elvis Presley.* Boston: Little, Brown & Co., 1994.

Jahn, Mike. *Rock.* New York: Quadrangle Books, 1973.

Kooper, Al. *Backstage Passes.* New York: Stein & Day, 1977. Amusing reminiscences of the rock scene by the pianist-organist-producer.

Laing, Dave. *One Chord Wonders: Power and Meaning in Punk Rock.* Milton Keynes, U.K.: Open University Press, 1985. A sociological view of the punk phenomenon.

Palmer, Tony. *All You Need Is Love.* New York: Grossman Publishers, 1976. A good history of the origins and evolution of rock.

Roxon, Lillian. *Rock Music Encyclopedia.* New York: Grosset & Dunlap, 1971.

Stambler, Irwin. *Encyclopedia of Pop, Rock and Soul.* New York: St. Martin's Press, 1976.

Street, John. *Rebel Rock: The Politics of Popular Music.* Oxford, U.K.: Basil Blackwell, 1986. One of the better social histories.

The Rolling Stone History of Rock & Roll: Rock of Ages. New York: Rolling Stone Press, 1986. A well-informed history, written by Ed Ward, Geoffrey Stokes, and Ken Tucker.

Walser, Robert. *Running with the Devil: Power, Gender and Madness in Heavy Metal Music.* Hanover, N.H.: Wesleyan University Press, 1993. An outstanding book.

POPULAR MUSIC IN GENERAL

Clarke, Donald. *The Rise and Fall of Popular Music.* New York: St. Martin's Press, 1995.

Ewen, David. *All the Years of American Popular Music.* Englewood Cliffs, N.J.: Prentice-Hall, 1977

Hamm, Charles. *Putting Popular Music in Its Place.* Cambridge, U.K.: Cambridge University Press, 1992.

Lull, James, ed. *Popular Music and Communication.* Newbury Park, Calif.: Sage Publications, 1988.

Nancy, Charles, ed. *American Music from Storyville to Woodstock.* New Brunswick, N.J.: Transaction Books, 1975.

Shapiro, Nat, ed. *Popular Music, An Annotated Index of American Popular Song.* 6 vols. New York: Adrian, 1964–73.

Whitfield, Ian. *After the Ball: Pop Music from Rag to Rock.* New York: Simon & Schuster, 1974. Entertaining and informative.

Wilder, Alec. *Popular Song: The Great Innovators, 1900–1950.* New York: Oxford University Press, 1975. A book about popular songs before the rock era.

SONGWRITING

There have been a large number of books written about songwriting in the last ten years. If you are particularly interested in songwriting, I suggest that you send to Writer's Digest for their catalog. They are the leading publisher in this field.

Braheny, John. *The Craft and Business of Songwriting.* Cincinnati: Writer's Digest Books, 1988. A comprehensive book discussing virtually all aspects of songwriting and publishing.

Citron, Stephen. *Songwriting: A Complete Guide to the Craft.* New York: William Morrow & Co., 1985. A good book, especially in the area of writing melodies.

Davis, Sheila. *The Craft of Lyric Writing.* Cincinnati: Writer's Digest Books, 1985.

———. *Successful Lyric Writing: A Step-by-Step Course & Workbook.* Cincinnati: Writer's Digest Books, 1988.

A friend of mine has sensibly suggested that the best thing to do with these books is to read them and absorb as much as you can and then be as spontaneous as possible in your writing rather than try to follow Davis's instructions too carefully.

Flanagan, Bill. *Written in My Soul: Conversations with Rock's Great Songwriters.* Chicago: Contemporary Books, 1987. A must for all songwriters; searching interviews with outstanding writers.

Gillette, Steve. *Songwriting and the Creative Process.* Bethlehem, Pa.: Sing Out Publications, 1995. A useful guide.

Laufenberg, Cindy, ed. *Songwriter's Market, 1996.* Cincinnati: Writer's Digest Books, 1996. An excellent annual guide to outlets for songwriters.

Mahonin, Valerie. *Market Your Songs: A "How To" Guide for Contemporary Songwriters and Performers.* Calgary, Alta: Songsmith Publications, 1986. A Canadian book that focuses on the Canadian market.

More, Paul. *When Originality Counts.* Nashville: The Discovery Lab, 1987. An interesting book on creativity as applied to songwriting.

Pickow, Peter, and Appleby, Amy. *The Billboard Book of Songwriting.* New York: Billboard Publications, 1988. Excellent.

Pierce, Jennifer Ember. *The Bottom Line Is Money: A Comprehensive Guide to Songwriting and the Nashville Music Industry.* Westport, Conn.: The Bold Strummer, Ltd., 1994.

Russell, Tom, and Tyson, Sylvia, eds. *And Then I Wrote: The Songwriter Speaks.* Vancouver, Canada: Arsenal Pulp Press, 1996.

Weissman, Dick. *Creating Melodies.* Cincinnati: Writer's Digest Books, 1994.

CAREERS IN MUSIC

A useful introduction to this field is the book *Careers in Music*, available from the American Music Conference, 150 East Huron, Chicago, Ill. 60611. It gives brief sketches of the various careers available today in music. See also *Exploring Music Careers: A Student Guidebook*, Washington, D.C.: U.S. Government Printing Office, 1976.

MUSIC EDUCATION

There are dozens of books available in the field of music education, and most colleges offer the music education major. I have therefore spent little time discussing music education careers in this book. Check with your local library or with a college offering a music education degree for more information.

MUSIC CRITICISM

Music criticism is not offered as a major in any college in the United States. A student wishing a career in this area should take writing, journalism, and music courses. Very few books have been written that examine the field, and most books about music criticism are critical works about specific forms of music. The following books are some of the available works on music criticism:

Graf, Max. *Composer and Critic: Two Hundred Years of Music Criticism.* New York: W. W. Norton, 1971.

Rosenfeld, Paul. *Discoveries of a Music Critic.* 1936. Reprint. New York: Vienna House, 1972.

Thomson, Virgil. *The Art of Judging Music.* New York: Alfred A. Knopf, 1958.

See the Music Critics Association in the Lists of Music Business Organizations in the Appendix.

MUSIC LIBRARY CAREERS

Bradley, Carol J. *Readings in Music Librarianship.* Englewood, Colo.: Service in Library and Information Services, 1973.

Redfern, Brian. *Organizing Music in Libraries.* 2nd edition. Hamden, Conn.: Shoestring Press, 1978.

MUSIC THERAPY

A few of the important available works in the field:

Alvin, Juliette. *Music for the Handicapped Child.* New York: Oxford University Press, 1976.

————. *Music Therapy.* New York: State Mutual Books, 1984.

Bright, Ruth. *Music in Geriatric Care.* New York: St. Martin's Press, 1976.

Bunt, Leslie. *Music Therapy: An Art Beyond Words.* London: Routledge, 1994.

Guston, E. Thayer. *Music in Therapy.* New York: Macmillan, 1968.

Gutheil, Emil. *Music and Your Emotions.* New York: Liveright, 1970.

Halpern, Steve, and Savery, Louis. *Sound Health: Music & Sounds That Make Us Whole*. New York: Harper & Row, 1985.

Herbert, Wilhelmina K. *Opening Doors Through Music: A Practical Guide for Teachers, Therapists, Students, Parents*. Springfield, Ill.: C. C. Thomas, 1974.

Michel, Donald E. *Music Therapy: An Introduction to Therapy and Special Education Through Music*. Springfield, Ill.: C. C. Thomas, 1976.

Nordoff, Paul, and Robbins, Clive E. *Individualized Treatment for the Handicapped Child in Music*. New York: John Day, 1976.

———. *Music Therapy in Specialized Education*. New York: John Day, 1971.

Priestly, Mary. *Music Therapy in Action*. New York: St. Martin's Press, 1975.

Purvis, Jennie, and Samet, Shelly. *Music in Developmental Therapy*. Baltimore, Md.: University Park Books, 1976.

Schullian, Dorothy, and Schoen, Max, eds. *Music and Medicine*. 1948 reprint. Plainview, N.Y.: Books for Libraries Press, 1971.

Storr, Anthony. *Music and the Mind*. New York: HarperCollins, 1992.

Tomet, Jean H., and Krutzky, Carmel D. *Learning Through Music for Special Children and Their Teachers*. South Waterford, Me.: Merriam Eddy, 1975.

Ward, David. *Hearts and Hands and Voices: Music in the Education of Slow Learners*. New York: Oxford University Press, 1971.

PIANO TUNING

Bradley, Jack. *How to Tune, Repair & Regulate Your Piano*. S. Charleston, W. Va.: Hill Springs Publications, 1986.

Fischer, Cree J. *Piano Tuning: Registry and Repairing*. New York: Dover Books, 1976.

Jackson, Jim. *Tuning & Repairing Your Own Piano*. Summit, Pa.: Tab, 1984.

Reblitz, Arthur. *Piano Servicing, Tuning & Rebuilding*. New edition. Charleston, W. Va.: Vestal, 1976.

CHURCH MUSIC

Consult your local church music staff for more information about the music of that specific religion.

A Guide to Music for the Church Year. 4th edition. Minneapolis, Minn.: Augsberg, 1974.

Bauman, William A. *The Ministry of Music: A Guide for the Practicing Church Musician*. Washington, D.C.: Liturgical, 1975.

Davidson, James R. *A Dictionary of Protestant Church Music*. Metuchen, N.J.: Scarecrow, 1975.

Davies, Henry W., and Grace, Harvey. *Music and Worship*. 1935 reprint. New York: AMS Press, 1977.

Hunter, Stanley A., ed. *Music and Religion*. 1930 reprint. New York: AMS Press.

Northcott, Cecil. *Hymns in Christian Worship*. Atlanta: John Knox, 1975.

Osbeck, Kenneth W. *Ministry of Music*. Grand Rapids, Mich.: Kriegel, 1975.

Pass, David B. *Music and the Church*. Nashville: Broadman, 1989.

Phillips, Henry A. *Singing Church: An Outline History of the Music Sung by Choirs and People*. Hamden, Conn.: Archon, 1969.

Pratt, Waldo S. *Musical Ministries in the Church*. New York: AMS Press, 1976.

Routley, Erik. *Twentieth-Century Church Music*. New York: Oxford University Press, 1962.

Schmitt, Francis P. *Church Music Transgressed: Reflections on Reform*. Somer, Conn.: Seabury, 1977.

Stevenson, Robert. *Protestant Church Music in America: A Short Summary of Men and Movements from 1564 to the Present*. New York: Norton, 1970.

Topp, Dale. *Music in the Christian Church*. Grand Rapids, Mich.: Eerdmans, 1976.

Westermeyer, Paul. *The Church Musician*. New York: Harper & Row, 1988.

LAW

Beiderman, Donald, et al. *Law and Business of the Entertainment Industries*. Westport, Conn.: Praeger, 1991, 2nd Edition. An absorbing book covering many disputes in music, theater, and other areas. Not recommended for light reading.

Berk, Eliot Lee. See Publishing, Performing Rights, Copyright.

Halloran, Mark, Ed. *The Musician's Business & Legal Guide*. Upper Saddle River, N.J.: Prentice-Hall Inc., 1996, 2nd Edition. Contains many useful articles.

New York Law School Review. See Publishing, Performing Rights, Copyright.

Shemel and Krasilovsky. See Recording.

Taubman, Joseph. *Performing Arts Management*. Book V: *Forms–Sound Copyright*. New York: Law Arts Press, 1977.

All of these books except Beiderman and the New York Law School Review book contain sample contracts.

ARTS MANAGEMENT

Chapin, Schuyler. *Musical Chairs: A Life in the Arts*. New York: Putnam's, 1977.

The Finances of the Performing Arts. Vols. 1 and 2. New York: The Ford Foundation, 1974.

Millions for the Arts: Federal and State Cultural Programs. Washington, D.C.: Washington International Arts Newsletter Editors, 1972.

Netzer, Dick. *The Subsidized Muse: Public Support for the Arts in the United States.* New York: Cambridge University Press, 1978. A well-reasoned and clear viewpoint on a complex subject.

Reiss, Alvin. *The Arts Management Handbook.* New York: Law Arts Press, 1974.

Rockefeller, David, ed. *Coming to Our Senses: The Significance of the Arts for American Education.* New York: McGraw-Hill, 1978. A useful study for teachers, administrators, and artists.

Salem, Mahmoud. *Organizational Survival in the Performing Arts: The Marketing of the Seattle Opera.* New York: Praeger, 1976.

Taubman, Joseph. *Performing Arts Management and Law.* 6 vols. New York: Law Arts Press, 1973.

Toobin, Jerome. *Agitato: A Trek Through the Musical Jungle.* New York: The Viking Press, 1975. Arts management through the informed eyes of the manager of the defunct "Symphony of the Air."

The following books are all published by the American Council of the Arts, 570 Seventh Avenue, New York, N.Y. 10018:

ACA Yellow Pages. 1200 U.S. and Canadian entries, a telephone directory for the arts.

Brownring, W. Grant. *Corporate Fund Raising: A Practical Plan of Action.*

Cities, Counties and the Arts. Information on what local governments are doing for the arts. Interbook, 1976.

Coe, Linda, ed. *The Cultural Directory: Guide to Federal Funds and Services for Cultural Activities.* Lists 250 federal programs.

Community Arts Agencies: A Handbook and a Guide. How to start and run an arts council.

Kreisberg, Linda. *Local Government and the Arts.* How to deal with local elected officials.

A Survey of Arts Administration Training in the United States and Canada. A description of college programs.

Wagner, Susan, ed. *A Guide to Corporate Giving in the Arts.* A detailed casebook.

GRANTS AND SCHOLARSHIPS

A Directory of International Scholarships in the Arts. New York: Institute of International Education.

Bauer, David. *The How-To Grant Manual: Successful Techniques for Obtaining Private and Public Grants.* New York: Macmillan, 1988.

Fandel, Nancy. *A National Directory of Grants & Aid to Individuals in the Arts.* 6th edition. Washington, D.C. Washington International Arts Letter, 1987.

Federal Funds and Services for the Arts. Washington, D.C. U.S. Government Printing Office.

Foundation Grants to Individuals. New York: The Foundation Center, 888 Seventh Ave., New York, N.Y. 10019.

Grantsy, R. O. *Register of Scholarships and Loans and Register of Fellowships and Grants.* New York: World Trade Academy Press, Simon & Schuster. Published annually.

Pavlakis, Christopher. *The Music Handbook.* New York: Free Press, 1974. Contains an extensive list of music grants and scholarships, lists of concert talent managers, musical instrument manufacturers, and a great deal of other useful information.

White, Virginia. *Grants for the Arts.* New York: Plenum Press, 1980.

The Foundation Center, which has national collections in 79 5th Avenue, New York, N.Y. 10003, offers much data on foundations, grants, IRS returns, foundation annual reports, and various reference materials regarding grants. It also has regional offices at 312 Sutter St., San Francisco, Calif. 94108, and 739 National City Bank Building, 629 Euclid Avenue, Cleveland, Ohio 44114.

The following publications are all available from the New York office listed above:

Comsearch Printouts. An annual computer printout of grants by more than 340 major foundations.

Foundation Center Source Book Profiles. An annual loose-leaf subscription service.

Foundation Grants to Individuals. 1977.

Margolin, Judith B. *About Foundations: How to Find the Facts You Need to Get a Grant.* 1977 Revised Edition, with 1978 addendum.

Martinson, Jean Alan. *International Philanthropy: A Compilation of Grants by United States Foundations.* 1978.

The Foundation Center National Data Book. 2 vols.

The following book is published by the Columbia University Press, New York:

Lewis, Marianna O., ed. *The Foundation Directory.*

WOMEN IN MUSIC

Chapple and Garafalo. See Recording. This book contains a good chapter on women in rock, but their percentage analysis of charts misses the point of the changes in women's music and its impact on the writing of men as well.

Cheney, Joyce; Diehl, Marcia; and Silverstein, Deborah. *All Our Lives: A Women's Songbook.* Baltimore: Diana Press, 1976. A fine study of women's music, yesterday and today. The focus is on American folk music.

Dahl, Linda. *Stormy Weather: The Music and Lives of Jazzwomen.* New York: Pantheon, 1984.

Drinker, Sophie. *Music and Women.* New York: Coward McCann, 1948. A brilliant historical study of the oppression of women in Western music.

Felixson, Nancy, et al. *Women in American Music.* Aptos, Calif.: Written Word Collective, 1975. The result of a seminar in women's music at Kresge College of the University of California at Santa Cruz. A compelling study.

Hixon, Don L., and Hennessee, Don. *Women in Music: A Bibliography.* Metuchen, N.J.: Scarecrow, 1975.

Jepson, Barbara. *You've Come a Long Way: Women in Symphony Orchestras.* Vienna, Va.: American Symphony League, 1975.

Juno, Andrea, ed. *Angry Women in Rock,* vol 1. New York: Juno Books, 1996.

Klever, Anita. *Women in Television.* Philadelphia, Pa.: Westminster Press, 1975.

Koskoff, Ellen, ed. *Women and Music in Cross-Cultural Perspective.* Urbana: University of Illinois Press, 1989. A series of essays on the role of women in the music of various cultures.

McClary, Susan. *Feminine Endings.* Minneapolis: University of Minnesota Press, 1991.

Neuls-Bates, Carol, ed. *Women in Music: An Anthology of Source Readings from the Middle Ages to the Present.* New York: Harper & Row, 1982.

O'Brien, Lucy. *She Bop: The Definitive History of Women in Rock, Pop & Soul.* New York: Penguin Books, 1996.

Placksin, Sally. *American Women in Jazz: 1900 to the Present.* New York: Wideview Books, 1982.

Raphael, Amy. *Grrrls: Viva Rock Divas.* New York: St. Martin's Griffin, 1996.

Reynolds, Simon, and Press, Joy. *The Sex Revolts: Gender, Rebellion and Rock 'n' Roll.* Cambridge: Harvard University Press, 1995.

Schwartz, Ellen. *Born a Woman: Seven Canadian Women Singer-Songwriters.* Winlaw, B.C.: Polestar Book Publishers, 1988.

Sorrels, Rosalie, ed. *Wine, Woman, and Who Myself I Am.* Sonoma, Calif.: Wooden Shoe, 1974. Poetry and song. A beautiful book.

Steward, Sue, and Garratt, Sheryl. *Signed, Sealed and Delivered: True Life Stories of Women in Pop.* Boston: South End Press, 1984. A useful presentation of women's perspectives on music, style, and politics.

Wenner, Hilda E., and Freilicher, Elizabeth. *Here's to the Women: 100 Songs for and About American Women.* Syracuse, N.Y.: Syracuse University Press, 1987.

OTHER MINORITY GROUPS

See also the book list on blues and jazz.

Abdul, Raoul. *Blacks in Classical Music.* New York: Dodd, Mead, 1977.

Brooks, Tilford. *America's Black Musical Heritage.* Englewood Cliffs, N.J.: Prentice-Hall, 1984. Covers folk music, jazz, pop, and classical.

Floyd, Samuel A., Jr. *The Power of Black Music*. New York: Oxford University Press, 1995.

Gerard, Charley, with Sheller, Marty. *Salsa: The Rhythm of Latin Music*. Crown Point, Ind.: White Cliffs Media Co., 1989.

Loza, Steven. *Barrio Rhythms: Mexican American Music in Los Angeles*. Urbana: University of Illinois Press, 1993.

Roach, Hildred. *Black American Music: Past and Present*. 2 vols. Malabar, Fla.: Robert E. Krieger Publishing Co., 1985. Vol. 1 covers everything except classical music, vol. 2 covers classical music.

Shaw, Arnold. *Black Popular Music in America*. New York: Schirmer Books, 1986.

Spencer, Jon. *Sing A New Song: Liberating Black Hymnody*. Minneapolis: Fortress Press, 1995.

POWER IN THE ARTS

Burns, Joan Simpson. *The Awkward Embrace*. New York: Alfred A. Knopf, 1975. Studies of some key figures who wield great power in the arts. Intelligent and well researched, not much material on music.

Frohnmeyer, John. *Leaving Town Alive: Confessions of an Arts Warrior*. Boston: Houghton Mifflin, 1993,

Levine, Faye. *The Culture Barons*. New York: Crowell, 1976. Some interesting material on the building of the Lincoln Center arts complex in New York and some colorful material about promoter Bill Graham, but written in a peculiar and irritating style.

Metz, Robert. *Reflections in a Bloodshot Eye*. New York: Signet, 1977. A book about CBS.

Monaco, James. *Media Culture*. New York: Delta Books, 1978. The most interesting part of this book is the series of tables and analyses in the back relating to conglomerates and their various holdings.

MISCELLANEOUS MUSIC AND MUSIC BUSINESS BOOKS

Altman, Richard, and Kaufman, Mervyn. *Making of a Musical: Fiddler on the Roof*. New York: Crown, 1971.

American Music Conference. *Music U.S.A. 1987*. Wilmette, Ill. 1988. An annual survey.

Amram, David. *Vibrations*. New York: Macmillan, 1968. Amram is an unusual musician in that he is active in jazz, classical music, and pop-rock.

Baskerville, David. *The New Music Business and the New Careers*. Revised by Tim Baskerville, 1990. Denver: Sherwood Press, 1995, Sixth Edition.

Beadle, Jeremy. *Will Pop Eat Itself?* London: Faber & Faber, 1993.

Bindas, Kenneth J., ed. *America's Musical Pulse: Popular Music in Twentieth-Century Society*. Westport, Conn.: Praeger, 1992.

Brabec, Jeffrey, and Brabec, Todd. *Music, Money and Success: The Insider's Guide to the Music Industry*. New York: Schirmer Books, 1994. Excellent information especially about music publishing royalties, but dry reading.

Burnett, Robert. *The Global Jukebox: The International Music Industry*. London: Routledge, 1996.

Dannen, Fredric. *Hit Men*. New York: Vintage Books, 1991. The best book about payola.

Engel, Lehman. *The American Musical Theatre*. Revised edition. New York: Collier, 1975.

———. *The Making of a Musical*. New York: Macmillan, 1977.

Farr, Joey. *Moguls and Mad Men: The Pursuit of Power in Popular Music*. New York: Simon & Schuster, 1994.

Field, Shelly. *Career Opportunities in the Music Industry*. 3rd edition. New York: Facts On File, 1995. An outline book of various careers, detailing responsibilities and job outlook.

Fink, Michael. *Inside the Music Business: Music in Contemporary Life*. Revised edition. New York: Schirmer Books, 1996.

Fox, Ted. *In the Groove: The People Behind the Music*. New York: St. Martin's Press, 1986. Extended interviews with key figures in the record business, especially producers. Excellent.

Frankel, Aaron. *Writing the Broadway Musical*. New York: Drama Books, 1977.

Frith, Simon, ed. *Facing the Music*. New York: Pantheon Books, 1988.

———. *Music for Pleasure*. New York: Routledge, 1988.
The first book is a series of interesting essays by various authors; the second is a compilation of Frith's magazine pieces.

Gibson, James. *How You Can Make $30,000 a Year as a Musician*. Cincinnati: Writer's Digest Books, 1986. Some good ideas for the sort of musician who takes naturally to selling himself; not so useful for the average musician.

Goldmark Peter C. *Maverick Inventor*. New York: Saturday Review Press/Dutton, 1973. Memoirs by the man who perfected the LP record. Contains amusing anecdotes about his struggle with the CBS bureaucracy.

Graham, Ronnie. *The Da Capo Guide to Contemporary African Music*. New York: Da Capo, 1988. Covers various regions of Africa.

Grindea, Carola, ed. *Tensions in the Performance of Music: A Symposium*. New York: Alexander Broude, 1984. Physical and related problems associated with various instruments.

Gurley, Ted, and Pfefferle, W. T. *Plug In: Guide to Music on the Net*. Upper Saddle River, N.J.: Prentice Hall, 1996.

Haring, Bruce. *Off the Charts*. New York: Birch Lane Press, 1996. An interesting approach to why record companies make money when artists don't.

Horowitz, Joseph. *The Ivory Trade: Music and the Business of Music at the Van Cliburn International Piano Competition.* New York: Summit Books, 1990.

Hustwit, Gary. *Releasing an Independent Record.* 5th edition. San Diego: Rock Pile Press, 1995.

Kishel, Gregory F., and Kishel, Patricia Guntel. *How to Start, Run and Stay in Business.* New York: John Wiley & Sons, 1981. A good basic guide for the beginning retail store owner.

Lambert, Dennis, and Zalkind, Ronald. *Producing Hit Records.* New York: Schirmer Books, 1980. A good guide, unfortunately no longer in print.

Lewisohn, Mark. *The Beatles Recording Sessions: The Official Abbey Road Studio Session Notes, 1962–1970.* New York: Harmony Books, 1988.

Littlejohn, Maureen, ed. *Music Directory Canada.* Toronto: CM Books. A terrific guide; I wish there was an annual guide as good as this for the United States. Look for the most recent edition.

Malm, Krister, and Wallis, Roger. *Media Policy and Music Activity.* London: Routledge, 1992. A survey of the music business in various parts of the world.

Marre, Jeremy, and Charlton, Hannah. *Beats of the Heart: Popular Music of the World.* London: Pluto Press, 1985. Enjoyable and well written.

Marsh, Dave. *The First Rock & Roll Confidential Report.* New York: Pantheon Books, 1986. Marsh is interesting to read, but often moralistic.

Muench, Teri, and Pomerantz, Susan. *Attention: A & R: A Step-by-Step Guide into the Recording Industry.* Los Angeles: Alfred Music, 1988. A sensible book, but not a terribly creative approach.

Musical Merchandising Review Directory of Musical Instrument Dealers, 1996. Newton, Mass. An annual list.

Naggar, David, and Brandstetter, Jeffrey D. *The Music Business Explained in Plain English.* San Francisco: DaJe Publishing, 1995. Very good for a brief survey.

O'Shea, Shad. *Just for the Record.* Cincinnati: Positive Feedback Communications Press, 1986. Some great stories; at its best when discussing promotional stunts. Long-winded, but funny.

Passman, Donald S. *All You Need to Know About the Music Business.* Revised edition. New York: Simon & Schuster, 1994. Excellent information by a top entertainment business attorney, marred by a wise-guy writing style.

Prindle, David F. *The Politics of Glamour: Ideology and Democracy in the Screen Actors Guild.* Madison: University of Wisconsin Press, 1988.

Pratt, Ray. *Rhythm and Resistance: The Political Uses of American Popular Music.* Washington: Smithsonian Institution Press, 1990.

Rapaport, Diane Sward. *How to Make and Sell Your Own Record.* 5th edition. Jerome, Ariz.: Headlands Press, 1995. An excellent book, with good, detailed information about packaging, graphics, and building a mailing list. Very practical.

Riordan, James. *Making It in the New Music Business*. Cincinnati: Writer's Digest Books, 1988. A useful book with an irritating habit of making lists about EVERYTHING.

Rockwell, John. *All American Music: Composition in the Late Twentieth Century*. New York: Vintage Books, 1984. Wide-ranging essays on everything from Neil Young to avant-garde classical music.

Rogers, Kenny, and Epand, Len. *Making It with Music*. New York: Harper & Row, 1978. Some interesting material about starting and keeping a group together.

Schaefer, John. *New Sounds: A Listener's Guide to New Music*. New York: Harper & Row, 1987. A rich guide to many musical styles.

Schuyler, Nina. *The Business of Multimedia*. New York: Allworth Press, 1995. A guide for CD-ROM developers.

Siegel, Alan H. *Breakin' in the Music Business*. Port Chester, N.Y.: Cherry Lane Books, 1983. Some good interviews and legal defensive tactics. Written in a very New York-ey wise-guy style.

Taylor, Barbara Zimmerman, ed. *National Directory of Record Labels and Music Publishers*. 5th edition. Atlanta: Rising Star Publishers, 1995.

Titon, Jeff Todd, general ed. *Worlds of Music: An Introduction to the Music of the World's Peoples*. New York: Schirmer Books, 1984. Surveys of world music by various authorities.

Vogel, Harold L. *Entertainment Industry Economics: A Guide for Financial Analysis*. Cambridge: Cambridge University Press, 1986. Good, but not easy reading.

Wacholtz, Larry E. *Star Tracks? Principles for Success in the Music and Entertainment Business*. Nashville: Thumbs Up Publishing, 1996.

Wallis, Roger, and Malm, Krister. *Big Sounds from Small Peoples: The Music Industry in Small Countries*. London: Constable, 1984. A superb book, hard to find but worth looking for.

Weissman, Dick. *Music Making in America*. New York: Ungar, 1982. A group of essays on various subjects.

Zalkind, Ron, and Stein, Howard. *Promoting Rock Concerts*. New York: Schirmer Books, 1979. Out-of-date, but still useful.

PERIODICALS

Music Trade Papers

Billboard, 5055 Wilshire Blvd., Los Angeles, CA 90036.

Cash Box, 6455 Sunset Blvd., #605, Los Angeles, CA 90028.

Daily Variety, 5700 Wilshire Blvd., #120, Hollywood, CA 90028. Some stories covering the music business; ads for musicians to play good-paying and rather specialized gigs.

Hits, 14958 Ventura Blvd., Sherman Oaks, CA 91403

Hollywood Reporter, 5055 Wilshire Blvd., Los Angeles, CA 90036
Music Row, P.O. Box 158542, Nashville, TN 37215
Radio and Record, 1930 Century Park W., Los Angeles, CA 90067
RPM, 6 Brentcliffe Rd., Toronto, Ont. 4MG 3Y2, Canada
Variety, 5700 Wilshire Blvd., #120, Los Angeles, CA 90036

Other Periodicals

Acoustic Guitar, P.O. Box 767, San Anselmo, CA 94979
Acoustic Musician, P.O. Box 1149, New Market, VA 22844
American Music, University of Illinois Press, 54 E. Gregory Dr., Champaign, IL
    61820
American Music Teacher, 441 Vine, #505, Cincinatti, OH 45202
American Songwriter, 121 17th Ave. S., Nashville, TN 37203
Audio, 1633 Broadway, 45th Floor, New York, NY 10019
Back Stage, 1515 Broadway, 14th Floor, New York, NY 10036
Back Stage West, 5055 Wilshire Blvd., 6th Floor, Los Angeles, CA 90036
BAM, 3770 Buskirk Ave., Pleasant Hill, CA 94523
Bass Player, 411 Borel Ave., #10, San Mateo, CA 94402
Black Beat, 233 Park Ave. South, New York, NY 10003
Bluegrass Unlimited, P.O. Box 111, Broad Run, VA 22014
Blues Access, 1455 Chestnut Place, Boulder, CO 80304
Blues Revue, 916 Douglas Drive, #101, Endwell, NY 13760
Broadcasting and Cable, 1705 De Salle St., Washington, DC 20018
Canadian Musician, 17 Mowat Ave., #350, Toronto, Ont. M6K 3E3, Canada
Chamber Music, 545 Eighth Ave., New York, NY 10018
Circus Magazine, 6 W. 18th St., 2nd Floor, New York, NY 10011
Coda, 64 Dundas St. E., Toronto, Ont. M5B 1C7, Canada. An excellent jazz
    journal.
Contemporary Christian Music, 107 Kenner Ave., Nashville, TN 37205
Country Weekly, 1225 17th Ave. S., Nashville, TN 37212
Dirty Linen, P.O. Box 66600, Baltimore, MD 21239. Folk music.
Down Beat, 102 N. Haven Rd., Elmhurst, IL 60126. Jazz and blues.
Electronic Musician, 6400 Hollis St., #2, Emoryville, CA 94608
Entertainment Law Reporter, 2119 Wilshire Blvd., Ste. 311, Santa Monica, CA
    90403
EQ, 939 Port Washington Blvd., Port Washington, NY 11050. A journal about
    music production.
Flute Talk, 200 Northfield Rd., Northfield, IL 60093
Goldmine, 700 E. State St., Iola, WI 54990. For record collectors.
Gospel Music Exclusive, P.O. Box 6, Riverside, CA 92505
Gospel Today, 2201 Murfreesboro Rd., #C-206, Nashville, TN 37217
Guitar for the Practicing Musician, 10 Midland Ave., Port Chester, NY 10573
Guitar Player, 411 Borel Ave., #100, San Mateo, CA 94402

Guitar School, 1115 Broadway, New York, NY 10010

Guitar World, 1115 Broadway, 8th Floor, New York, NY 10010

Heartsong Review, P.O. Box 1084, Cottage Grove, OR 97424. New Age music.

High Fidelity, 825 7th Ave., New York, NY 10019

International Musician, 1501 Broadway, New York, NY 10036. Musicians' union journal, information about symphony jobs, articles.

Jazz Educators Journal, Box 724, Manhattan, KS 66502

Jazz Player, P.O. Box 206, Medfield, MA 02052

Jazz Times, 8055 13th St., Silver Spring, MD 20910

Jazziz, 3620 N.W. 43rd St., #D, Gainesville, FL 32606

Journal of Country Music, 4 Music Sq. E., Nashville, TN 37203

Journal of Jazz Studies, Rutgers University, 135 Bradley Hall, Newark, NJ 07102

Keyboard Classics, 223 Katonah Ave., Katonah, NY 10536

Keyboard Magazine, 411 Borel Ave., #100, San Mateo, CA 94402

Living Blues, Center for the Study of Southern Culture, University of Mississippi, University, MS 38677

Lost Highway (The Alternative Music Magazine of Country Music), P.O. Box 22299, Nashville, TN 37202

Maximum Rock 'n' Roll, P.O. Box 288, Berkeley, CA 94701

Metal Edge, 233 Park Ave. S., 5th Floor, New York, NY 10003

Millimeter, 122 E. 42nd St., #900, New York, NY 10168. Motion picture, TV, and commercials.

Mix, 6400 Hollis St., #12, Emoryville, CA 94608

Modern Drummer, 12 Old Bridge Rd., Cedar Grove, NJ 07009

Music City News, P.O. Box 22975, Nashville, TN 37203

Music Connection, 5640 Sunset Blvd., Hollywood, CA 90028. An excellent magazine with many useful articles and interviews.

Music Educators Journal, 1806 Robert Fulton Dr., Reston, VA 22091

Music Trades, 80 West St., Box 432, Englewood, NJ 07631. Music stores.

Musical Merchandise Review, 100 Wells Ave., Newton, MA 02159. Music stores.

Musician Magazine, 1515 Broadway, 11th Floor, New York, NY 10036

New York Times, 229 W. 43rd St., New York, NY 10036. Read the Sunday arts section to keep abreast of contemporary music.

Option, 1522-B Cloverfield Blvd., Santa Monica, CA 90404. Reviews many obscure albums.

Pastoral Music, 225 Sheridan St., NW, Washington, D.C. 20011

Popular Music, Cambridge University Press, 40 W. 20th St., New York, NY 10011

Popular Music and Society, Bowling Green State University, Popular Press, Bowling Green, OH 43403

Producer, 25 Willowdale Ave., Port Washington, NY 11050

Pulse, 2500 del Monte St., Bldg. C., W. Sacramento, CA 95691. Tower Records' monthly. Contains considerable regional news.

Rap Masters, 210 Route 4 East, #401, Paramus, NJ 07652

Rap Sheet, 2601 Ocean Park Blvd., #200, Santa Monica, CA 90405

Recording, 7318 Topanga Canyon Blvd., #200, Canoga Park, CA 91303

Release, 404 BNA Drive, #508, Bldg. 200, Nashville, TN 37217. Christian music.

Relix, P.O. Box 94, Brooklyn, NY 11229. Commemorates the Grateful Dead and the San Francisco scene.

Right On, 233 Park Ave. S., New York, NY 10003. Black entertainment.

RIP, 8484 Wilshire Blvd., #900, Los Angeles, CA 90211

The Rocket, 2028 5th Ave., Seattle, WA 98121. Covers the Seattle scene.

Rolling Stone, 1290 Avenue of the Americas, 2nd Floor, New York, NY 10104

Saxophone Journal, P.O. Box 206, Medfield, MA 02052

Sing Out, P.O. Box 5253, Bethlehem, PA 18015. Folk music journal.

Song Talk, 6381 Hollywood Blvd., #780, Hollywood, CA 90028

Strings, P.O. Box 767, San Anselmo, CA 94979. Covers bowed string instruments.

OTHER RESOURCES

The Album Network's *Yellow Pages of Rock* is available from The Album Network, Inc., 120 N. Victory Blvd., 3rd Floor, Burbank, CA 91502.

Billboard publishes annual directories that cover a variety of subjects including Touring, Retailing, International Buyers' Guide, etc. Write to Billboard Directories, P.O. Box 2015, Lakewood, NJ 08702.

The Nashville Red Book is an annual directory for the Nashville scene. It is published at 1207 Faydur Ct., Nashville, TN 37210.

Performance Magazine also publishes a series of annual guides to Booking, Managers, Touring, etc. The address is Performance Guide Series, 1101 University, Ste. 108, Fort Worth, TX 76107.

The Recording Industry Sourcebook is an annual guide available on disk or in hard copy from Cardinal Music Entertainment Group, 6400 Hollis St., Ste. 12, Emeryville, CA 94608.

RECENTLY DISCOVERED OR LATELY ARRIVED RESOURCES

Buttwinick, Marty. *How to Make a Living as a Musician So You Never Have a Day Job Again!* Glendale, Ca.: Sonata Publishing, 1993. Contains some interesting strategies for survival.

Garaofalo, Reebee. *Rockin' Out: Popular Music in the USA*. Boston: Allyn and Bacon, 1996. An excellent new book on rock and roll.

Hall, Charles W., and Taylor, Frederick J. *Marketing in the Music Industry*, Needham Heights, Ma.: Simon & Schuster, 1996.

Shagan, Rena. *Booking & Tour Management for the Performing Arts*. New York: Allworth Press, 1996. A valuable guide to touring and tour management.

Stanfield, Jana. *A Musician's Guide to Outrageous Success: Making & Selling CDs and Cassettes.* Nashville: Jana Stantunes Music, 1996. Useful if somewhat over-hyped strategies for making and selling your own recordings.

COPYRIGHT OFFICE

United States Copyright Office
    Library of Congress, Washington, DC 20559 (202) 707-3000

You can order free copyright forms by calling (202) 707-9100, but you must know the specific forms that you are requesting.

ACKNOWLEDGMENTS

My thanks go to Rick Abramson, Diane Deschanel, Cathy Hourigan, and Tom MacCluskey for initial encouragement and support. Jim Campbell, Dan Fox, Ed Hinshaw, Ron Lockhart, Andy Robinson, and Harry Tuft contributed specific ideas and comments that influenced my thinking, but they are in no way responsible for my conclusions. My thanks go to The Bookstore in Woodstock, New York, the Woodstock Public Library, Craig Liske, and the library at Colorado Women's College for various favors.

I enjoyed working with Pat Winsor and Brandt Aymar, my editors, who made a number of useful suggestions that helped me organize and complete this book.

I would like to thank my students at the Colorado Institute of Art. Their questions and comments provide a constant evaluation of my own ideas.

Because I have taught at a women's college, I am particularly conscious of the usually exclusive use of the pronoun he, especially in reference to people in professional jobs. In an attempt to avoid this stereotyping, in this book I have alternated the use of *he* and *she*.

INDEX